Edge of the Sound

Edge
of the Sound

MEMOIRS OF A WEST COAST LOG SALVAGER

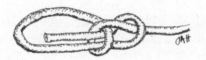

JO HAMMOND

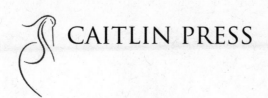

CAITLIN PRESS

Caitlin Press Inc.
8100 Alderwood Road,
Halfmoon Bay, BC V0N 1Y1
www.caitlin-press.com

Text and cover design by Pamela Cambiazo.
Edited by Rebecca Hendry and Betty Keller.
Illustrations by Jo Hammond.
Cover photograph by Chris Shepherd.

Printed in Canada.

Caitlin Press Inc. acknowledges financial support from the Government of Canada
through the Canada Book Fund and the Canada Council for the Arts, and from the
Province of British Columbia through the British Columbia Arts Council and the Book
Publisher's Tax Credit.

Canada Council for the Arts **Conseil des Arts du Canada**

BRITISH COLUMBIA
ARTS COUNCIL
We acknowledge the support of the Province of British Columbia
through the British Columbia Arts Council

Library and Archives Canada Cataloguing in Publication

Hammond, Josephine, 1941–

    Edge of the Sound : memoirs of a west coast log salvager / Josephine

Hammond.

ISBN 978-1-894759-49-6

    1. Hammond, Josephine, 1941–. 2. Hammond, Josephine, 1941– —Family.

3. Log salvagers—British Columbia—Howe Sound—Biography. 4. Boats and

boating—British Columbia—Howe Sound. 5. Howe Sound (B.C.)—Biography.

I. Title.

SD537.52.H34A3 2010   634.9'8092   C2010-904459-

Dedicated to Dick Hammond, friend, lover, husband, log salvor,
author, philosopher, and father extraordinaire.
(1929–2008)

Contents

1

The Ocean Calls

I have always been fascinated by the sea. I was born and reared a stone's throw from the English Channel, and while the sea and its beaches only spelled danger to my parents, my eccentric maternal grandmother showed me that it was something wild and beautiful that must be explored and experienced.

Her apartment, one block from the ocean and four from our house, would be my port-in-a-storm until I left high school. She was so passionate about the sea that when I was a young child she would scoop me out of bed at dawn to accompany her for nude swims off a deserted Bognor Regis beach. It didn't matter to her that the classy hotels overlooked the shore.

When I was eight years old, she took me for a walk on the old Victorian-built pier. Reconstructed several years before, after the end of World War II, the pier was on my parents' list of forbidden places because they thought I'd fall from it and drown, and with their constant warnings they had me almost convinced. What if the pier collapsed?

I did want to go with my grandmother, but … "Come on, Jo," she said, taking my hand. "I want to show you something very special."

For a while, the hollow clapping of our feet over the weathered grey planks distracted me a little from the butterflies in my stomach. I deliberately kept my head up so that I wouldn't see the water beneath the cracks.

"Gran, what's on the other side of the sea?"

"France."

France. Daddy. I had heard my mother mutter those words in the same breath when some German planes had flown over our house a long time ago. Perhaps he was living there. Why would no one tell me where my father had gone? But by then, four years after he "ran away," I had grown tired of asking questions that none of my relatives, not even my grandmother, could answer.

Glancing back over my shoulder at the sunburned town we had left behind, I thought we had almost walked far enough to see France. But still the horizon revealed nothing.

"Nearly there," Gran encouraged, leading me around the circular pavilion near the end.

Moored to the landing stage on the far side of the pavilion was a ship that seemed to have sailed straight out of one of my storybooks. A carved bird's head rose from the prow of its dark wooden hull. Below the gunwales were rows of holes for the long golden oars that now lay neatly inside across the benches. The vessel was partly rigged, its red and white striped sail hanging motionless in the hot summer air, while seated in its shade, several bronzed, fair-haired men wearing animal skins were splicing ropes. They spoke in a strange but happy-sounding language. Lilting and forward in the mouth, it was nothing like the ugly nasal French my father's aunts spoke when they didn't want me to understand what they were saying.

"It's a Viking boat made from oak trees, copied from long ago," explained Gran. "Those men have sailed and rowed all the way from Denmark without a motor."

Squinting, I searched the long line between the sea and sky but I still couldn't see France, nor any sign of land. And then, as my gaze lit on the boat again, I was overwhelmed by a strange sense of yearning.

I let go of my grandmother's hand and ran up the ship's gangplank. But she chased me, calling my name, grabbed my arm and led me back to the landing stage.

"I want to sail away," I sobbed. "I want to go away on that boat!"

"I know you're unhappy at home," she said, "and one day you will escape on a ship, but not this one. Not yet."

At twenty-two, after graduating with a diploma in secondary education specializing in music and science, I was in my first year of teaching at a Catholic secondary school when I received a note from my parents telling me that Gran had died. By this time I was estranged from my parents because they disapproved of me living with my first and only boyfriend, Gordon—a fellow student from college whom I would later marry. That night I had a vivid dream about the Viking ship she had taken me to see, and it was as real as it had been on the hot summer's day I had set eyes on it.

In my dream the ship was tied to a dock in a small harbour surrounded by rolling hills, its oak hull glowing richly against the blue sea, while fastened to the mast in the centre of the vessel, a partly furled crimson-and-white-striped sail fluttered in the breeze. Swirling knot-like designs had been carved into the gunwales, and a remarkable figurehead, a swan, had been intricately carved from the same red-coloured wood. But its eyes were not those of a swan. They were human, a pale olive-green with rivulets of real tears falling from them. Not only did I realize that these sad eyes were my own, I somehow knew that this exquisite ship would be my escape from England and my only route to happiness.

Surrounded by a crew of silent, expressionless men, the captain handed me aboard. As the men readied the boat to leave, the azure sky dimmed to an ominous red streaked with black, the sun faded, and the breeze died. The sail stilled and the air became oppressive. I asked the captain how long we might have to wait for departure, but he did not answer. His eyes stared vacantly at me like those of a corpse. The sailors, too, were transfixed, their eyes dull pearls, their bodies now mummified.

Within seconds, the pitch-black sea had drained away, exposing dried mud and spears of dead grass that protruded upwards through swirls of white vapour. Fingers of fog crept over the side of the ship then oozed along the deck, engulfing and assimilating each body before slinking noiselessly over the gunwales and out of the ship.

I was paralyzed by fear, unable to fight this all-consuming evil because I could not understand it. But as the wooden deck began to crack under my feet, I found enough power to scramble back onto the dock.

Then, to my dismay, the ship silently disintegrated into a stark, grey skeleton surrounded by wisps of the sinister vapour.

I awoke crying silently, certain I would never escape England.

This was the first of many similar boat dreams that would trouble my sleep until two years after I had arrived in Canada. Their plots were never quite the same. The vessels were sometimes as small as a dinghy or as large as an ocean liner, but in all of them I never left the dock because as soon as I climbed aboard, the sea always vanished, the boat disintegrated or it metamorphosed into a building. In spite of their promising beginnings, I would awake from these dreams disappointed and frustrated, often with tears in my eyes.

Then in the summer of 1967 my dreams of an escape on a ship and Gran's promise were fulfilled at last. Gordon and I had signed teaching contracts with the school district in Sechelt on the Sunshine Coast, a rural area of British Columbia accessible from Vancouver only via car ferry or float plane. Why Sechelt? Gordon had made an extended visit to a record collector friend there several years before he had become a

The *Canadian Star* fulfilled a lifelong dream, bringing me to Canada in 1967.

teacher. As for me, I had hopes that our immigration to Canada aboard the six-thousand-ton freighter *Canadian Star* would end my search for something stable in my life. But I was also hoping that once we were in a new country Gordon might free himself from his addiction to alcohol and his daily doses of pot.

However, the depressing *idée fixe* of my unpleasant boat dreams caught up with me even as we were driving from Manchester to the Glasgow docks. Because Gordon had miscalculated the amount of petrol we would need for the journey, our rental car ran dry around midnight beside a field of sheep in the Scottish Lowlands and we almost missed our freighter. And again, four hours later, after the *Canadian Star* had glided down the hundred-mile stretch of the River Clyde, past banks lined with lights and dark shapes of buildings, only to stop at Gourock, so obsessed was I that this ship, too, might not be going anywhere, that I asked one of the officers what was wrong. When he explained that Gourock was where the local pilots leave the ships after guiding them down the river, I spent the rest of the night standing on deck, too excited to sleep.

At Horseshoe Bay we board the BC Ferries' vessel *Langdale Queen* in our rented truck. The ferry looks top-heavy compared to the sleek lines of the *Canadian Star* and I have the impression that if any more than its half-load of forty-three cars were to join us, it might sink. But it is a ship and, in spite of the spitting rain, I can't wait to explore. On the lifeboat deck I shake off the city's fumes and inhale fresh sea air. To starboard, steep forested mountains arise from the greenish, almost opaque sea, their peaks encircled by soft drapes of moisture-laden clouds. About a mile or two away on the port side sits a tree-covered island large enough to have its own mountains, and beneath them along the water's edge, I can just make out a sprinkling of small houses. Ahead of the ship as far as the eye can see, mountains lie upon mountains, some partly covered by dissipating mists. As the ship turns to port, my gaze is drawn by more green islands and their promontories, and I feel as lost as I had on the *Canadian Star* sailing through Haro Strait en route to Crofton.

At last the sun emerges to give me a clue as to our direction of travel. Armed with this knowledge, I locate a nautical map in the passenger lounge and learn that the first large island I had seen on our port side is Bowen.

Driving off the ramp into the Langdale ferry parking lot, Gordon pulls up beside a shirtless, well-built man standing beside a red Ford truck. "There's Gib. Must've just got off work."

Gib is Gordon's record collector friend and we will be lodging with him until we find a place to rent. Gib is about forty-five and the first thing that strikes me about him is his amazing tan. It makes his dense, white crew-cut hair quite shocking. "What on earth does he do to get burned like that?" I ask.

"He's a boom foreman. He makes up log booms out on the water."

I am still none the wiser. After a brief exchange of greetings with our host and his Adonis look-alike passenger—also shirtless and brown—we tailgate the red truck for a mile, where Gib drops his passenger off before continuing up a steep road. After twelve meandering miles through forest, we turn left into a narrow tunnel of dense conifers. Although I haven't glimpsed the water since Gib dropped his passenger off, I know that it can't be far away. "Does Gib live on the waterfront?" I ask Gordon.

"No idea. He's moved into another rental since I last saw him, and that was eight years ago."

We park beside some exotic-looking trees with curvaceous yellow-green branches partially covered with thin, peeling reddish skin. I pull off one of the shiny bright-olive leaves, a perfect backdrop for the tree's sprays of green-orange berries.

"Arbutus," Gib tells me when I ask what they are.

Seconds later, when I stand on the side porch, my question about waterfront is answered.

The house is atop a hundred-foot-high bluff that faces south over the sunny Strait of Georgia. Our viewing angle is such that, if I were to paint the scene, the sea would fill at least the lower two-thirds of the canvas. In spite of having just spent five weeks living aboard a ship, I am speechless at such a sight.

The south side of the whole length of the living room is a series of floor-to-ceiling panes of glass. And hanging over a red brick fireplace on the opposite wall, a slightly angled mirror about six feet wide and four feet high reflects the view back again with me caught in the middle.

As the late afternoon sun blazing through the porch door, Gib shows us to our bedroom. "I've found you a rental cabin," he tells us, "but it won't be ready for another week. And it's waterfront."

Definitely a plus.

Gordon hands him a gift of a few classical records. "How about your Wednesday music evenings?"

"There's one tomorrow. There'll be a couple of different regulars since you were here. A Dutch garage owner … and there's a beach-comber from Gibsons. But I don't think he'll show up because I told him you would be here."

"What difference does that make?" Gordon asks.

"He's an oddball. Doesn't like groups. Won't allow smoking in his house because he says the tar coats his record collection."

Gordon shrugs.

"What kind of stuff does he find on the beaches?" I ask Gib.

"Logs. I guess his proper job description is log salvor."

I can't wait to see what a log salvor looks like, particularly an "oddball."

2

The Music Listeners

Andy, the greying, bespectacled Dutch immigrant, is first to arrive. Listening to classical music is one of this garage mechanic's hobbies, and he soon lets us know in his clipped accent that he would rather hear the higher fidelity of LP records than the crackles and pops of the fragile 78 rpms that Gordon prefers. Minutes after finding a comfortable chair, Andy is embroiled in a discussion with Gib about a Swedish neo-romantic composer, "who," he complains in a staccato Dutch accent, "never goes anywhere with his music." Gib is about to put his new recording of the offending composer's music on the turntable when there is a rap at the glass door. Gib beckons the visitor in.

From our host's "Ah, Dick! I didn't expect you tonight," I know it's the oddball.

The newcomer unties the laces on his black running shoes and places them neatly out of the way behind the door. His close-fitting jeans and black skin-tight T-shirt reveals a muscular body and his short, dark hair is balding. There's nothing about him that would make him stand out in a crowd. Quite the opposite. The teacher in me suspects he had been one of those children who learned how to blend into the background in the classroom, but once outside had got up to mischief.

His handshake is firm, his skin calloused and rough. But his voice does not match his build or handshake; it's extremely quiet with a kind of lilting burr. And as his sea-coloured eyes flash brief unease at meeting me, a stranger, I find myself averting my own gaze from his face in sympathy. Then, cat-like, in one seemingly continuous movement, he glides across the green Chinese carpet and lowers himself gracefully onto the wooden chair beside Andy.

Gib pours each of his guests a glass of port and invites us to help ourselves to the dishes of peanuts, chips and cookies. He places the tone arm onto the disc, and talking stops until we've heard both sides of the record.

After my six-week musical fast, I am hungry for the language that talks to me without words. I wonder if my fellow listeners' perceptions are the same as mine. But while there is an interesting group discussion and argument about the music and the performers afterwards, I keep my opinions to myself.

Andy turns to the latecomer. "Dick, surely you see vhat I'm getting at?" he demands. "It doesn't go anywhere."

Dick glances at him then stares down at the worn Oriental carpet. "How do you know where it's going if you don't know where it ends?"

The Dutchman snorts. "Ach ... you and your tricky vords!" he retorts. He and the beachcomber seem to be quite at ease with each other.

Dick grins. "The trouble with you," he banters, "is that you listen like a car mechanic. You're trying to hear problems instead of just allowing the music to wash over you."

He has a very good point but I keep quiet.

Andy ignores him and turns to me. "So, Jo," he asks, "vhat do you think?"

"I'd have to listen to it again then let you know," I reply, quite taken aback that a man, and a relative stranger, would be interested in what I think.

Dick nods. "Sensible answer."

Gordon pronounces the work "interesting."

The rest of the evening is spent playing and discussing several 78 rpm recordings of old opera singers. Although neither the beachcomber nor Andy specialize in this type of collecting, they're very forthcoming with their opinions, and it leaves me puzzled as to why our host thinks that Dick is strange. Compared to Gordon he uses words sparingly, and since he has hardly said a word to me all evening, I suspect he also feels ill at ease with strange women. But he is certainly no oddball. If I lived on my own, I wouldn't want people to smoke inside my house either.

As the half-moon's rays fall through the south-facing windows, our host hands us mugs of hot chocolate and passes around a dish of Danish pastries. Then, perhaps as an afterthought, he starts playing Beethoven's Romance for Violin and Orchestra and turns the lights off.

I find a spot on the floor and gaze out at the sequined sea and the twinkling lights of Nanaimo on the other side of the Strait. If I had to choose a moment to lose myself in eternity, this would be one.

Our West Sechelt rental, a cedar cabin only twenty feet from the high-tide line, seems idyllic, but public transport on the ribbon-developed Sunshine Coast is almost non-existent, with only two express buses a day between Powell River and Vancouver. My two-roomed elementary school is within easy walking distance, but Gordon's is twenty miles away in Langdale. He buys a new VW Beetle from the local dealer, but a month later on his way home after an evening in the Legion, he upends it in a ditch and forgets to turn the engine off. Awakened by the crash, the inhabitants of a nearby house leave their beds and roll the car back on its wheels. But the engine needs a complete rebuild, and Gordon has to make do with the school bus for about a month.

When the cold November weather arrives, our uninsulated cabin hovers around forty degrees Fahrenheit in spite of the constantly running propane heater. Complaints to the landlord have no effect, so we start looking for a warmer place. Meanwhile, we wear winter jackets indoors and tell ourselves it could be a lot worse.

One of these icy mornings—a Sunday—I leave Gordon hungover and walk out onto the porch where my attention is caught by the sturdy trunk of a cedar tree ten feet away.

There's something familiar about the way the winter light defines its buttress-like ribs that arise from the ground, gradually narrowing before disappearing under opulent valences of green boughs. As I stare at it, I recall a vivid oil painting that had been lying against some stage costumes in my art-critic grandpa Eric's cluttered cellar. Even though I was only eleven years old at the time, I remember being struck with the picture's glorious swirls of evergreen branches, windswept and powerful, above columns of dark trunks and waves of ferns, and by the unadorned signature in small capitals in the corner: "EMILY CARR."

No wonder the tree has jogged my memory. Grandpa's second wife, Stella, now widowed, has just written to tell me that she had rediscovered the painting, one that Grandpa had brought back from his trans-Canada lecture tour in 1937. She added that after giving a lecture on modern art in Victoria, he had visited Miss Carr in hospital before selecting several canvasses from her home for the Canadian National Gallery in Ottawa. Interestingly, Stella's comment near the end of the letter had been, "Eric once told me that if he were to emigrate, he would choose to live in Canada."

But I think he might not if he'd been living under my present conditions.

I sit on a large driftwood log near the tide line and watch the sea making little runs toward my rubber boots, miniature waves, clear, curling over like the large ones at Bognor, noiselessly and without foam. But after a while I realize that as each wavelet forms, mounts and falls, it sighs … just like my own breath. Over and over again each sigh travels along the pebbly beach until, to my ears at least, it fades to nothing.

My hopes have faded, too. Gordon's addictions continue to scuttle our relationship, and it is only the occasional musical weekend in Vancouver that helps to distract and recharge me. Sharing live music at a concert or opera reminds me of our first couple of years together when things were better between us. We had both been singing in world-class choirs in Liverpool and Manchester with world-class orchestras, and only now do I realize what a huge and vital part of my life I have left behind. So far, there is nothing to fill this void.

Slowly creeping around my boots, the sea now invites my tears. So right, so natural seems the blending of these salty liquids that I feel drawn into a kind of symbiosis, and it eases me. I try to tune in to its own music, to understand its own peculiar language, but while I hear the sea's vague songs of promise, there's nothing more.

At last I raise my head and stare across the Georgia Strait at the wintery mountains of Vancouver Island, twenty-five miles away. Their powerful grey presence comforts me, just as the pinpricks of light from the settlements at their feet console me at night. Unlike the French coast beyond the English Channel, this one is visible, tangible.

At bedtime a couple of days later the weather changes. A wind begins to blow off the Strait from the southeast, hammering against the cabin. Every so often the walls crack and startle me. If I stand beside the windows, I feel its chilly breath against my hand and face, hear it hissing, forcing its way through the ill-fitting wooden casements. Sometimes, like dark snow, leaves from the cedar tree fly erratically past the porch light and litter the ground. I peer out the door, listen to the waves, then check the tide table on the fridge to discover that the sea is on its way out and won't be high again until the morning.

Around dawn, I awake to a strange rattling that seems connected to a series of rumbles. At first I think it is part of my dream until I hear the unsettling clatter of crockery. Then, as the next series of thumps sets the bed and the whole cabin shaking, I freeze. The wind is still howling in the big cedar, but the crashing surf now sounds dangerously close. I leap out of bed and run to the windows.

"What's going on?" Gordon demands, following more sedately. He watches for a few seconds before wandering toward the bathroom. "I don't think it'll come any closer," he says, "or they would have built a seawall."

I open the window a crack but the wind snatches the hinged pane from me, forcing it open to its full extent, while spray-laden gusts almost blow me backwards. I grab the frame, wresting it shut, then stare out at the whitecaps rolling toward us. But it's not just the waves that alarm me. Carried atop the curling swells, huge logs, roots and pieces of driftwood thunder against the fifteen feet of mowed lawn that separates us from the beach. With each hit, the cabin trembles. Chunks of turf have already been undermined and torn out by the sea's force. Ten feet further along the beach, two gigantic logs are sucked out by a swell that tosses them up, smashes them together and throws them down onto our muddy lawn. They are dragged out again only to be swept closer to the cabin.

Then quite unexpectedly my fear dissipates, and I find myself empathizing with the sea's anger as it had empathized with me, singing its promises that cold, calm morning two days earlier. Is this storm one of those promises?

The tide table taped to the fridge shows the tide has reached its highest point.

Back at the window again, I hear the pulsing growl of an engine. A couple of hundred yards off the beach a little black speedboat passes by, riding the swells before disappearing around the promontory to the right of our cabin. Moments later, bucking the waves, the boat returns, stops, and its hooded driver stares in our direction.

This is no pleasure boater. Standing alert, head slightly forward, he is all business as he steers his craft over the whitecaps toward our cabin.

I'm tempted to run outside, to wave him back and shout that it's dangerous to come ashore in this storm. Can't he see that a single wave could flip that small boat? Those two giant logs could crush it and him easily. What if one landed on his head? He turns the craft 180 degrees, heaves a bundle of thick rope over his shoulder, vaults over the stern and carries the rope ashore. His boat will be swept up the beach. Swamped!

"Quick!" I shout against the closed window. "Hurry!"

Waves and driftwood break about him, foaming up to his chest as he throws a chain that is attached to the other end of the rope over the two logs, blindly adjusting it under them while they bounce as high as his shoulders. One more second and he'll be crushed. But he turns, flees. How can he move so fast in such deep water? He chins himself back onto the boat, leaps—almost flies—to the steering wheel, guns the engine and the rope straightens. As the following swell hurls the logs up again, the rope pulls taut, stretches, the boat halts, and a five-foot wall of water collapses inside its stern. The engine roars, the boat charges forward again, dragging the logs through the water, out beyond the swells. The man steers slowly southeastwards, toward Sechelt, waving as he disappears around the point.

In the kitchen, Gordon is getting ready to go to work. He slides his bagged lunch into his briefcase. "That's what Gib's friend does for a living," he says. "Log salvage. Beachcombing."

That same evening at Gib's, Dick asks us if we'd seen him wave.

"That was you?" I exclaim.

"Who did you think it was?" he replies in his quiet, measured way.

Andy the Dutchman laughs. "See," he chides his friend, "you're not as infamous as you think you are."

"Alas, to my great regret," Dick agrees without missing a beat.

Gib hands him a glass of port. "Just listen to the man! You'd never know he was the best log salvor in BC ... Mr. Hammond, your reputation has never been in question."

Dick glares at the floor. "It had better not be," he growls, obviously embarrassed.

"Why was the tide so high this morning?" I ask him.

He stares intently at me—just for a second—then averts his eyes toward the sea. "It's a combination of high winter tides and a storm surge."

"What do you mean—storm surge?" I persist.

"Sorry," he says, shooting a glance my way again. "Usually it's a strong southeaster that pushes the water up the Gulf for four days without stopping. It doesn't have time to drain out properly so the normal high tides are even higher."

"A few inches?"

"More like a couple of feet," he says. "Enough to rip out your West Sechelt lawn." Why does he look away when he starts to talk? Does he feel awkward?

Gordon leans forward in his chair. "How many logs did you find up there?" he asks, "and what will you do with them?"

"Twenty-three," Dick replies. "I'll wait till I've got enough for a four-section boom."

"A log boom?" I ask.

Gib regards me patiently. "Those thousands of logs you see behind the tugboats, they're log booms. It's the cheapest way of bringing them from the forests to the sorting grounds and from there to the mills."

Dick nods. "And some mills only take certain sizes and species."

I am now beginning to realize just how much of this area's wealth is tied up in trees.

3

Comet over the Sound

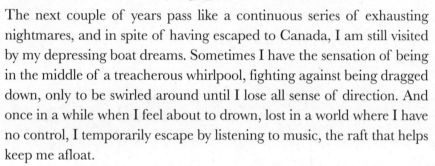

The next couple of years pass like a continuous series of exhausting nightmares, and in spite of having escaped to Canada, I am still visited by my depressing boat dreams. Sometimes I have the sensation of being in the middle of a treacherous whirlpool, fighting against being dragged down, only to be swirled around until I lose all sense of direction. And once in a while when I feel about to drown, lost in a world where I have no control, I temporarily escape by listening to music, the raft that helps keep me afloat.

But Gordon's crazy behaviour escalates and our domestic crises become more frequent. Something has to change or I will have a breakdown. Thinking he might be one of those men who needs fulfillment as a father, I quit teaching, and consider starting a family. I can always get a substitute-teaching job if I change my mind.

On a Saturday that same month, Dick invites Andy the Dutchman, Gordon and me over for an evening of music and also to view Comet Bennett through his telescope. Knowing our host never cooks, I volunteer to bring a casserole of Boeuf Bourguignon.

When Gordon has not shown up at home by 4:45, I pace about the room until I find myself gazing at my favourite miniature painting, one of seven given to me by my grandpa Eric's second wife, Stella. Painted *circa* 1850 in oil on a two-and-a-half-inch oval of ivory, the green-eyed young woman in her mid-twenties returns my gaze with a meek and forgiving expression. Her close-fitting, off-the-shoulder emerald dress is bordered with frilled white lace—almost three-dimensional in effect—

that echoes the delicate paleness of her breast. Two gold chains encircle her neck; from the longer one an ornate gold and ruby cross rests on the lace frill. The miniaturist was a master. So exquisite is the workmanship that, under the lamp, I can see where he had used one hair of a sable brush to paint the young woman's gleaming locks. The links of the chain must have been executed in the same way, each one reflecting the light as a single, almost microscopic, entity. Her skin is remarkable. Not only has it been coloured with a mixture of pink, beige, and white, it has been subtly mottled with blue and brown tints to give an incredibly lifelike sheen. This dappling, barely evident to the naked eye, suggests a flawless peaches-and-cream complexion. But what fascinates me most is that, beneath her expression of resigned forbearance, the Lady in Green seems to be hiding her soul. Why hadn't I noticed this deception before? Since the artist has now convinced me of a further truth, I can't help wanting to know more about her.

Around five I phone Gordon, who has already been in the Wakefield Inn for three hours, to remind him we should have left for Gibsons five minutes ago. And when he tells me he'll make his own way there, I pack the dish into my recently acquired rusted-out 1962 VW and leave without him.

Darkness is falling as I drive down the asphalt driveway past Dick's blackberry-covered workshop. His house and garden, bought from his parents the previous year, sits at the bottom, conveniently next to Hendricksons' "Boatworks" with its fuel dock, tanks, boat ways and live bait pond.

Andy is already in the kitchen when I arrive, and knowing Gordon's habits, he persuades the three of us to eat while the food is hot.

Over Andy's donation of ice cream, the three of us watch out the window as a tug roars into reverse and docks alongside the Boatworks' fuel pumps.

Dick's house beside the Boatworks in Gibsons.

Andy gives a contented sigh. "Now you must agree that this is a most pleasant way to spend an evening. Full belly, good company, bottle of port and looking forward to music." Then he turns to Dick. "See what you're missing, Mr. Hammond? How much longer will you be finding yourself a vife, for goodness sake? Time won't wait for you, you know, in spite of you thinking that you're so different from everyone else."

Dick usually takes Andy's needling with equanimity, but since this dig seems to be more of an attack, I wait for a sarcastic reply.

"I keep telling you," Dick calmly insists, "that I haven't found what I want."

"And I keep telling you," Andy responds impatiently, "that people can't always get vhat they vant. Mr. Hammond, you are far too fussy. Look, you're already forty years old."

"I am quite aware of that, thank you, but what about you?" Dick counters, staring out at the tug. "Can you honestly say you're happy with your marriage?"

Andy snorts and glares at the floor. "Ach-ch! Nothing's perfect." It's obvious from his intent expression that he's not finished. He raises his head and demands, "So tell me vhat it is that you vant in this imaginary vife?"

"Well, since I don't cook, it would be very nice if she knew how to make a tasty supper. And, of course, she'd have to be interested in music ... life in general, someone to discuss things with ... " He pushes his plate away.

"Go on, Mr. Hammond, I'm listening," encourages Andy.

"And ... well, I couldn't live with one of those aggressive women, and naturally she'd have to be reasonably attractive ..."

"So you think you vill find such a woman around here?" Andy asks sarcastically.

"Not necessarily. Anyway," Dick adds abruptly, flashing his friend an annoyed glance, "that's enough of such talk." He stands. "Let's listen to some music."

The Dutchman shoves his chair back impatiently. He hates to be fobbed off with a change of subject. "Ach," he repeats in disgust. "You'll never find one because you never go anywhere."

As we pass the unfinished living room Andy notices that the wall

between it and Dick's parents' old bedroom has recently been demol-
ished and a raised ceiling added. He stares up at it. "Not bad. Who did
you get to do that?"

"A couple of Hungarians. It's designed to bring the best out of
those JB Lansing speakers."

"What else have you planned?"

"Record shelves, cabinets. And a fireplace. But I haven't made my
mind up about its facing."

We spend the next forty minutes listening to Schumann's piano
concerto in the bedroom where Dick has temporarily set up his expensive sound system. Then, adjourning to the enlarged living room and the
telescope, Andy and I wait in the dark to accustom our eyes while our
host feeds his cat in the kitchen. There's still no sign of Gordon and no
reply when I phone home.

"You must be vorried," Andy remarks to me. Over supper he had
confided that he was concerned about the suitability of his twenty-two-
year-old daughter's fiancé as marriage material, so now I am prepared
for him to tackle me about my own marriage.

I shrug. "Worrying doesn't do any good."

"For goodness' sake!" he bursts out. "How on earth do you put up
with the man? I mean, don't you ever think of …?" He pauses.

"Leaving him?" I'm shocked that I have actually said it.

"But of course!" he sputters. "It's for certain he's not getting any
better."

Trust honest Andy. He's the only one of our acquaintances to
comment on Gordon's behaviour. "I didn't think you'd noticed," I tell
him, relieved that at last someone sympathizes. "No one else has."

"Of course I notice!" he explodes, but Dick's entrance into the
room silences him on the subject.

As I peer through the binoculars at the magnificent sight above
the harbour, the first comet I've ever seen, my heart pounds with sub-
dued excitement. But I can't concentrate on anything. My mind is leap-
frogging so wildly that I suspect I must be overtired.

One symphony later, we all sniff pot in the air and Dick finds Gordon, supine and reeking of booze, on the spare bed in the basement. We

leave him to sleep it off while I drive home alone.

Coincidentally, one of the local school principals half-jokingly confides in me the following day, "I told Gordon to smarten up, because if he didn't, you'd go off with some old logger." To which I retort, "Not a chance."

However, at Wednesday's music evening, I follow fifty-year-old grandfatherly Gib into his record library and ask if his spare room is going to be vacant in the near future should I need respite from Gordon.

He doesn't bat an eyelid. Has he been talking to Andy? "Sure. Any time," he says casually. "My niece used it last year under similar circumstances."

I don't tell him he has quite a reputation for helping young people in a crisis.

Mine takes place less than three weeks later. After preparing a dinner of two stuffed Cornish game hens, scalloped potatoes and peas, with a dessert of stewed pears in wine, I wait ... and wait ... It's after six-thirty and Gordon's still not home from school. I locate him—by phone—in the Peninsula Hotel, but in spite of me telling him the meal is waiting, he insists that he's not ready to come home.

How will I know I have arrived at the moment when mind and body have reached breaking point? As my gaze falls on the clock in the bedroom—one of our wedding presents—I think, who will keep that after everything's over? The hour hand is on eight, and the minute hand stands just past the vertical of the number twelve. Off balance. Ready to fall. I see the fall storm waves eroding the grass in front of the cedar cabin, and my marriage a disintegrating muddied mess sweeping out to sea with the driftwood.

Three minutes past eight ... Something in my brain quits. Driven by fury, there's no room for a conscious decision. Suddenly—not knowing how I got there—I am sitting on the floor in front of the fireplace, love letters and photo albums in my hands. The blackened hole swallows the letters. I tear out every photo of Gordon and throw them on top. My hands find the matches and set fire to the lot.

I pack my bags, remembering to take the antique miniatures my step-grandmother had given me. The first one I wrap is the young woman in the green dress. She catches me with her eyes, won't let me go. As I turn the picture slightly, a distortion in the old glass seems to move her head a little, urging me on.

In a fit of practicality I force myself to gulp down the dried-up meal I had prepared, but I can only taste my salty tears. Knowing that Gib is an early riser I phone to warn him that I'm on my way.

The five-minute drive to his house is fraught with guilt and I feel like a naughty student playing truant. But Gib greets me with, "Good for you," and hands me a mug of his overly sweet hot chocolate. Then with a slight smile he adds, "Knowing Gordon from a way back, I'm not surprised."

As soon as he has gone to bed, I wrap myself in a jacket against the light frost, sit on the mossy bluff in front of the house, and stare at the almost full moon. The first theme of Beethoven's violin concerto plays in my mind, a flashback to my first summer evening here on the Coast, two and a half years earlier. The beautiful but simple melodic line has a calming effect, but I refuse to hear the troubling second theme that modulates into the minor key. Across twenty-two miles of cold, dark water, the lights of Nanaimo and its environs sparkle as they had done then. I'm not so alone … But what next? I can't even try to think about the future; it is hard enough to make sense of the present.

Two evenings later, Gordon comes around with some hippies. He is so drunk and stoned that I wonder if the pot he's smoking has been mixed with something else. In spite of me telling him otherwise, he insists that my move is temporary. "You must realize I can't promise I won't drink anymore," he mumbles, adding, "You'll be back … I know it."

I sneak out of the house and hide behind the arbutus trees until he drives off. Gib tells me that he had to order him to go home. "God knows what he was on," he mutters.

4

Jet Boat Ride

When Dick phones the following day and invites me for a ride in his boat, I suspect Gib of telling him I need some distraction. I accept Dick's offer, knowing he won't get personal and ask questions about my leaving Gordon.

"Where are we going?" I ask as he lets me through the back door. Not that I care. It is enough that we are going out on the water.

"You'll see," he says, leading the way down his basement stairs, then handing me a pair of waterproof trousers and some gloves. "You might need a Helly Hansen jacket too," he adds. I am not prepared when he helps me put it on because he has never seemed concerned before about other people and their needs.

I follow him down the long chain of floats, stepping carefully across the gap between each one to avoid tripping over the bouncing float ahead. Tied to the end float is his new boat, a strange-looking craft. It reminds me of a manta ray with its black hull, large built-in, nose-like searchlight—a swiveling aeroplane landing light from Germany, he tells me—and running lights that look like eyes on each side of the squared, grey, flattened bow. It is perhaps a foot or two longer than his old black speedboat, but the windshield is obviously from an early '50s car, rounded and curved at the sides. A large metal cleat is bolted on the top of the boat's wide, flat-topped stern.

"Is that what you tie your towropes to?"

He nods. "There wasn't room for a proper towpost, so I invented this. If I need to suspend the boat from a lift, that and the bow ring are strong enough to bear its whole weight."

"I've never seen anything like it," I tell him.

"It is unique," he agrees casually. "I built most of it myself."

"What's it called?"

"The *Snark*."

"After T.S. Eliot's poem?"

"Yep. But I haven't got around to painting its name."

"What happened to the old boat?"

"Burned to the water line."

Strange I hadn't heard about that at Gib's. "How? Were you in it?"

He nods and unties each end of the boat from the float. "It happened here, in the dark … rain torrenting down, so I was in a hurry, monkeying with the starter, trying to get it going … I'd spilled fuel in the bilge and the fibreglass was already oil-soaked … The hull acted like a wick in spite of the rain. A spark from the starter was all it needed."

"I never noticed any burns on your face."

"Just a few singed eyebrows … but no insurance," he adds wryly. "Luckily I'd already started building the *Snark*. The fire just made me finish it in a hurry." He jumps lightly down in front of the dash and holds out his hand to help me in. Spurning his manly politeness, I grab the gunwale and step clumsily over it. But thinking my action must have seemed rather rude, I give an embarrassed laugh and apologize.

Adding another log to the morning's tow.

He smiles, sits beside me, turns the key and we're off. It's not until we pass the creosoted breakwater and dock at the end of the government wharf that we speed up. The engine growls with effort as the boat angles upwards for a couple of hundred yards then levels off until it's running flat on the water's surface almost like a hovercraft. Clearing the bluff to our starboard, we aim in the direction of an island. "Keats," he shouts, nodding toward it, and we charge alongside a series of rocky outcrops on top of which summer cabins perch, their ramps drawn up like drawbridges. He steers to port, around the westernmost point of Keats. Then just as I think we're going to hit a group of rocks, I see a tiny gap between them and a very small rocky island to starboard. But it's too narrow for us! Gripping the starboard gunwale, I hold my breath and wait for the crunch as we speed through, missing the rocks on either side by mere inches. He catches me glancing at him and grins. I've never seen him like this before. He's always been serious and understated, speaking only when he has to.

"That was close!" I yell.

"Only draws a few inches," he explains loudly.

"Did you say 'draw'?"

He decelerates so he doesn't have to shout. "The hull depth under the water. It's called draft. This boat doesn't have a prop to worry about. It's jet-driven, like my old Dowty Turbocraft."

"What kind of jet?"

"A Hamilton three-stage. It's a tunnel under the boat with three impellors in a row linked to the engine. It sucks the water through a grid from under the hull and shoots it out through a nozzle in the stern. Think of a firehose under water propelling the boat."

"Must be easier to get close to the beach without a propeller."

"That's right. But it's not efficient for towing." He depresses the accelerator with his right foot, and we speed away from Keats toward more islands a couple of miles to the south. The cool air brushes against my face and makes my eyes water.

He must have noticed my discomfort. "Rest your hand, palm forward, so it sticks up above the windshield to deflect the air," he shouts, demonstrating. "Like this."

After the shock of passing between the rocks, I try to absorb my surroundings. But this is a speedboat, and I'm so overloaded with scenes and sensations that I can't pay attention to all of them, particularly the direction we're taking. The constantly shifting centre of gravity compels every muscle to tense in response. The roaring engine is a pure, continuous growl that sets my bones vibrating when I lean back against the fibreglass engine cover. The mass of ropes and chains at my feet and the tools rattling in a rubber bucket beside him. The dashboard with busy needles on dials, one seemingly non-functioning. And what is that aroma? Sometimes of Bognor Beach, and sometimes of St. Michael's Mount off southern Cornwall where the Atlantic winds blow in … and then a rude whiff of gasoline exhaust from the stern, caught somehow in a back eddy behind the windshield.

He grimaces. "Pee-yoo!"

But it is mainly the sea that acts like a magnet to my eyes, forcing them to constantly focus, near, far, to starboard, to port, and everywhichway between. My companion seems to have a remarkable way of blending into our surroundings so that they take precedence. Under the cloudy sky the water is calm, almost black, its surface crowded with small ripples, just like the sand ripples on Bognor Beach at low tide. Something ahead splashes. A seabird? A fish? A piece of driftwood? Perhaps a submerged rock? But by the time we reach one of the islands, there is no reflection, just a dark shadow indicating the treed bluffs above. A breeze has blown in. Why can't I remember the sea from my freighter trip through Haro Strait? Have I washed that part of my life from my mind already? Or perhaps I never really paid attention. This world that now surrounds me in the beachcomber's boat has a dream-like quality about it.

Dick stands then decelerates. "Warm enough?" he asks.

Even though I know by now that his question is not just a formality, I would never admit to being anything else. Besides, my body temperature is one of the furthest things from my mind.

After rounding a rocky point he steers toward a narrow float in a small bay. This time I allow him to help me out, but I turn my face so that he can't see my embarrassed smile.

I follow him up a grassy bank and past a summer cabin. "Do you know the owner?" I ask.

"I fix his floats and ramp when they need attention," he replies, pushing through some leathery green salal bushes, then stopping to hold back the springy branches so they won't hit me.

"Thanks," I say, again taken aback by his thoughtfulness. Climbing a few more feet the path becomes a barely passable gap between the salal and a plantation of stunted evergreen trees. "Where are we?" I begin.

He turns and holds his finger to his lips. "Sh-sh. Nearly there."

Twelve more steps and we're almost at the top of the little rise. My companion halts, kneels, and peers over the other side, then backs off.

"Your turn," he whispers. "Slowly, now. No sudden movements."

I crouch so that I can just see over the rise. A quick glance tells me it's just another bay with a few grey lichen-covered rocks with patches of seaweed. But when I turn my head questioningly toward him, he nods and points in the same direction. "Keep looking," he whispers.

At last I understand why he has brought me here. As a child I used to search out the camouflage puzzles in annuals and magazines in which the reader is instructed to find the number of animals or items. Here in 3-D colour, framed by salal and the cedar boughs, about twenty seals gradually materialize. No wonder I had missed them. Even though I am only thirty feet away, they are almost invisible, their speckled or blotched dark brown or black skins, some with silvery spotted heads, blending perfectly with the dappled rocks. Like a collection of freshly plumped cushions tossed upon the hard granite, a few of the animals lie asleep. Others seem to be playing or feeding in the water. One head pops up and swivels like a periscope while its huge black marble-like eyes take everything in. It sees me and for a moment there is some kind of exchange between us.

"See that smooth bank over to the right?" Dick whispers. "It's an otter slide."

There's a ten-foot-long muddy slope a few feet up from the water. But since there aren't any otters, I stand and turn to leave. "Their escape route?"

Dick follows. "No, they play on it."

"You must be joking." Even though I'm becoming familiar with the Canadian sense of humour, I am never quite sure.

"I never tire of watching them. They slide on their chests head-first, over and over again, just like kids."

As the path widens slightly, he informs me there's a wild lily plantation near the otter slide. "They'll be blooming in a couple of weeks."

"White ones?"

He nods. "Erythroniums. We call them Easter lilies. I transplanted a couple of them outside the basement door. There's a rare pink form, too."

Is this interest in flowers one of the things that give Gib's logger friends reason to suspect that Dick is gay? That and the rather beautiful oriental *objets d'art* he has in his listening room. And of course, his appreciation of classical music and other art forms, all pursuits considered by ignoramuses as too effeminate for "real men."

"Did the lilies take?" I ask.

Again he holds a salal branch back for me. "The white ones did, but when Father tried the pink ones that same year, they never made it."

And while Dick is thinking about lilies, my thought returns to the gossip of this small community. I have heard that he has never been seen out with a woman. But he does keep his cards extremely close to his chest. I have seen the way he infuriates Andy with his wicked game of playing devil's advocate so that by the end of the discussion no one can tell which side he is really on.

"You never know with wild plants," he continues, falling in step beside me now that the path is wider. "They'll wither and die if you don't give them the right environment ... like the Indian paintbrushes I kept transplanting from Bowen Island. They just wouldn't take."

"No wonder," I tell him. "They're hemiparasites. I learned about them in grade thirteen botany."

He laughs. "If I'd studied botany, I wouldn't have wasted my time on them."

We walk down the ramp in silence, and I wonder what it is about his manner of speech that is so different from other Canadians I have met.

Perhaps it is because he reads a lot and socializes little.

Back at the boat, I feel awkward again. It must be the relative quiet in this bay. "What have you got under there?" I blurt out, pointing to the engine cover.

"A Shelby Cobra 289." It sounds as if he should be proud of it, but I can't hear that in his voice. "It's powerful," he adds, "but it's not working out the way I'd hoped."

"Will you get a bigger engine?"

"Possibly, but first I'll try modifying the hull." He unties the ropes from the dock and grabs the side plank. "Had enough sightseeing?"

"Don't you want to look for logs?"

"I've already done my morning rounds ... but if you want to see more ..."

I think, *of course I do*, but I say, "I don't want to take up your time."

He halts, pausing for a moment as if to make his point. "Jo, I wouldn't have offered if I didn't enjoy your company."

"Then I wish you'd asked me ages ago." *But would I have gone at that time?*

Without a word he unties the rope, pushes off from the float and aims for the southernmost island in the group. As he speeds past it and turns to follow its outer shore, I have the odd sensation of being on the edge of some *thing*, that if we left here and now in this small boat and tried to cross what appears to be the vast expanse of the Georgia Strait, we'd never reach Vancouver Island on the other side. Then it dawns on me that this is an illusion caused by our sea-level viewing angle. Vancouver Island appears far closer when viewed from Gib's house on its high bluff.

"Worlcombe Island!" Dick shouts in my ear.

Atop a wind-distorted pine that grows between two bluffs, an eagle balances, its head slightly cocked as if it's watching something below. "Bald eagle!" I call back.

He points to a few ducks busily pecking at the seaweed-covered rocks. "Eagle dinner!"

I am not sure I believe him.

As we turn around the rocky promontory back into the island

group, a huge head rears from the sea ahead of us. I nudge Dick and ask what it is.

"Sea lion," he tells me, easing his foot off the throttle. "It's their time to go north to breed. Most have already left."

"How big are they?"

"This one's a Steller. The males can weigh as much as two thousand pounds."

"Dangerous?"

He shrugs. "Can be." Turning the boat, he steers northwards away from the sun then in an S shape, so that after leaving the small islands we end up facing Bowen Island's steep shore with a good view of the highest mountain above it. He stops the engine and allows the boat to drift. "Mount Gardiner," he says, nodding toward it, then points toward a dark M shape of evergreen trees on either side of a gully, halfway up the steep mountainside. It's surrounded by what looks to me like scrub or brush. "See the darker green area?"

I nod.

"That's where my father and I handlogged. Other loggers had already clear-cut around it."

"How come only your patch has trees growing? And what is 'clear' logging?"

"Clear-cut," he corrects. "That's when loggers fall every single tree. They cut all the trees down and it takes ages for new ones to colonize, but a handlogger selects certain trees he wants to fall and leaves the smaller ones to grow. The idea is to fall the big trees without knocking down the ones you want to leave. That requires precision. Father was an expert. Of course, you can't use machines on that steep mountainside. That claim has two huge ravines. No one wanted to touch it until Father heard it was available, and he knew how to peel the bark in the spring and slide the slippery logs downhill."

"You could use those saws with motors, couldn't you?"

"Chainsaws? You could, but we didn't on that claim. We only used crosscut saws and logging jacks."

About half a mile off the harbour, it starts to pour. With the drops hitting my face at about forty knots, it feels as if it's being blasted with dried peas, and I duck below the windshield.

"Doesn't the rain blind you?" I ask as he draws alongside the dock.

He throws the boat's mooring rope over the float cleat. "You get used to it," he says then jumps in his running shoes onto the planks and ties the stern. I've never seen a man move so gracefully.

"Thanks very much for the ride," I tell him as he helps me up over the gunwale.

"I've enjoyed your company," he responds quietly.

Inside the basement, he takes my borrowed Helly Hansen jacket and hangs it near the furnace duct. "You in a rush?"

"Gib's expecting me to help out with supper."

"Well, I won't keep you … but if you feel like another ride, give me a call. And don't forget you're always welcome to listen to music."

"How did you know I was staying at Gib's?" I ask.

"Ran into one of his friends at Kenmac Parts."

"It's only until I find a place of my own."

"My parents have a small place a couple of blocks away," he says. "Their tenants are leaving in a few days. Would you like me to ask about it?"

"If it's cheap."

Driving back to Gib's place I feel strangely carefree. The boat, the man who drives it, the sea, I can't seem to separate the three of them in my mind and I can't think of anything else. No man has ever been so genuinely considerate to me. At Gib's music evenings Dick and I would barely exchange more than a few sentences. Likewise during his occasional visits with Gordon and me, always for supper and music afterwards. It was at the end of one of those visits that Dick had demonstrated his strong-mindedness, his resoluteness. Peter, an eccentric strong-willed doctor friend who had helped me to conquer my fear of diving so that I could swim underwater, was also present. And it was he who tried most passionately to persuade Dick to stay longer. But Dick had stood his ground as if his life depended on it, clearly but quietly stating he had to get up before dawn. Where Peter's remarkable powers of persuasion had always succeeded with Gordon—and anyone else for that matter—they failed dramatically with Dick.

5

Gibsons

I meet Dick outside his parents' rental the following afternoon. "It's nothing special," he warns as we walk up the cement path, "but at least you'll be on your own." He then explains it should be ready to move into within a week.

The single-bedroomed cottage can't be any larger than seven hundred square feet. Although there's no more view of the sea than the sliver I could see from my grandmother's Bognor Regis apartment, I tell him it will suit me fine. I'll have to be extra careful now that I've quit my job, but the six hundred dollars my great-aunt has left me in her will should last a few months, particularly if I work as a substitute teacher.

"Doing anything?" he asks.

"I have to set up a lawyer's appointment in Vancouver," I tell him. "Why?"

"A new record set came in yesterday's mail. The *Flying Dutchman*. I was thinking of playing it."

"Doesn't Andy want to hear it, too?"

"He has the same set. Highly recommended it."

After using Dick's kitchen phone, I find him in his bedroom—his temporary listening room—where I tell him my appointment is for legal advice, in a week's time. "I want to divorce Gordon."

He moves the easy chair to a central place in the room so that I might hear the full stereophonic effect then indicates for me to take a seat. "You sound pretty certain."

"I should have done it years ago. I kept threatening to leave, always hoping things would improve … what with everyone telling us how much we had in common … And then Andy said—"

"Don't listen to others," he advises. "Only you know how you want to live your life." Without further prying, he hands me the libretto. "It's the first of Wagner's mature operas." Then he sits on the bed and waits silently until I've finished reading.

Wagner, who wrote the music and libretto, based his plot on a multitude of versions of a medieval story about a ghostly Dutch captain condemned for his sins to ride a phantom ship around the world for eternity. For hundreds of years, sailors have claimed to have seen his ship during storms. Wagner, who sets the opera's first act off the Norwegian coast, has the sea cast the captain onto land every seven years to search for a woman who will be faithful to him unto death. Only then can the curse be broken.

Like Gib, Dick is half Norwegian, so I ask if his Norwegian grandfather had ever mentioned the legend.

He laughs. "Doubt he ever heard of it. He came from farming stock on my mother's side."

"What about your paternal grandfather?"

"Now *he* could have seen the Dutchman," he jokes. "In the 1890s he built *The Crusader*, a seventy-eight-foot schooner, in Pender Harbour. His plan was to make money delivering freight up and down the BC Coast."

"But there wouldn't have been enough settlements to make it worth his while, would it?"

"Actually, there were, but he was too late. Steam vessels had started to come into their own by that time."

"More reliable."

He nods and picks up the record player's tone arm. "So he and his family used the schooner for a couple of years, travelling up and down the coast, living off the land until they settled on Texada Island. That's where my father was born, and from there they moved to Nelson Island."

"What happened to the schooner?"

"Sold. Cut in half and rebuilt as a tugboat. One of these days I'll show you the drawings he did on the schooner and some of his ship's logs from the 1890s." Carefully he lowers the stylus onto the record.

This is the first time I have listened to music alone with Dick and it is different from listening to music with anyone else. I sense an acute receptiveness in the room, as if he is processing the musical language on a far deeper level than others I have shared my listening with. I'm surprised how it heightens my own enjoyment and understanding, even of a Wagner opera that I have only heard once.

Every day at Gib's, around lunchtime, I find myself anticipating Dick's phone calls, but I tell myself that a call might mean nothing other than that he is feeling sorry for me. However, our hour or so of conversation passes so fast that it is hard to believe that he and I have so much to share and discuss. Why haven't we communicated like this before? We can't both have changed that much since we first met at Gib's two and a half years previously.

While Gordon waits for me to come back to him, my friends tell me he continues to socialize in the pubs and the Legions. Even when I phone to tell him that I am seeking the advice of a lawyer, he does not take me seriously until I give him the date and time of my appointment.

During the second ferry crossing that particular day I stay inside my Beetle, parked beside an open door that leads to the engine room on the car deck. Against the background of a clackety diesel powerhouse I start rehashing the past, reflecting how I have made a mess of my life. Suddenly the passenger door opens and Gordon pokes his head inside, face sunken, eyelids heavy. Remembering the time of my lawyer's appointment, he had guessed that I would be on this ferry.

He sits beside me. "So you're determined to go ahead with this stupid idea?"

"I'm going for some advice."

"We'll get over this, believe me."

"It's happened too often," I say in a monotone. "We're not suited."

"Please, just one more chance."

I shake my head. "You don't understand. How can you know what I'm going through when you black out after two drinks?"

"We could go for counselling."

"I'd be willing, but it wouldn't make any difference."

"I can't live without you ..."

Broken only by his sobs, Gordon's incessant pleading drags me down until I feel the most horrible guilt. But why should I? Searching for a mental lifeboat, I tune in to the gritty sound of the ship's hard-working engine. This ferry hasn't broken down for years. I, too, have always been reliable. Gordon has chosen his own destructive lifestyle, and it has almost destroyed me. Six years of compromise is far too long.

For the rest of the journey, nothing new is said, and Gordon returns to Langdale on the same ship.

After hearing about my husband's behaviour, the lawyer can suggest no immediate solution. "It would be a lot easier if he'd beaten you up," he says, "otherwise, the three-year separation period for desertion would be the simplest ... and of course, there's always infidelity."

Either way, I have left Gordon for good. The following day I move into the vacant cottage.

Less than a week later, Dick phones to tell me that he is about to start work on the *Snark*'s hull. Curious, I visit the workshop at the top of his driveway where I find the manta ray-like boat cradled in its trailer. "What are you going to do to it?" I ask.

"Add some fibreglass strakes. Longitudinal ridges. Should help it plane better."

"Being without a boat must drive you crazy."

He nods. "Sure does. My partner does my rounds in the *Styx*— that little iron tug—but it's so slow. You can't work the beaches with that thing."

"Your competitors will be happy," I joke.

"I'd just as soon not be reminded," he growls then turns to the workbench and points to a block of blackish-grey rock the size of a four-gallon milk carton. "Here, come and look at this."

I gaze at it and feel its cold, waxy surface. "What is it?"

"Soapstone ... and so is this," he adds, lifting something out of a small box nearby. He hands me a heavy little ornament about six inches by three, a greenish-grey seal on a rock. Apart from the different colour, the graining in this piece is finer, almost non-existent. "I thought you might like to try to make one of your own."

I am taken aback. "What a wonderful idea." I slide my hands over the sculpture, stroking it, imagining the bones and muscles that gave it form, exploring the cold, smooth soapstone with its flowing lines. When I close my eyes for a moment, it feels complete, perfect, well-balanced. The carver must have spent days sanding, rubbing, working the roughness out of it. Even though the seal is resting on a rock I sense how its fluid shape helps it move through the water.

"It's carved by an Eskimo," he tells me. "I borrowed it from the Hendricksons next door." Then he explains that the previous owner of the soapstone block was Alex Znotin, an artist who lived in a shack three lots down from the Boatworks, and who had once been a foot soldier in the White Russian army. "He told me that Rasputin was a smallish man with a big moustache and the biggest feet he'd ever seen ... and that his eyes burned right through you." When I plead forgetfulness about the Rasputin/Tzar Nicholas history, Dick reminds me of it in such an interesting way that I wonder if he's making some of it up.

"Did you learn about him in school?"

He shakes his head. "I learned very little in school. I hated it, probably because they accelerated me by two years."

"They wouldn't do that today," I tell him. "It tends to encourage bullying."

"At least it forced me to learn self-defence ... Even though I took grade thirteen by correspondence and graduated when I was sixteen, most of what I know I learned myself. Reading."

"What kind of stuff?"

"Philosophy attracted me when I was twelve. I'd borrow stacks of books at a time from the huge library in Victoria. They'd send them by mail. There were a lot of interesting people around here, most of them highly educated, and I'd borrow their books, too. My employer, Pop Jackson, was one. We'd have discussions about all kinds of things."

"Did you go to university?"

"After my teachers had tested my IQ, they tried to persuade me to go to Cal Tec, but I knew I'd never be able to cope with the crowds." Turning to adjust something on the boat, he finishes, "But that's enough about me."

"When can I start carving?" I ask.

"Whenever you want. I never lock the door."

As usual, my curiosity gets the better of me, and before I leave, I casually ask—stating it was purely from a teacher's point of view—what his IQ was.

"It's not important," he says, "but they told me it was 169."

We spend at least a couple of hours a day working side by side in the workshop. Carving my seal from the soapstone block is very therapeutic, even if it is against my impulsive nature. Using chisels, rasps and sandpaper to make the basic shape is challenging and slow, and I am forced to think well ahead because once I have chiselled a piece out, I can't replace it. Construction by removal ... Isn't that what I've done with Gordon?

Dick, however, is constructing his boat by addition. He lies on his back on the newspaper-covered floor, sticky resin dripping down his arms, painstakingly fabricating strakes onto the hull. He places fibreglass strips soaked in resin, adding them layer by layer, covering them with a piece of polythene and applying pressure with thin plywood sheets propped by sticks. A heat lamp accelerates the hardening process. He never complains when a piece of plywood falls out of place before the resin has hardened; he takes it all in his stride—a challenge, he tells me—and tries again.

Then one day after we have finished in the shop, as he takes the hand whisk and gently brushes the fine grey soapstone dust off my clothes, I sense that something different has entered our companionable relationship, that he is feeling the shape of my body in a way that is both remote yet intimate. I say nothing, order myself to feel nothing, but I do not back off. While this tacit connection between us makes me want to communicate to him in a far deeper way, I am fearful. His eyes attract me, but I am afraid to gaze into them. I don't think I am quite on his wavelength ... yet. His quietness often makes me wonder what he is thinking. Perhaps it's just that I am used to Gordon's louder and frequent vocalizing; seven years with one person is a long time.

The fibreglassing is completed in ten days, and as soon as the last strake has been dried and sanded, he phones me. "Ready for the trial run? The sea's calm."

I wander down to the public launching ramp a block away and watch him back the *Snark* into the harbour. After parking car and trailer, we go for a two-mile test run from the beacon to Langdale ferry dock. There he makes a tight U-turn at high speed so that the boat skips scarily sideways, then he steers, still at top speed, toward the dock at Hopkins Landing.

"Duck!" he yells, aiming for one of the gaps between the pilings. But I am prepared. We miss the planks above by at least a couple of feet.

"Getting braver!" he yells. He must have seen the grin on my face.

"Do you want me to tell you how it looks from the dock?" I ask.

"Sure." He doubles back to drop me off before making a straight run at high revs. Even with my inexperienced eyes, the *Snark*'s jet wash viewed side-on and from a distance looks so different from those of propeller-driven boats. The powerful but narrow column of water emerging from the nozzle travels beneath the surface for about ten feet behind the boat's stern then gradually rises in a long and graceful curve before falling back into the sea, where it spreads out into two extended, foaming waves enclosing a flat wake. This boat's unique hull adds its own signature to the way it rides the water. If someone ever asked me what speed looks like, I would tell them to watch the *Snark* doing forty-five knots. Its beauty brings a lump to my throat.

"Impressive!" I shout as he collects me.

"Let's take a run around the islands," he says, and wheels the *Snark* toward Keats' northern shore.

Within fifteen minutes we're about half a mile off Pasley Island when he suddenly slows to an idle. I look around for an explanation. Then I see it. A few feet from the boat, a deer—a doe, its head barely visible—bobs aimlessly. It is obviously close to drowning.

Dick pulls one of his shorter, thicker ropes from under the bow.

"We'll give her a bit of help," he says. But the deer is scared and the adrenaline has given it a second wind. Dick manoeuvres the hull to pull alongside the animal and fastens the rope loosely around its neck. "Put the loop over the side cleat!" he directs, then slowly tows the exhausted animal alongside the gunwale toward the shore until its feet hit the sea-covered boulders. He shuts off the engine, hands me the long pole to keep the boat still, then jumps out to untie the rope. "I'll try to guide it to shore," he says. The deer just stands there half out of the water, swaying for a moment before falling.

"It's hypothermic," he explains. He picks it up, hoists it over his shoulders, and clambers over the submerged boulders toward the low grassy bank. After lowering the stricken doe gently to the ground, he retreats twenty feet and watches for a minute before returning to the *Snark*.

"She'll make it," he assures me, pulling himself up onto the stern. "Probably been chased by dogs. Must've lost her sense of direction after being in the cold water so long. It happens sometimes."

Outside the harbour he slows, and I ask if he is happy with the strakes. "Definitely," he replies, "but there's still room for improvement."

As I walk back to my cottage, I hear myself singing a Mozart aria I had learned for my final music exam at college. But when I answer the phone later that afternoon, a mutual friend who has been boarding Gordon informs me that he is recuperating from an overdose of sleeping pills or tranquillizers. Knowing that he has friends for support, I steel myself against guilt and order myself not to become involved.

6

Mount Elphinstone

Friday, May 1, 1970, dawns bright and hot. Gazing up at my favourite miniature hanging beside my bed, I try to will at least some of the Lady in Green's beauty into my own face. The sparkle in her eyes must surely be an illusion caused by the early morning sunlight.

After breakfast, Dick's Citroën Pallas DS21—the only one in Gibsons—pulls up. He wants to show me a view of the Georgia Strait from yet another angle, the top of Mount Elphinstone. Two days earlier when I had run into Gib at Ken's Lucky Dollar store, I told him that Dick was taking me up the mountain, and he had warned, "Don't get your hopes too high. His type's not interested in women." To which I'd responded, "Oh, I'm only going for the view." Why is Gib so certain about Dick's sexual preference?

I sling my duffle bag on my shoulder and meet Dick at the gate. "I hope you took the morning off?" I remark, referring to his daybreak log salvage "rounds."

"Of course not," he replies. "Glad you're wearing jeans. It can be quite brushy up there … Did you pack a lunch?"

"Enough for two." Why is my breathing shallow? Why does the sun seem exceptionally brilliant? Even the chink of sea between the houses opposite has a startling glow. There is something different about Dick's manner, too, a tenseness perhaps.

Five miles out of the village we turn right off the highway onto a dirt logging road, and Dick pulls over to raise the lever that hydraulically lifts the chassis. "That'll avoid most of the rocks," he explains. Several minutes later we begin to climb, but we pass so many crossroads and turnoffs that I am hopelessly lost, mainly because I can't see the sea for the tall conifers that curtain both sides of the logging road. Their shadows tell me that we are travelling north until we turn east onto a steep, almost undriveable creek-bed-like road.

"How do you know where you're going?" I ask.

"I helped put in most of these logging roads for Pop Jackson."

"Jackson's Logging in Wilson Creek?"

He nods. "Father was his boom foreman. I lived with them and did a few things in the camp, including work as a timber cruiser, and I helped Grandpa Mart, the strong Norwegian. He was their blacksmith."

"I've never heard of a timber cruiser."

"They're forest surveyors. You walk through a stand of timber to identify species and size for prospective loggers." He stops the car on the edge of a huge rut that diagonally crosses the ascending road, climbs out, glances at it, then throws a couple of large, flattish boulders into it before driving the car across.

A few yards on, another deep rut presents itself. "Why don't they fill these in?" I complain.

"They're cross-ditches, necessary for drainage. Otherwise the roads would wash out." He finds several old shakes on the side of the road and throws them into the rut before driving very slowly across. "But if they're not maintained, the cross-ditches themselves get washed out, particularly on disused roads like this."

Three of them are so deep that, even with its extra height, the car scrapes its exhaust pipe. A couple of hundred feet further on, he stops in front of another, gets out, surveys it from both sides, then leans in the window. "Good place to leave the car."

He lifts a couple of rugs out of the back and throws them over his shoulder, while I carry the lunch bag.

"Not far now," he says as we make our way uphill, pushing through dense waist-high alder saplings that are recolonizing the logging road.

He has made the right decision because the next two cross-ditches are impassable, even for a Jeep. But when we come to a fifteen-foot log— all that remains of an old bridge across a steep ravine and turbulent creek—I wait for guidance. Further upstream, a series of small rapids intermittently pushes a cooling breeze down to us.

"Hmm," he says. "Didn't expect this." He takes my duffle bag and carries it across with the rugs. With cat-like steps, he pads back toward me, stops suddenly over the middle of the ravine and stands motionless for a few moments, as if he and the log were one solid statue. Six more wide steps then he leaps off and alights beside me. "How's your balance?" he asks.

"I'll be okay as long as I don't look down." The water is several feet below the log, but I know it will feel twice that once I'm crossing it. "Is it slippery?"

"You should be okay with those shoes." With one foot on the log, he holds his hand out to me. "Here. Grab my hand."

I think about the time when he first helped me into the boat after showing me the seals. But this is completely different. As I stretch toward him, my hand seems to act independently, pulling the rest of me over the icy torrent. We touch … Gone is the firm politeness of his first handshake. Although it is supplanted by tenderness, there is power too, a strength, both physical and mental. He is to be trusted. Even if I were to lose my footing, he would not let me fall … And then he seems to sense my sudden wish to pause halfway, so that I can feel the exhilarating cool draft from the rapids against my red-hot cheeks in this midday heat. But it is not enough. Gazing down at the greenish turbulence, I know that my face will not stop burning as long as I stand here holding his hand.

On the other side I thank him and let go of his grip. He regards me quizzically, smiles, then adds, "You did well."

I laugh, trying to make light of it. "Only because I knew you were strong enough to stop me falling if I lost my balance."

Rather than give the impression that I am attracted to him, I step away and pick up the duffle. Just past the creek, around a bend in the road, I catch sight of a steep boggy bank crammed with miniscule plants of various kinds. My guide follows me and listens to my exclamations of delight as I investigate this miniature vertical water garden close up. Tiny waterfalls no more than two inches wide and less than a foot long tumble down the bank. Underneath them, constantly fed by drops and trickles of water that exude from the gravelly clay, various ferns, mosses and liverworts crowd together, their brilliant and multi-hued greens set off from the patches of pale lichens amongst them. It must be the sunny clear air up here that gives these plants such an exquisite vibrancy. Then, thinking of my patient partner, I turn away. "Sorry. I'm holding you back."

He seems a little embarrassed. "You're not. I brought you here to show you these things."

"Everything's so new to me."

"I think there's more to it than that," he says quietly. As we continue our climb, I wonder what he means.

"Here we are," he declares at last.

But there's nothing around us except two thick walls of trees either side of a slight widening in the road, a place, perhaps, where a logging truck might stop to allow another to pass. He turns off to the right and, beckoning me to follow, pushes into the brushy perimeter. A few hundred feet into the dark forest, too dark for brush to grow, chinks of sky peep through distant tree trunks. I hesitate beside a twenty-foot-high conifer growing from the top of an old stump. The young tree has sent out several muscular-looking brown roots that snake straight down its rotting host's remains before disappearing into the ground.

"It's growing from a nurse tree," he explains. "The seedlings don't always do well after the nurse rots out." He holds his hand up. "Listen!" And as we stand motionless, the faint sound of the wind in the treetops filters downwards to my ears.

"How would you describe that?" I whisper. "Fir trees don't rustle, they don't sigh."

"True. But there is an old word that fits," he says. "Soughing."

"Soughing," I echo. "Longer and gentler than sighing."

Moments later we come upon a clearing.

While he lays the rugs a couple of feet apart under a tall pine, I stare at the view, briefly distracted by a long-forgotten memory from the time my family left Bognor and moved two miles inland. So intensely did I miss my connection with the sea that I'd often stand and stare from my bedroom window across the farmers' fields and use strange tricks of light and perspective to transform the distance into what I really yearned for. It worked so well that I would sometimes awake thinking I was still living by the sea.

But this view from the mountain is real and mesmerizing. And it is mine.

In front of us the logging slash falls steeply away into a vast forested plateau—a magnificent green carpet that extends for miles. And beyond it, the Strait of Georgia is a glowing, shimmering liquid. We must be on a mountain shoulder because, if I turn my eyes from the Langdale ferry dock in the east, I can follow the pale body of water all the way to the west where grey-blue Lasquiti and Texada islands arise from it. And protecting it all from the wildness of the Pacific Ocean, the mountain range of Vancouver Island stands on the far side of the Strait … So this is where the *Canadian Star* has brought me.

A curious raven wings its way noisily past us then catches a hot air current. As it begins its hovering circular ascent, I set the duffle between us, and sit cross-legged on one of the rugs.

For a while we both gaze out at the Strait. The silence feels natural, as if both of us know that conversation will detract from the moment. I attempt to subdue the underlying excitement that threatens to spring up in my mind, try to relax. The warm air rises from below, wafts against my skin, begs to be inhaled, but not too deeply. I close my eyes, smell the forest's perfume set free by the sun's heat, of green needles, pitch oozing from bark, moss and fungi amongst soil moistened by water fresh from the winter snows.

A buzzing over our heads shocks my eyes open. A hummingbird hovers, then faster than I can follow its movements, it dives lower and hovers again, this time only a couple of feet in front of us, squeaking and squawking. Then, without warning, it rockets upwards to repeat the diving and hovering manoeuvre.

Dick laughs. "Belligerent little beasts," he says. "He's telling us we're too close to its nest … or he's putting on a display for his mate."

"You mean showing off," I tell him.

After a short pause he says, "You know, I really enjoy your company. You never feel compelled to fill the silences."

I explain that I feel the same way about him, but I don't mention that his silences seemed strange at first because I was so used to Gordon.

The hummingbird dives a little closer. "I suppose you've guessed," he says casually, "I have been looking for someone."

"Andy says you're too fussy," I tell him.

"I've had a couple of girlfriends, but ... well, I couldn't imagine spending my whole life with them."

"Were they bad cooks?" I ask, recalling what he had told Andy the night we had watched the comet.

He turns to me and smiles. "It's not just that."

"Classical music?"

"Naturally ... and other things ..."

The hummingbird actually brushes my hair with its wings. Dick pretends to try to catch it. We laugh.

"What about you?" he says, stealing a glance at me. "Are you looking for someone?"

My cheeks are aflame. I can't think. "Yes." I didn't mean to say that. I wanted to say, *Yes, you,* but the words I speak seem to be bypassing my brain. "But I'm not interested in shallow affairs."

"Neither am I," he says, his voice barely audible. "I've been waiting for you to make up your—"

"But I'm not a virgin," I blurt out. When I hear the blatant despair in my voice I realize that my deeply ingrained fear has held me back from him.

He snorts, laughs and leans back, face up to the cloudless sky. "Neither am I!"

"But I thought all men wanted to marry virgins. Gordon did."

"That's just a lot of stupid religious nonsense. He's a lapsed Catholic, isn't he?"

I nod. "I went to a convent too ..."

He sits up. "I've been wondering what was going on in your mind." Shaking his head, he explains, "Virginity is absolutely irrelevant to me, it is so ludicrous ... you have no idea."

With a few tears of relief I turn away from the view just in time to see him leaning toward me. We grab for the duffle bag at the same moment, but he allows me to move it out of the way. And as he curls his arm around my shoulder, I look long into his eyes for the first time "I hadn't noticed," I whisper.

"What?"

"Your eyes. They're sea-washed ..." Even his face smells of the sea.

"Hungry?" he asks after our first kiss.

"I can wait ..."

Taking pity on the frenetic but surely tiring hummingbird, we carry our rugs beneath the next tree and place them together.

"Happy?" he asks.

I bundle the empty sandwich bags. "That's not the right word. It's happier than happy," I try to explain. "I've never felt that way before. Not with anyone or anything. Believe me."

He lifts my left hand, twists a piece of fern about my naked ring finger. "And ... I do want to marry you."

The distant waters of the Strait lie quiescent, suspended in place and time, waiting.

I snatch a breath. "I thought you'd be the unconventional type."

"Marriage isn't convention," he argues. "It's a commitment."

Commitment. From the way he lingers on the word, weighs it—but not blatantly so—I know he has considered it at length. That's the way he is. He chooses his words carefully, sparingly. He is the only man I have ever trusted. I know he would lay down his life for me.

Gordon's interpretation of commitment flashes alarmingly. "I agree ... but ... what about the divorce?"

Spotting a spider on his leg, Dick picks it up, taking care not to squash it, and throws it out of harm's way. "We can always let Gordon cite me as co-respondent. It's no skin off my nose."

The rest of my afternoon on the mountain is a blur of unalloyed happiness, an enchanted state so unexpectedly powerful that it overrides most of my physical sensations, and on the hike back to the Citroën it even supplies one of its own: the oddest feeling of weightlessness, of soaring.

Then as we begin the drive down the mountain in near darkness, Dick asks, "So how come you didn't have a problem crossing that old log bridge just now?"

I tell him the truth, that I can't even recall my surroundings during the hike back, that I was only aware of the sky. He stops the car beside a tree stump, and as we embrace again a thought flashes through my mind: So much for those under the illusion that only gay men appreciate fine arts. It can mean the total opposite.

A sudden movement on the stump catches my eyes. I nudge him. "There's something outside your window!"

He turns his head so slowly that it is almost imperceptible. As he does so, we hear the sound of metal being sharpened. "A saw-whet owl," he whispers. "That's its call. Like a saw being sharpened. Flashlight's under your seat. Don't move. I'll get it."

He must be used to tracking or watching animals because he manages to slide the flashlight out so stealthily that I am not aware he is holding it until he aims the beam at the tiny owl. It is about eight inches long with its stubby tail, and I can clearly see reddish-flecked discs around each staring yellow eye, and a white chest with reddish streaks. It seems to be mesmerized by the light.

"It looks angry."

Laughing, he turns the light off. "It is. We've interrupted its evening hunt."

We continue the night drive down the logging road. "I remember watching a large owl hunting vermin in a Scottish sheep pasture almost three years ago," I begin. But as I tell him about Gordon running out of gas on our way to the *Canadian Star* at Glasgow Docks, it feels as if I'm talking about another person.

After much procrastinating, I write to my mother and stepfather to inform them, without any explanation, that I have left Gordon. When their return aerogramme reply exhorts me to return to England to stay in their house, I explain I am quite happy where I am, that everything is under control, and that they should not be concerned.

I have only been living in my cottage a couple of weeks when my next-door neighbour stops me in the driveway to inform me that I have a peeping tom. He shows me a couple of wood blocks stacked outside my high bedroom window and describes how, two nights ago, he had returned late from visiting a friend and had seen someone in shorts running out of my yard. The following night he had seen the stranger actually looking in through the same window before driving off in an open sports car. The neighbour hadn't phoned the police because he had thought it might have been my ex-husband.

As soon as I tell Dick that afternoon, he frowns, pauses, then mutters, "I don't like the idea of you in that place alone. I think it best if you stay here tonight."

I don't argue. I just ask if I can come out with him on his morning round.

"Sure," he says, "but you might change your mind when it's four o'clock and still dark outside."

"So an early rising wife wasn't on your want list?"

He shakes his head. "Not at all. That's my job."

"But you wouldn't mind if I came?"

"'Course not."

Under the gold-coloured bedspread that night, the sea enters my sleep again, but unlike the old dreams where the sea prevented me from escaping, it is warm, dark and filled with phosphorescence. As consciousness returns, the overwhelming feeling that I am cherished lingers.

His work-roughened hand alights softly upon my breast. "Are you sure you want to get up this early?" he whispers.

With an energy I have never felt before, I leap out of the twin bed. "Got any cornflakes?"

7

My First Morning Round

The Boatworks' pale yard light is just bright enough to illuminate our way along the chain of floats leading to the *Snark*. Dick's waders slap and brush noisily together, disturbing the sleeping mallards and Canada geese who cackle their annoyance and flutter off the planks into the black water. Moored to the other side of the end float lies the dark and silent *Styx*, Dick's partner's tug.

I hold the flashlight over *Snark*'s engine while Dick tops up the engine oil. "Do they stay open all night?" I ask, noticing that the fuel dock's office is also brightly lit.

He slams the engine cover shut, startling a pair of mallards observing us from the Boatworks' live bait herring pond. "Nope. But they'll open for emergencies … if a boat's sinking or has a line tangled in its prop. Okay," he says looking up to me on the float. "Let's do it right this time. May I, Madame?"

And I grab his arm, thrilling to test his strength as I climb in beside him.

He steers to port around the government dock and out of the harbour, but the boat is still moving slowly, barely planing. "Warming the engine," he explains.

A refreshing land breeze gently dusts sleep from my face, and within a minute we're travelling about thirty-five knots due east, straight into the darkness.

"No lights?" I shout into his ear.

"See better without."

It takes only a few seconds for my eyes to adjust and then, against the navy sky, the Coast range presents itself, a mere suggestion of glow revealing its stark peaks. Something inside me switches on and my senses suddenly become super-acute. Even my tongue tastes salt in the air. Dew melts on my cheeks, tingling, evaporating, as the fleeing night rushes past. There is an urgency to our travel, an appointment to be kept, a meeting with the morning.

The engine sounds different, too. It must be the slight swell lingering on the calm surface from the previous day's westerly that causes the boat's pulsing movement, affecting the jet's wash behind us. And it might be an echo from Keats Island to our left, a sound barely audible over the engine that generates it. I lean back and gaze up at the sky, from the northeast to the east, and over Bowen to the south.

An unusually bright shooting star arcs above Keats. I nudge Dick. "Meteor!"

He'd caught it, too. "An Eta Aquarid," he yells over the engine. "Lucky to see one. Average five an hour."

Aquarid from Aquarius, another name for Ganymede, the shepherd boy captured by Zeus to become the water bearer for the Gods on Mount Olympus. I had watched the Perseid shower from the *Canadian Star* as we sailed northward from Panama, past the Mexican coast. They were far more prolific with fifty to eighty an hour, but this lone one, seen on my first night with Dick, is far more symbolic. I make a wish.

After turning a few degrees to port just past the ferry slip, my attention is drawn far up the inlet by some lights so bright that their reflection shimmers with the power of a full moon.

Without warning, Dick flashes his hand-held searchlight at a log only a few feet away. He stops the engine and grabs—with his left hand—a yellow rope several feet long from the rubber bucket at my feet. As the *Snark* half turns from inertia and gently heaves-to, he swings—right-handedly—a large single-bladed axe into the log to stabilize it. He pulls the blade out, changes hands and uses the flat side to tap something metal into it before leaping behind the seat to fasten the end of the rope to the stern cleat—a perfectly linked series of manoeuvres totalling less than eight seconds.

"What did you do just then?" I ask.

He shines the light into the rope bucket and points at several of these half-inch-diameter ropes, each one connected by a triangular stainless steel coldshut link to the eye of a metal spike about five or six inches long. The other rope end has been spliced into a loop. "Pickup lines," he says. "That metal spike is a 'dog.'"

"How did you know that log was there?"

"Reflections from the lights."

And we're off, aiming for the two tiny islands near the ferry route off Gambier Island where he ties his log to an anchored buoy, stamping the end of it with a long-handled hammer. "My licence number," he explains, depressing the accelerator with his right foot. I grab the stamp hammer and shine the flashlight at a square face with a mirror image of LS 608 cast in high relief. As we turn east, hugging Gambier's shore, I lean back against the engine cover again and watch the dimming stars.

Another stop. In the calm lemon sea of dawn, a black strip turns into a log with two more close by. I hand him a pickup line.

And after the three logs have been secured over the stern cleat, he lifts a bundle of long, thicker rope from beside the engine cover and threads one end of it though all three eyes, tying them together before throwing them and the knot overboard behind the stern. The other end of the long line is looped over the cleat.

"Why the long rope?"

"If they're further away from the jet wash," he explains, "they'll tow faster."

Over the steep, black mountains the glow intensifies so relentlessly, so dramatically, I imagine trolls running for cover under the craggy hanging valleys above. But when I gaze back to Shoal Channel twelve miles away to the west, the pale-blue Strait beyond is already glimmering, calmly preparing itself for the day.

Dick steals a glance at me. He smiles—perhaps a little abashed at being discovered—turns the engine off, then curves his right arm about my shoulder to pull me close. I smell only the sea on his skin ... taste the salt on his lips. "You're a sea troll, a *sjötrollet*," I tell him. Being half-Norwegian and interested in folklore, he'd know that a *sjötrollet* cares for and protects the sea. That is his job, too.

"Lucky for you *sjötrollet*s are benevolent," he quips, slowly steering the *Snark* past a large bay, toward another buoy in a small cove.

"I wouldn't be here if they weren't," I retort.

Just short of the cove, he reverses to stop the *Snark*'s forward motion, shoves the gear lever into neutral and leaps back to the stern. As he neatly gathers up the long towrope on his arm, the three logs on its far end continue to drift toward us under their own inertia. Swiftly he unties them and slips the loops their pickup lines over the stern cleat before towing and tying them to the buoy. The rocky beach behind it is gentle enough, but the brushy bank rises steeply. There's no sign of a house here.

He coils the long rope and stows it beside the engine cover. "Alan'll pick them up in the *Styx* later."

"How many buoys do you have?"

"Including the ones out at the islands, eleven … and a couple of tie-ups hammered into the cliffs up the inlet."

I point back to a large bay that we had barely entered, one filled with log booms and, lying peacefully alongside one, a couple of tugs. "Nothing in there?"

He decelerates so that he can make himself heard. "Log owners don't like salvors in storage areas. They think they steal."

"Do they?"

"A few. And those usually rationalize their behaviour."

Does he? Gib has always said he has a reputation for being a truly honest log salvor. "It's one of the things that makes him a loner," he had told me the day I left his place to move into the Hammonds' rental cottage. "Makes the other kind feel second class, if you know what I mean."

Anxious to get going again, Dick steers out of the cove, around the next promontory and into a half-mile-wide bay, where several large pleasure yachts are moored to the little rocky island in its centre. "Alexandra Island, Vancouver Yacht Club's moorage!" he shouts, zooming past them. Ignoring the log booms tied near the head of the mile-and-a half-long bay, he aims for the rocky shore below a summer cabin on the far side, where he collects a couple of floating logs. He tows them for a short distance then ties them to a buoy inside a shady, protected cove.

Not far above the tide line stands a grassy orchard of several fruit trees, their delicate half-blown blossoms echoing the paleness of the early morning. But moments later, after securing the anchored logs, we emerge staring straight at the sun now blazing on top of the mountain ridge.

As Dick steps on the accelerator, it is my turn to steal a glance at him. His face is gold. I hold up my bare arm, golden too. Assuming that he is totally preoccupied with his search for logs, I'm surprised when he comments, "Yes," he says. "I never tire of it."

Surely he can't know what I'm thinking. "What?"

"The early morning light," he replies then makes a sharp, high-speed turn left into another longer bay. "Long Bay!" he shouts, pointing upwards to starboard where a steep mountain plunges into the still green water, shading it from the early sun. "Mount Artaban!"

Along the shore below the forest to our left, a few shuttered cabins and houses wait for their owners to return and set their rooms echoing again. Almost each dwelling has its own dock because there are no roads on this part of the island.

But one house is inhabited. Smoke drifts straight upwards from its chimney, and considering today's warm weather it must be from a cooking stove. The dock is the same type as the one at the Boatworks, a planked walk on creosote pilings that leads to a mooring float via an articulated ramp. It is painted the same dark green and grey as the house—an old one by Canadian standards, perhaps from the 1920s. Tied to the float is another piece of history, a wooden boat with cabin, also grey and green. An old man waves from the deck as we pass by.

"Cece Huggins," says Dick, aiming for a large log about three hundred feet away. He shuts the engine off and waits until the hull drifts against the log. "And this is one he won't get," he mutters, hammering the dog into it.

"Is he a log salvor?"

"For years," he says, nodding towards the stored booms further inside the bay.

As we drive across the ferry route, I glance back at Langdale ter-minal, a few miles to the northwest, where the day's first ferry awaits

its release. And facing south toward Bowen to our port side, I have no trouble picking out the M-shaped forest on Mount Gardiner. Between it and Keats' southern shore the water is still wave-free, and while the swell from the previous day's westerly is more pronounced here, the sea's surface is smooth enough to mirror the green islands of the Pasley group. But as the *Snark* accelerates, it flies off each watery mound and lands with an uncomfortable and noisy thump. Every time we are airborne the jet sucks air through the grill underneath, causing the impellors and the engine that drives them to over-rev until the hull sits on the water again. "The jet's cavitating," he says.

I don't mind the roaring but the landing scares me. It feels as if the whole boat is going to split open. Dick must have seen me wincing because he eases off the throttle pedal until the hull remains in constant touch with the sea. "Blowing out in the Gulf all night," he explains.

"Gulf or Strait?" I shout.

"Either."

Then, without warning, he accelerates until we are travelling even faster than before. There is an urgency in the way he stands, a rigidity in his body, head jutting forward, eyes squinting straight ahead. He is silent. Is there something wrong? With me? I daren't ask.

He just stares ahead, tense, isolated … a glance to starboard, then forward again. White-knuckled hands grip the black steering wheel. What has he seen? A white wake two miles to starboard. From a speed-boat? Two or three miles straight ahead of us, not far from Bowen's southwesterly point, a dark strip glints in the sun. I grab the starboard gunwale with my right hand.

Has my presence delayed him? If I hadn't asked so many questions, he would have been out here earlier.

The other boat—an avocado green—is also heading that way. It seems to have a speed advantage because it's in the lee of a relatively long island where the water is flatter. But moments later as it hits the heaving Strait, it slows, sending great sheets of white water flying from each side of its bow each time it lands in the deep troughs.

Inside *Snark*, meanwhile, ropes, buckets, axes, tools, chains and other items I'm ignorant about fly up and crash down with every leap.

Dick obviously has only one thing on his mind: the large log ahead. For the first time I notice the black rev counter in the dash. Its white needle has passed the 4,500 mark, spiking even higher with each jet cavitation. We must be travelling at forty knots or more. Even though we're approaching the log from a different angle, we are definitely gaining on the green boat.

But as soon as we are within a quarter of a mile of the log, the speedboat—more than twice that distance away from it—turns abruptly and disappears behind one of the islands. Immediately Dick decelerates, shuts the engine off and lifts the cover, asking me to hand him the old plastic milk jug under the bow. "Just in time," he mutters, pouring water into the expansion tank. "Must have a slight leak in the cooling system."

"Competitor?"

He nods. "He knew I'd beat him to it." Job done, we're off again, slower this time, until he draws alongside his prize. Even to my uneducated eye this log is fatter and longer than the others he has found today. It is also very smooth, without knots, and the diameter at each end appears the same.

He swings the axe blade into it. "You brought me luck."

I'm very relieved.

"A fir peeler," he volunteers.

Underway with it at the end of the long towline behind us, he explains, "The mills pay extra for these. Special machines 'peel' them longitudinally from the outside in. Makes good, knot-free plywood veneer."

He ties it to his buoy inside one of the island bays, stamping it several times in different places, adding, "Just in case it decides to roam." Then he explains that his competitor's boat is also a jet, but unlike the *Snark's* three-stage coupled to a V8 engine, it only has a two-stage model connected to a smaller V6 in a deep V hull.

Two bays further on we spot another log, but it's high above the tide line on a rocky beach. "Hard pull," he says. "I'll have to put a roll on it and set up a skid to get it over that large boulder."

Whatever he means, it must be the reason why his competitor had not bothered with it.

He turns the engine off and allows the *Snark* to drift. From under the gunwale he pulls out a long aluminum pole with a double prong on one end, and sticks it down into the shallow water until it hits boulders. "Could you hold the boat? If the tide's too strong for you, just let it go."

Carrying the chain end of the long thick pulling line, he vaults into the waist-deep water and wades quickly toward the beach, practically running over the boulders above the tide line. He threads the large hook under the log, encircling it with the chain before hooking into a link to close the circle. After he has rolled the chain circle three times, I can see its purpose. Then he places a flat piece of driftwood to make a skid-like ramp against the obstructing boulder.

It is not easy to keep the boat stationary. A powerful current swirls around the bay, trying to sweep the boat out of position, but I'm more than a match for it.

Hauling himself aboard, he loops the other end of the pulling line around the cleat on the stern and grabs the pike pole from me to slide it back under the gunwale. He starts the motor. "Sit down and hold on!" he warns.

I grip the edge of the dash, tense myself and turn to watch. As the line pulls taut, the log—parallel to the water's edge—rolls downwards, gathering momentum. It hits the driftwood skid with full force, flying several feet into the air and over the boulder before crashing down into the water with a huge splash. But its slightly wider butt catches against a partly submerged rock. The *Snark* comes to an unforgiving halt then recoils as the stretched line retracts like a rubber band. My head nearly hits the top of the windshield and a deluge of sea water cascades over the stern, sloshing against my seat and back. In spite of the warning, I am taken by surprise.

He turns off the engine. "Bilge pump'll take care of the water. It's automatic."

Aiming the boat out at a different angle on the next pull solves the problem, and seconds later the log is lying next to the gunwale a few hundred feet offshore. He unhooks the heavy line, and as he coils it into the back of the boat, I grab the axe and a pickup line.

Climbing over the bench, I lean over the gunwale. "Can I try?"

"Go ahead."

Holding the dog point down with my left hand, I place it two feet from the end of the log as he had done, and with my right hand I grip the axe halfway up the handle so that its flat back hovers just a foot above the dog's eye. As I tap it, the log bounces up and down and rolls from side to side. Must be a swell, perhaps from a distant ferry. The spike falls out. I pull it up and try again, hitting harder, but driving it in barely half an inch. And when I raise the axe higher I miss completely because I hadn't gauged the right moment. "Bloody HELL!" I curse, swinging the axe a fourth time. He laughs. Although I use more force, my anger allows intuition to do the thinking, and it's a bull's eye.

"That's it!" he yells enthusiastically.

I must have hit it slightly off centre because the dog bounces out again and the log floats away out of reach. "Ugh!"

"It's fir," he explains. "Tough and dense. And the dog's new ... with a rounded top so you have to hit it exactly right." He starts the engine and manoeuvres alongside it again. "I'll take over," he says, his

Dick pulling a large log over a boulder above the high-tide line.

hand out to grab the axe.

I shake my head. "I'll try again." Watching the log's movements intently, I hold the dog and tap it in before transferring my left hand to the axe handle, bringing its head down onto the eye as the swell bounces the log upward. There's a satisfying, dull, metallic thwack as I hit it just right, embedding its point about an inch or more into the resisting wood.

"And again!" he hollers.

I gauge the log's upward movement to coincide with the descending axe.

"Two more!"

At last the pickup line is looped over the cleat, but by now the *Snark* is almost on the rocks. Dick poles the boat away from them and restarts the engine.

"Never knew you had it in you," he says.

After the island's circuit yields no more, he allows me to drive the *Snark* back to Gibsons Harbour.

A couple of hundred yards off the government dock, I shift back to the passenger seat on the right, allowing him to take over.

"Don't you want to steer back to the float?" he asks.

"And make a fool of myself?"

"Just joking."

We enter the harbour as Dick's business partner, Alan Jackson, is leaving in the *Styx*. Dick turns the *Snark*, waits until the tug has cleared the northeast breakwater pilings, then draws alongside the cabin. The tantalizing fumes of super-strong coffee waft past my nose.

A chubby, clean-shaven face pokes out of the tug's open window and grins ear to ear, probably because it's the first time he's seen Dick with a girlfriend, one who, from circumstantial evidence, has obviously stayed the night. "'Mornin', Boss! Passenger bring you any luck?"

"Naturally," replies Dick, hurriedly reeling off the list of tie-up buoys from which his partner has to collect today's harvest, strange names, some of which I suspect the pair of them have made up: "Thieves' Bay," "Hjorthoi's," "Pasley tie-up," "Twin Islands," "Goodies'." Then he reminds Alan about delivering a summer float out to one of the islands.

"Will do, Boss," replies Alan, flipping his hat from his pale balding head and slapping it on the tug's dash. "Another hot day," he adds with a grin.

As Dick nods and wheels the *Snark* around the breakwater into the harbour, I'm certain he was too embarrassed to introduce me.

After the last three and a half hours of turmoil the basement's static environment is shockingly quiet. Out in the boat I have been shown a place where sounds are magnified and where—except for towing respites—everything moves at high speed, and if I don't keep up, chaos will result.

As the sudden transition from such surroundings hits me, I am overcome by tiredness. Now I understand why, on my first trip in the boat where Dick had shown me the seals, there had been no time to think of my problems.

I turn to him as he follows me upstairs. "I thought you were Alan's partner, not his boss."

"He always calls me 'boss'," he explains. "It's his idea of a joke."

"Does he ever drive the *Snark*?"

"Only if he has to. He hates fast boats. Not so long ago he took the jet boat out … landed up on top of a log boom in the dark … said his mind couldn't think as fast as the boat. Guess that's why he prefers towing." He checks the kitchen clock. "Time for a couple of hour's shut-eye."

In spite of the bright sun outside I fall asleep easily in the pitch-black bedroom and wake, sweating, around ten, wondering what to do about my living arrangement. But for some reason—perhaps it's the overwhelming memory of the morning's run—I do not feel concerned.

Over brunch, Dick tells me he's not used to eating in the middle of the day.

"I couldn't starve that long," I remark.

"I always eat supper at my parents' place. Which reminds me. How do you feel about moving in here permanently?"

"How do *you* feel about it?" I would not want him to think I'm pushy.

He fixes me with his gaze. "You should know the answer to that," he replies quietly.

I really don't need to think about it. It's something I had occasionally fantasized about for weeks before the mountain picnic but had always put it out of my mind because I never thought that there'd be the remotest possibility of it happening. Now I feel as if I have known Dick intimately for ages. Perhaps we have been subliminally communicating for the two and a half years during Gib's musical evenings.

"Of course I want to stay, but only if you—"

Laughing at my seeming inability to make up my mind, he phones his parents to tell them that I have moved in with him. His mother promptly invites me around to their house, four blocks away, for tonight's dinner.

As Lil Hammond takes me up on my offer to dry the dishes, she confides that she had given up on her son ever being married. "He's just turned forty-one and never had any girlfriends, you know." Then she tells me that the Boatworks' owner's wife has been keeping her informed of my comings and goings, including the time she had seen me leaving Dick's house after midnight. No wonder the inquisitive old postmaster at the post office opposite had smirked as I handed my change-of-address form to him the previous Saturday. He is probably another local who wondered why Dick had never married. By now, everyone in the village must know about me, the local scarlet woman.

While Lil gossips to me in the kitchen, Dick has prompted his father, Hal, to reminisce. And as we join them in the living room, Lil— soon to go to bingo—disagrees with a date Hal has mentioned regarding the time he was boom boss at a certain logging camp in Hotham Sound. Trying to prevent an argument, Dick flies to his father's defence. But his mother loses her patience with the pair of them and flounces out for her evening's entertainment.

On the way home I ask, "Is she always like that?"

He shrugs. "They're both very strong-willed. Even though they know their boundaries, they still test them occasionally."

"So who do you think should have the final say in a marriage?" I ask.

"Well, a ship can only have one captain, but that doesn't mean he won't listen to his first mate!"

Even though he sounds as if he is joking, I sense a potential mine-field. "My stepfather made my mother's life miserable because he had total control of the finances. She never dared touch a bank book."

"I want nothing to do with money," he says. "I just go out and make it." Then he laughs, adding, "And I wouldn't dream of telling you how to cook!"

"Go on," I urge, "explain further."

"Well," he begins, "You may think I don't socialize much, but I do pay attention to what's going on around me, and I've noticed that successful marriages are the ones where the roles are defined."

"Because males and females are basically different?"

"Something like that. But I'm not saying that they can't trade. As long as they know what to expect from their partner."

As we turn into the driveway, I ask, "Does your mother know I'm technically married?"

"Of course," he replies. "It doesn't bother her, and even if it did, I'd tell her that's just too bad."

"She said you never had any girlfriends before me."

"Just shows you how well I've kept them hidden," he says, turning the engine off.

He laughs when I tell him how Gib warned me about him. "Like many of us," he says, nodding at me accusingly, "Gib tends to be nosey. So every time he prodded me about my private life, I'd toss it off ... make a joke about it."

"You kept him guessing?"

"It gave me a lot of amusement!"

That evening he plays me a recording of an aria sung by his favourite lyric tenor, the Ukrainian Ivan Kozlovsky. "You might want to shut your eyes for this one," he suggests as he lowers the tone arm.

It is Lensky's aria, "Kuda, Kuda vi udalilis," from Tchaikovsky's opera, *Eugene Onegin*, sung as he yearns for the happy days of his youth, and also his acceptance of whatever fate might throw at him—even death—as long as the love of his life will remember him with fondness.

The aria overwhelms me to tears. Although I have no reason to feel the emotion of yearning, Kozlovsky's interpretation now elicits a depth of devastating pathos and longing I have never experienced before. To whom do I owe this response? The composer, the conductor, the singer, or the man listening beside me?

"Didn't you play this for Gordon and me a couple of years ago?" I ask.

He nods. "Good memory. But all you both said was that you thought it was well sung."

"I wasn't listening to it with the right person."

At the end of the early morning rounds the following day, Dick navigates the *Snark* through the twenty-five or more pleasure boats of various sizes that clog Shoal Channel and approaches a fisherman anchored about a hundred feet outside the main group. It takes me a while to recognize that the slender, white-haired man sitting alone in an old clinker-built boat is his father, Hal, whose apparent quiescence belies his activity. In fact, he's anything but idle. With one rod on a holder and another in his hand, he might appear relaxed enough to a casual observer, but as we draw nearer, I notice that his sinewy body is constantly compensating to balance against the westerly swells. He reels in the line he is holding, and even though unpredictable waves from passing vessels continue to buffet his boat, he rises and stands without holding on, seemingly glued to the floor for several seconds before grabbing the *Snark*'s gunwale to prevent a swell-driven collision.

He smiles a welcome. "Thought you'd check up on me, did you?" he says and asks his son how he fared "this beautiful morning."

As I observe this brief interaction, I am conscious of the enviable easiness and warmth between father and son. I had also been aware of it the previous evening, but only now, here on the water, does it remind me of what I have missed from my own childhood, and I feel sad.

While Hal's voice is not that of a young person, he speaks slowly with a powerful sound that surges from the diaphragm then resonates inside the sinuses before exiting through a high, open throat. Known as the "support" that classical singers train for, with him it is the result of an iron-hard midriff formed by years of falling trees and wielding an axe. It is a sound that carries over water and through wind, a voice accustomed to giving orders to the boom men who worked under him.

He lifts a salmon from an aged wooden box under the stern seat. "Jo, how'd you like to take a fish home for supper?" he asks.

I'm taken aback, shocked, by his reference to home. "Sure," I say, my Canadian speech coming easier now, "What do you think it weighs?"

Dick takes the fish by its gills, hefting it. "A fifteen-pounder. Perfect size." He lays it on the floor beside the engine cover.

Hal beams as I thank him profusely. "You're most welcome," he says with utmost sincerity. "Now get it home before it rots."

Home? Yes, I think I believe that now.

As Dick pulls off his waders in the basement, I ask how he feels about teaching me to run the *Snark*.

"I've got a little flat-bottomed ten-footer and twenty-horse outboard you could have," he says. "My first beachcomb boat. Untippable too. But it needs a bit of work."

Is he trying to put me off? "I'd rather learn how to deal with the *Snark*."

"Sure, but jet boats are much harder to manoeuvre. It'll take you at least a couple of weeks to master."

And it feels even more like a perfect home that evening as we settle down to listen to music. My stepfather—for some extraordinary reason unknown to me—would never allow me, a sixteen-year-old, to play my own LP records of Beethoven's Fifth and Ninth symphonies.

"Chopin?" Dick suggests.

I nod. "Surprise me."

He does. Although I've only heard the piece once, the amazing circumstances surrounding my first hearing of it replays vividly in my mind. Aged thirteen, I'd just arrived at my art-critic and author grandpa Eric's house for one of my frequent and fascinating holidays with him and Stella. The sound of piano music had drawn me from my room to the living room where Stella's old mother, Georgia, was playing one of their two Steinways. Not wanting to disturb her, I had hidden in an alcove to listen. As she began a new piece, I remember blanking out my surroundings—my grandfather's hand-painted faux-marble walls hung with more originals than one might see in a small art gallery—while all sense of myself was completely taken over by some kind of overwhelming tragedy. It was as if a new but wordless language had suddenly become accessible to me, revealing unknown emotions so intense that I could not comprehend them. I only knew that they had been important to the composer, who had been able to convey them through the old lady's expertise. As the sound of Stella's footsteps broke the spell, I hurriedly wiped my sleeve over my eyes and asked Georgia what she had played. "Chopin's posthumous nocturne, but," she explained, holding up her strangely bent ring finger, "I can't play it the way it should be played." When I told her the music had made me cry, she smiled contentedly.

Now alongside Dick, the piece affects me the same way. He seems to understand that there is no need for words at this moment, choosing instead to grip my hand and gently kiss my eyes. I could not wish for more.

Afterwards, I explain my reaction, adding Georgia's later revelation to me that she, as a piano student, had seen Liszt play.

"Did you hear her play any Liszt?" Dick asks.

I nod. "One of his transcendental etudes. I'd always thought of him as a historical figure, something ethereal and long gone … you know, represented by dots on paper, but when she played it …"

"Yes …?"

"I was taken aback. Don't laugh, but it felt as if he'd passed through the room."

"I understand."

I believe him.

8

The Docking Lesson

"Feel like coming for a short drive?" Dick asks after lunch.

Turning left out of the driveway, he follows the road around the bay for a few hundred feet, then changes gear to climb the steep, arbutus-covered Gibsons' bluff. At the top, he parks in the cul-de-sac, and we climb out and gaze at the panoramic view framed by the tortuous red-limbed trees. Although the elevation is perhaps only a few feet higher than Gib's house, I have never seen the Strait from this particular view-point. Directly below us, Shoal Channel, locally known as "The Gap," is speckled with anchored boats. On its far side is the western point of Keats Island, and only a stone's throw further west from that is the one-acre grassy Salmon Rock, the narrow, granite-lined passage separating them, reminding me of my first trip in the *Snark*.

"Father and I had to fight a fire on Salmon Rock," he recalls. "Must've been all of twenty years ago. He was local fire marshal at the time."

"How did it start?"

"A boater's cigarette, I guess," he says, adding, "We had to remove a lot of smouldering moss afterwards."

He pulls the binoculars out from under the seat and we sit on a patch of grass to make for steadier viewing. "Should be a good freshet this year."

"What's a fresh't?"

"Fresh-et," he repeats carefully. "Fresh water running off the mountains. Hot sun on a heavy snowpack after a cool spring. But it has to be suddenly hot and last for a few days to make the rivers race." He scans the Strait for a few seconds. "That's what sweeps the logs out of their storage areas and from booms in the river. If the current is right, they'll end up here."

"Those miniature waterfalls up Elphinstone ..." I recall.

He nods and squeezes my hand. "That was just the start," he says.

With my naked eye I gaze past Keats and the outermost Pasley islands to the eastern part of the Georgia Strait or "the Gulf" as he usually refers to it. There, in the far distance, the unseen Fraser River delta and hinterland is covered by a heat haze. But to the right of it lies pure drama. Oily, opaque, olive-green river water swirls intrusively against the Gulf's translucent, blue-green salt water forming a distinct boundary, a meeting of yin and yang. What is happening out there under the surface where plants and animals from the freshet meet the salt? Do they die?

Dick hands me the glasses and I tell him what I see. "There's a mess of old stumps with curly roots just beyond the islands, and ... it looks like an old piece of float with squared timbers sticking up ... but out toward the west along the water delineation are two conifers complete with roots ... and further on ... three logs, two next to each other and the third on its own ... all on that same line. Must be at least a couple of miles off Gower Point."

He nods. "Good for you. Let's go get'em."

The water is calmer here off the Gibsons' side of Keats as I tow our freshet harvest toward the Shelter Island storage grounds. I set the engine to idle, and Dick lifts the towline from the cleat and ties it to one of the standing boomsticks that surround his grounds. River reeds and fern fronds still cling to the logs, and there is a different type of furry algae growing on one of them—a freshwater variety—and a downy bird's feather, still dry, caught in an uprooted bog plant.

He watches me examining the river stuff and laughs. "You're lucky we didn't find a stinky dead sea lion."

I suspect he's joking. He's always catching me out with his sense of humour, telling me I'm too easy to fool, that my mind is far too literal.

But in a no-nonsense voice, he adds, "Last year, a dead cow washed up on Gower Point."

He restarts the engine and drives the *Snark* around an antique-looking contraption, a giant corkscrew attached to an old Briggs and Stratton motor on a ten-by-twelve-foot float. "There's your practice dock," he points. "A boring machine from 1910. The engine's so old the dealer couldn't find any of the numbers in his ancient parts book."

My docking lesson at last? Afraid I'll make a fool of myself, I'm having second thoughts. "It doesn't look boring," I joke.

"True enough," he agrees. "It bores big holes in boomsticks so they can be chained end to end to contain loose logs or bundles. Doing it this way is easier on your back than the hand augers or chainsaws they use today. Want to see how it works?"

"Only if you have time."

"Jo, will you stop that?" he chides. "I enjoy showing you these things."

Floating nearby, a row of extra long logs of similar lengths lie side by side. Each one has a metal dog embedded in it halfway along its length, and running through all of the dog eyes is a long wire drawn so tightly that the logs have no space between them. "Potential boomsticks," he explains, hitting one of the dogs out with the back of his dogging axe. "Dogline keeps 'em in order."

By deft use of the front part of the *Snark*'s keel, he manoeuvres one holeless boomstick away from its neighbours and shoves it toward the boring machine float. Now I see that the float has a wide gap straddled by a couple of crosspieces in the middle of it, and it is into this gap, under the crosspieces, that he shoves the end of the log. He wraps a chain around that end and winches it up a few inches so it can't move, and starts the old engine with a rope. A long belt connects the engine to the auger gear which, of course, turns the auger. With the motor at full throttle he uses a lever to lower the giant screw—its diameter a little bigger than a man's hand—onto the secured boomstick. The motor hesitates momentarily and the auger bores into the wood, sending pieces of spiral-shaped shavings upwards to eventually fall into the water. It only takes thirty seconds for the auger to drill right through, when Dick raises it and shuts off the motor.

"If the auger hits a knot," he points out, "it won't go through so easily." He lowers the chain and boomstick into the water, frees it and with the boat guides the stick back to the others.

"Those boomsticks," I say, partly as a delaying tactic. "Are they always the same length?""

"Yes, about sixty-six feet, because they're often reused or sold as such to make more log booms … Now, ready to concentrate?" he asks, shifting to neutral, and we drift. "Don't forget, if you're in neutral you'll keep drifting in the same direction because …"

"There's no brake," I finish.

"Put the engine in reverse if you need to stop. Like this." And with his left hand he shoves the lever backward.

"How does the jet reverse?"

"Just in front of the nozzle there's a pair of gates that swing either side of it to change the steering. This reverse lever drops a metal scoop over them, deflecting the water jet frontward under the hull, making the boat go backwards." He makes his left hand into a nozzle end and cups his right hand, palm down, before changing its angle so that it almost covers the nozzle.

"So that's why the throttle influences the way the boat handles."

He nods. "You can turn the steering wheel all you want, but if you don't give it enough gas it won't change direction. Watch."

But I am distracted by a fairly large and dumpy bird that sits absolutely motionless on an arbutus branch overhanging the water. Its colours had attracted my attention, blue tufted head with a vicious-looking beak, blue wings, and two stripes around its white body—one blue and the lower one red. I grab Dick's arm. "What that?"

Missile-like, the bird dives into the water and returns to the branch with a small fish crossways in its beak. In two seconds the fish is disappearing headfirst down the bird's throat.

He nods toward it. "A kingfisher. That red belt means it's a female."

"It's much bigger than the kingfishers in England, and the colour's different."

"They're noisy brutes, but they're slatternly. They foul their own nests."

"Sorry," I say. "I shouldn't have interrupted you."

"That bird's worth an interruption." Returning to my lesson, he circles and steers the *Snark* toward the dock. "Right now the water's coming straight out of the jet nozzle at the stern and past those two moveable gates ... When I steer forty-five degrees to the right toward the dock, the gates each side of the nozzle redirect the water flow. Now I ease off the throttle and steer the other way so that I'm parallel to the dock, quickly change to reverse, and immediately step on the throttle."

The boat growls and comes to rest gently alongside the boring machine float.

It looks so easy, and it is fascinating to learn the mechanics, but while I understand the theory behind this series of manoeuvres, like learning to dance, it'll take ages before I learn to apply it. "Remember your 'road' is liquid," he continues. "The winds and currents will work against you, but once you get the basics, intuition takes over." He steers away from the float and we trade places. "Main thing is to use reverse and gas to stop forward movement."

With the wheel in my hand I remember the violent docking three years earlier by the *Canadian Star*, the freighter that had brought me to Canada. Without assist tugs we had to dock at Crofton pulp mill against an uncooperative tide. The engine slowed, drifted, then changed to reverse. We approached it at a slight angle, but with only forty feet to go it was obvious that inertia—and the tide—had won. The reverse revs had not been high enough to halt the ship at the critical moment. As the *Canadian Star*'s port fo'c's'le hit, I fell out of my deck chair. The iron gunwale crunched against the solid diagonal creosote timber facing. It splintered and broke several, displacing others from the drift bolts that held them against the pilings, and with an ear-splitting screech, gouged out a ten-foot horizontal scar. The ship slid a further thirty feet while deckhands hurled the mooring ropes at the dock workers who caught them and deftly fastened them to the bollards ...

Snapping to the present, my mind blanks in panic. I'll be found out and found wanting. And what will my teacher do then?

"First thing, angle of approach," he says, demonstrating with his hands.

"Forty-five degrees," I mutter. "Slowly ... Now what?"

"Steer parallel to dock, reverse and give a shot of gas."

That works until …

"Not so MUCH!" The stern corner hits the float. "Circle left and try again."

I wait for him to lose his temper. I'm sure he wants to hit me.

This time I use too little gas with reverse and the boat stops at least four feet from the dock. Another circle, another try. Too much gas forward and the bow hits it. I cringe.

He's amazingly calm. "Reverse earlier," he advises.

"I KNOW! I know!" I yell. The next pass is better. The speed is almost perfect but I'm too slow with the steering wheel and he throws his right arm around mine to correct the motion. Again I cringe. But I reassure myself I'm being helped and stop the *Snark* three feet away from the little float, grabbing the axe from the bin and sticking the blade into the small platform to pull the boat to it.

Laughing, he ties the *Snark* to the boring machine. "Cheater!"

Dick is using his axe to remove dogs from a boom under construction. Howe Sound and Gambier Island are in the background.

"I'd rather practise on my own," I explain, fighting the welling tears.

"Let's quit. You've done well."

"You're just being polite."

He frowns. "Would I let you drive my boat if I thought you couldn't?" Then he turns to me and asks quietly, "Are you afraid of me?"

Old habits, I reason silently. *You're the only one I can trust.*

"It's not you!" I blurt out. "It's any man. My stepfather used to strap me until one of my grade nine friends showed the class teacher my welts."

As he slowly, firmly puts his arm around my shoulder and draws me close, I turn my head away so he can't see my tears. But it is too late. He pulls me beside him and, seizing my face between his hands, kisses my eyes. "One day you'll know I'm not 'any' man. And didn't I warn you it would take at least two weeks? You're already ahead of the game." Then he hands me a crumpled handkerchief. "Don't be so hard on yourself," he reproaches. "Let intuition take over."

He's right. Whenever I am challenged, I spiral into self-doubt. By then, intuition is beyond reach.

Suddenly he laughs, rubs a finger over my cheek and shows me a gob of black and bronze-flecked molybdenum bearing grease. I laugh too when I see what he had given me to wipe my eyes, the rag he uses to clean the excess bearing grease off the jet. I pull a Kleenex out of my back jeans pocket and ask him to do a better job.

Later, steering toward a tier of logs on pickup lines, he says, "Got a job to do here. Drop me off and practise on your own. I'll wave when I'm finished." He jumps off *Snark*'s gunwale and alights on a standing boomstick, one of the many chained together end to end that surround his storage area. "Think positively!" he yells as I slowly accelerate to avoid knocking him off with the jet wash.

It is here, off Shelter Island, while I have control of the *Snark*, that I recall my frustration as a toddler at being denied the chance to drive a tiny paddle boat. Even as a ten-year-old on a school field trip to Arundel's famous little Swanbourne Lake, my wish to go rowing with the other children had been thwarted by my parents who had refused to give me permission to do so. But when my teacher saw me alone on the shore, watching the rest of my class in boats, she took me for a ride herself assuming my parents wouldn't mind. She was wrong. My thrilling account was later met with stern words, bedroom confinement and a strapping.

Presented at last with this powerful boat, my time has come.

During the ensuing twenty minutes, I must have dislodged all the marine growth from the underside of the little float. With the theory understood and practice under my belt, I now leave it to my brain to deal with. At last things seem to be under control.

"Now you've got it!" Dick yells, beckoning me over. He is standing on a single, free-swinging narrow log connected to the standing boom by a fifteen-foot-long pickup line. This, then is a sign that he trusts me. I must do everything right.

Gripping the steering wheel tightly, I circle, preparing for the approach.

"The current!" he warns.

Too late. Because I have never experienced how the *Snark* behaves with currents, I have to stop and think. Already committed, I freeze. As the stern swings too far, it crashes against the log and my teacher is thrown into the sea.

I turn the engine off. When he ignores my proffered hand and swims instead to the stern, I prepare myself for his rage. Placing his feet on the jet guard, he grabs the towing cleat and pulls himself, dripping, into the boat. But instead of the shouts and curses I had been dreading, he's laughs loudly. "I'm pretty good at log birling, but not if a boat runs into me!"

"I—I'm so sorry," I stammer. "I'm hopeless. Beyond teaching."

"If you don't stop kicking yourself," he says, the grin still on his face, "I'll throw you overboard too!"

How could I have ever doubted his forgiving nature?

Steering through the harbour entrance, he nudges me and points to our house. "You have a visitor." Parked behind it on the hilly driveway is Gordon's red Beetle.

"I don't want to see him."

"Take a book into the living room," he advises. "I'll talk to him in the kitchen—as soon as I've changed these wet clothes."

After the two men's voices have droned on for more than an hour, I hear the back door open and close.

Dick joins me on the loveseat. "He still thinks there's a chance you'll go back to him."

"He doesn't have a clue."

"And he's set up ten counselling sessions for both of you."

"If that's what it takes for him to divorce me, I'll go, but it won't change anything."

"He also warned me that the fact you left him means you won't last with me either—"

I groan.

"So," he continues, "I tactfully pointed out that you had good reason to leave."

"It took an hour for all that?"

"If I'd been in his position, I'd fight for you too."

After today's experience, I think Dick has already proved his commitment to me.

The first counselling session—a joint one—is held next to the cabin where Peter, the crazy Brit doctor, had taught me to swim and dive the previous summer. Until that lesson, even submerging my face in water would cause a panic attack. Now, however, with Gordon present, I stare out the counsellor's living room window at the glittering sea and the same feeling of drowning rushes over me. If Peter hadn't led me below the sea's surface, convinced me to open my eyes and deal with my fear, would I still be trapped with Gordon? Surely Peter must have known how bad things were between us? He has left the country on a sabbatical, so I can't ask.

At the end of ten sessions, the counsellor tells us that while she does not recommend we try to patch up our marriage, she suggests that we wait awhile before embarking on a new relationship. But because my marriage had ended years ago, eroded in much the same way the sea had ripped out the turf in front of our first rental cabin, I feel that I am more than ready for my new relationship.

9

Dog Damage

A dog.

This morning we begin our rounds twenty minutes late. A few days earlier, Dick's partner, Alan, had been joking to him—privately—that he was surprised that my moving in had not changed Dick's early morning schedule. "Now you've got a nice warm woman in your bed I thought you'd have a lie-in at least once a week," he'd said—or words to that effect. "He should know you better than that," I had retorted, remembering that Dick prides himself on never taking mornings off, not even on holidays. "Besides," I added, pointedly, "two in a twin-sized bed in summer is rather sweaty." Nodding in agreement, he'd admitted we should buy a larger one the next time we go to Vancouver.

But today, neither of us hears the alarm. Since those extra twenty minutes could mean missing out on several logs, maybe even a bundle of them, Dick barely manages to tie his running shoes. So when he suddenly accelerates after steering to port around Twin Islands en route to Gambier Harbour and the Bays, I know he's seen something.

I'm slower than he is at spotting merchantable logs or log salvors' boats in the dawn light, mostly because the surroundings are still unfamiliar to me. Learning the forty-mile morning route will require a lot of repeated journeys, particularly since there are so few buildings to use as landmarks. But he has been working this area for years, and if I were to show him a close-up photo of a thirty-foot expanse of virgin beach within a twenty-mile radius of Gibsons or even further, he would be able to point to the place on a map.

At last I see what he's aiming for. Two hundred yards away, parallel to the tide line and partly in the water, lies a log not quite afloat, and another close by on the same beach. Meanwhile, in the distance from the opposite direction, I can barely make out a small boat speeding in our direction.

We stop alongside the closest log, a mid-sized fir with a slight flare on its butt end. Instead of using the pulling chain and its long, thick rope, Dick hammers a yellow pickup line and dog into its narrow end and throws the loop over the stern cleat. From his lightning-fast movements and snatched glances at the approaching competitor's boat, I can tell that he intends to collect the second log before the other salvor reaches it.

He leaps back to the wheel and accelerates slightly. The log's narrow end swings out over the water toward the boat, and stops. The slightly curved butt end is hooked into the gravel.

He pulls again sharply and with more power. The *Snark* jerks, there's an explosion, a shattering of glass, and the boat charges straight out from the beach without the log. Pea-sized glass fragments litter the bow, bilge and seat. Only the aluminum U-frame that held the windshield remains.

"Your neck!" I yell.

Blood pours from just below his jaw on his left side. The broken glass is forgotten. He sits on the shards, grabs a dirty rag and hands it to me. "Press this on it," he orders calmly.

I do as he says, then take his hand and place it on the rag. "Here, you keep the pressure on. I'll drive. Then it's the hospital."

"The clinic's closer," he says.

"Won't be open for hours."

He insists he's all right, but he's as white as a sheet.

Since the rusty floor under the driver's seat had completely fallen out of my Beetle the previous week, I'm forced to drive the Citroën. I stall it twice not only in panic but because I have never driven a column shift before, neither am I used to the car's unique and extraordinarily positive brake button. Luckily there is very little traffic at this early hour, and fifteen minutes later we march into St. Mary's small emergency ward in Sechelt.

The nurse glares at the filthy rag against Dick's unshaven neck, glances at his oil-soiled, dead mussel juice-stinking jeans, grimy, holey runners, and shakes her head. "Onto the bed with you."

A bleary-eyed doctor takes over, cleaning the wound to expose a thick flap of skin and a three-inch gash to one side of the patient's Adam's apple.

"You're extremely lucky," he says, drawing anaesthetic into a hypodermic. "You missed the carotid artery by a quarter of an inch … How did you try to kill yourself?"

Dick waits until the doctor has withdrawn the needle then explains how the metal dog had pulled out of the log like a slingshot, hitting him and the windshield, but missing me. Then he adds sheepishly, "Those ropes have a lot of stretch …"

Out in the hospital parking lot afterwards, I ask, "Why didn't you use the pulling chain?"

"In a hurry. Didn't you see the other boat?"

He gets in on the passenger side and puts his hand on my thigh. "I should never have done that. What with you in the boat, too."

"You gave me a real scare with all that blood."

"Me give you a scare?" he protests. "Your driving scared me!"

"Oh well," I tell him huffily, "if you want to drive back …"

"Hey, where's your sense of humour?"

Of course, as soon as we get home, he insists on driving the *Snark* to the Boatworks dock to install the spare windshield, "in case we're called out on a spill."

10

Thieves and Violence

Knowing how wary I am about manoeuvring the *Snark* in public, Dick encourages, then insists I try out my new skill by refuelling at the Boatworks next door.

I dread it almost as much as I had the docking lesson. The attendant appears a little surprised to see me and is obviously concerned because, as I approach the tie-up rail, he leans so far out over the water to grab the *Snark*'s gunwale that I'm afraid he's going to fall in. Fortunately everything goes as planned. While I stand there in the boat with the nozzle in my hand, waiting for fifty dollars worth of gas to pump into the tank, Walt, the Boatworks owner, drives down the ramp on his lawn tractor. Using crutches, he gracefully swings himself and his polio-paralyzed legs off the tractor and into the float office.

His struggles remind me of another similarly challenged man I had met when I was seven. My mother and Mr. Evans, one of the five lodgers she had taken in after World War II—and her divorce—had dropped me and my five-year-old sister off at a craft shop in Chichester. They introduced us to the owner, Mr. Sisman, sitting on a cushion on the floor with an unfinished woven basket beside him. "Mr. Sisman makes willow baskets to sell in the shop," my mother told us, and promptly left with Mr. Evans. I shall never forget what happened next. With the basket in his lap, Mr. Sisman picked up his legs as if they were floppy rags and wrapped them tightly around the basket to keep it in place while he worked. I could not stop staring at those horribly limp, useless legs. When I asked him why they wouldn't work, he explained that he had caught polio as a boy. Around tea time my mother and Mr. Evans returned, and Mr. and Mrs. Sisman gave them a beige pottery vase with an envelope inside. As Mr. Evans drove us back to our house, my mother, sitting beside him, stared straight ahead and, in a voice that sounded as if it came out of an empty barn, stated: "From now on you can call Mr. Evans 'Daddy.' We've just got married." I remember how I had held my breath for a very long time, and how I had tightened my body to try to make it very small. *Mr. Evans. He scares me. Daddy? He isn't. How can I call him that? I am afraid to be in the same room with him.* All the way home my thoughts kept oscillating between that idea and poor Mr. Sisman trapped with his useless legs, and I empathized with him even more.

"Are you Dick Hammond's girlfriend?"

I look up from the *Snark* at the long, wader-clad legs of a tall, skinny, elderly man looming above me. He's obviously a log salvor. His old beaten-up salvage boat is moored at the far end. Since his LS number is a low one, it stands to reason that he's been at it for a long time.

"Yep," I reply, hoping my substitution of a 'p' for the 's' will break the culture barrier.

"Rocky Grey. Glad to meet you."

Rocky Grey. Dick has mentioned him. He's a part-timer whose usual job is to drive the little ferry that connects Keats and Gambier islands with Langdale ferry terminal. Occasionally he phones to tell Dick of a good log he has spotted while out on his regular job.

After we have exchanged a couple of brief sentences about the weather, he surprises me with a shake of his head and suddenly comes out with, "I dunno ... I'd heard Dick had got a girlfriend at last ... But how on earth can a girl like you deal with a man like that?"

"What do you mean?" I ask, trying to keep my curiosity at an unreadable minimum.

"Well ... How are you going to know what he's thinking if he never talks to you?"

I climb out of the *Snark* and hang up the pump nozzle. Then I turn to Rocky and break the secret gently. "Well, he says plenty to me."

Rocky just shakes his head again and ambles off to another gas pump.

"Jo!" Walt calls through the office doors, "will you please tell Dick

I heard a skipper on the radio talking about a log spill the other side of Sechelt."

After hearing the message, Dick suggests we investigate by car.

"What's wrong with the *Snark*?" I enquire.

"Too far to go on spec," he explains. "It could be all over by now."

As we leave, the Citroën is hammered by a gusty rain shower that clears up within twenty minutes. On the way I mention Rocky's comments, and Dick laughs loudly. "Good!" he says, "That's the way I want 'em to think."

"Why?"

"The less your competition knows about you, the better. You should've heard about the rumours flying around when I was building the *Snark*."

I refrain from asking for examples.

Dick and I with oily hands after finishing another oil change at our dock beside Boatworks.

"Probably that curved windshield I ordered. And the aircraft landing light on the bow ... This is a small place. You know how even boring news gets around."

Thanks to Dick's knowledge of the local area, we find a good parking place on a high bluff overlooking the sea.

From the car we spot three logs floating about half a mile offshore amongst the litter of small whitecapped waves from the recent squall. Dick pulls the binoculars from under the seat and we hike over the sodden grass to a better vantage point against a backdrop of arbutus where we find a natural seat, a large exposed piece of granite already dried by the sun. Below us, in the shimmering waters of a protected bay, men in two outboard boats are busy gathering several loose logs scattered near a large boom. Two boats with cabins are rafted to a tug alongside a boom. One is a white pleasure cruiser, and the other dark grey with white LS licence numbers on the side.

Gib had already explained how a log boom is made in sections, each one an oblong of parallel logs surrounded by extra long logs—boomsticks—chained together, and from this height I can see the structure quite clearly, except that one of the sections at the tail end is empty, and the end boomstick seems to be missing.

"They've lost quite a few," I remark.

Dick hands me the glasses. "Tailstick must've let go."

"The white boat doesn't have LS numbers on it."

"It belongs to the spill coordinator. He represents the logging insurance companies. Usually wears a green parka. He'll be on the tug."

As I focus the glasses on him, he staggers to the side of the tug. A few seconds later another man exits the cabin and hands him a mug. I return the binoculars with a bit of sarcasm. "Quite a party."

"You've got that right," growls Dick. "The other guy's a log salvor."

"That must be his big salvage boat."

"It's good camouflage at night."

A third man lurches out of the tug's wheelhouse, says something, and throws a bottle overboard.

"The skipper," Dick indicates as he hands over the binoculars again. "Back inside for more ... Keep your eye on the guy in the outboard near the tail end. Any minute he'll undo a boom chain."

He is right. As a result the logs from inside that section begin to float into the bay and out toward the Strait. The salvor in one of the outboards drives further along the boom opening more sections, so that within twenty minutes, hundreds of logs have been freed. Having accomplished what he'd obviously set out to do, the man accelerates out of the broken boom into the bay where he joins the other salvor collecting those logs.

More mutterings from Dick. "What they've spent on booze is peanuts to what they'll get for this haul."

"I suppose you won't be joining them."

He sneers. "Work with these crooks? It's the difference between going fishing and robbing a trout farm."

"Those men in outboards are taking a chance," I point out.

"They've planned it." He looks as if he's just tasted some bitter aloes. "The grey boat owner gets the tugboat captain and deckhand drunk as well as the spill coordinator. It's happened before and it'll happen again."

"Whose logs are they?"

"Some logging company up the coast, perhaps. Or even worse, could belong to a gyppo logger."

"Gypsies?"

"They're *like* gypsies. Loggers who travel around trying to make a living off small logging claims. Sometimes with a wife and kids in tow. They'll usually log with initiative rather than capital and can't afford to insure their booms. They're the ones I feel sorry for ... A few years ago, one of my friends lost big-time from something like this. He never got over it."

I nod toward the boom. "Do you think some of those could belong to a gyppo logger?"

"Very likely ... C'mon, let's go."

As I take one last look at the dramatic sky to the east, billowy rain clouds tinged pinkish-white by the sun, something over the Strait makes me catch my breath. "Hey! Look at those birds. They're fighting!" Raising the wide-angled binoculars to my eyes, I watch, fascinated, as a herring gull is chased by three pale-brown birds of similar size. In an effort to outmanoeuvre them, it drops almost to the water, soaring off to one side then climbing a couple of hundred feet. But it is no match for the darker birds with their more powerful, rapid wing beats. Incredible divers and flyers, they attack relentlessly, repeatedly fanning their strange pointed tails to help them make abrupt changes in direction.

"Those three brown birds are parasitic jaegers," says Dick. "Keep watching. They haven't finished with that gull yet."

"Jaegers. German for hunter," I remark, recalling he has been teaching himself German to help his comprehension of Lieder.

"Yep. Hunting for a fast food outlet."

I soon see what he means as the terrorized gull regurgitates the contents of its crop in mid-flight. Ignoring the fleeing bird, the three robbers follow their airborne meal with amazing speed and agility, one of them scooping some in its beak on the way down, while the other two gobble the rest of the predigested food from the water.

"That's immoral and repulsive," I say.

"Not for jaegers. It's their instinct."

"But not yours."

He squeezes my thigh. Then, as we drive through Sechelt, he explains that his father reared him to be totally honest, even though others around him were not. "He said I'd be one of the few who'd be able to live with my conscience."

"But aren't you tempted?" I ask. "I mean, you go past thousands of logs every day and no one's looking."

"Sure. But if I stole, I'd be admitting I was incompetent … a failure."

I am beginning to see why he has a reputation as an expert. "But salvors wouldn't steal from each other," I remark.

"Not usually. They know their victims would come looking and recognize their own logs, and things could get very nasty. Some of the Fraser River beachcombers had guns aboard. Years ago, one of them was found dead on the riverbank. He'd been shot and his boat was found sunk, riddled with bullet holes."

I ask him if someone has ever stolen his logs, or had attempted to.

"A couple of times," he admits. "During the late '50s, it got to the point where some of us up here felt we had to protect ourselves with a weapon."

I am taken aback until I recall how shocked I had been at the Long Beach dock in California on seeing my first American policeman with a gun in his belt.

"Did you ever …?" I begin.

He nods. "I had a good tow behind me off Worlcombe. An old slow cabin cruiser—a river beachcomber—came alongside. He yelled something obnoxious, reached up to grab something above him—I could tell it was a gun—but I was faster, grabbed mine, yelled 'drop it!'"

"And?"

"He took off. Never saw him again."

"What about the other time?"

When he hesitates, I press him.

"I don't like talking about it, but since it's you … This happened long before Alan's time. I was working with Father, and we'd already towed our logs to the grounds that morning because they were especially good ones. But when I returned after my morning nap, they'd gone."

"You'd tied them up properly?"

"Naturally. We'd taken extra precautions. Put them inside the standing boom, too. Right away I had my suspicions who'd taken them. As I said, most salvors don't steal from each other, but this character was known for it, although he'd never tried it on me before. Besides, earlier that morning, he'd seen us with our tow. So I paid him a visit—by boat—up the inlet to his cabin. His own boat was tied up, engine still hot. My logs were there all right, hidden behind his float with its load of junk.

"I marched up the ramp, knocked at his cabin door—it was one of those old, rundown shacks, mounds of wine bottles in the yard, bits of old machinery parts, mangy dog tied to a rotting doghouse. A woman opened the door. The look on her face … I felt sorry for her. She must've thought the devil had come to get her. I was full of adrenaline, fighting mad, must've seemed unstoppable. I yelled, 'Where's Ivan?' and charged straight past her."

"What did she say?"

"Can't remember exactly. Didn't matter at the time. Something about him being sick in bed. As soon as I saw the only closed door inside that shack, I knew he was there. Can't even remember opening it. For all I know it could have fallen off its hinges when I tried the doorknob."

"Was he there?"

Dick nods. "Lying on the bed under an old grey army blanket he'd pulled up to his chin. Forehead beaded with sweat. He had one of those coarse-featured faces, florid, unshaven, topped with matted greasy hair … I'll never forget it. Guilt personified. And to cap it all, he'd pulled the blanket up so far that I could see he hadn't had time to pull his work boots off!"

"A giveaway!"

"I ripped the blanket off. Of course he was still dressed in his work clothes. I remember yelling, 'Sick, are you?' You should've heard his excuses, then the threats. Violent. Vicious. He must have been prepared for trouble because he leaped up, grabbed a crowbar on the far side of the bed and came after me."

"Weren't you scared?"

"Jo!" The tires squeal as he speeds around the bend. "Wash your mouth out! If anyone ever threatens me or my family, they'd better watch it. No, I was ready. He stood there for a moment with that bar in both hands, waving it, threatening me. A middle-aged, flabby man like that? He hadn't a hope and he knew it. Besides, I learned early on how to defend myself."

"Couldn't you just walk away?"

"And let him think he'd intimidated me? He'd only steal from me again. No way. He needed a lesson, so I egged him on a bit, 'C'mon! Try it,' that kind of thing. He came at me, 'Get de hell out or I kill you!' I picked up a chair. He swung the bar again, dropped it, then tried to grab the chair from me. It's hard to remember exactly what happens in those situations, but he and the chair somehow ended up on the floor. That's when I delivered my lesson."

While he pauses, he continues to exceed the Coast's 50 mph speed limit.

I turn my face expectantly toward him. "What d'you mean?"

"I just leaned over him and told him quietly, 'Don't you threaten me. If you touch any of my logs again, it will be for the last time. Got that?' And I walked out, followed by a stream of Russian oaths."

"Poor woman," I sigh. "Imagine being married to a man like that."

"Yes, she certainly had my sympathies."

My own thoughts immediately turn to the violence aboard the *Canadian Star* as we approached the Mona Passage, the shipping channel between the Dominican Republic and the island of Puerto Rico. We were en route for the Panama Canal prior to the Pacific leg of the journey. I had been leaning against the fo'c's'le gunwale listening to the whispers of a warm breeze in my ears and the hiss of the water as the bow cleaved through it, when something in my peripheral vision grabbed my attention. Half a dozen glistening grey dolphins shot out of the sea about a hundred feet in front of the ship, suspending themselves in zero gravity for a second before diving. Like miniature silver torpedoes they streaked along under the glassy surface before leaping up, cycling again and again. Raising my head to see where they were headed, I spotted the blue-grey island of Puerto Rico, thirty degrees to port. As we drew closer, it slowly elongated, turning, chameleon-like, to a dull green, while several degrees to starboard on the other side of the channel, the Dominican Republic arose in the distance. I climbed down the fo'c's'le steps to search for Gordon to tell him about the dolphins, but as I made my way between the gunwale and a container I heard the slap of running footsteps coming from the other side of it. More footsteps followed, quicker, chasing away from the superstructure. Adult feet ... rubber soles skidding, dodging, changing direction. Crew, deckhands perhaps. As I reached the end of the container, two figures in white whizzed past the gap on its far side, between it and the next container ... returning to the superstructure, with no more than half-a-second's distance between them. "I'll KILL you!" a man shouted. A door slammed.

I froze. His voice stiffened the hairs on the back of my neck. It rekindled the thrilling memories of bitter fights—usually about money—between my mother and Mr. Evans. At the first sound of their raised voices I used to creep out of bed and listen from halfway down the stairs.

I worried constantly that if we didn't pay the bank overdraft, we'd all be thrown out of the house. Even so, I longed for these dreadful scenes. They gave me hope that my mother's second marriage would fail and life would be happy again.

A scream snapped me back. From where? inside? outside? Something about its partly falsetto sound made me want to vomit. Then, above the ship's engine, a dreadful silence. Had I really heard a scream? And why the silence afterwards? I ran into the superstructure. A few yards in, near the inside staircase, drops of blood. A trail of them. I had to tell someone on the bridge. Blood on the staircase, too … but it stopped on the second flight. Whoever had been injured must have come partway up before doubling back down. On the stairs I almost collided with one of the officers. A brief exchange between us revealed he knew something was up. I ran to the lounge and explained to a couple of passengers what I'd seen and heard, when the ship suddenly slowed and swerved to port, banking so steeply that the inertia tipped me sprawling onto an easy chair. Rows of books slid off the shelves onto the floor and the ship juddered violently, rattling light fixtures, ashtrays and setting other loose objects vibrating in sympathy. Ten minutes after the ship's dramatic change of course, another officer entered, explaining that there'd been a brutal attack on one of the kitchen staff, and that we were going to deliver him to hospital and his attacker to the British Consulate in San Juan, Puerto Rico. At dinner, an officer told me that the hospitalized man had been slashed with a broken wineglass and would lose his eye.

With the ship anchored off San Juan Harbour that evening during a raging tropical thunderstorm, I remember the other passengers' apparent indifference to the horrible drama. While they seemed to regard the incident as a welcome diversion, I cannot imagine my new partner reacting like that. He learned the language of confrontation the hard way, in logging camps. However, it's not until we drive into the carport that I realize the seriousness of Dick's threat to Ivan, and instead of being wary of his potential for violence, I feel safer and more cared for than at any other time in my life.

11

Monkeys and Boxcars

One breezy afternoon Dick and I continue work on the four-section boom that he and his partner have already started. Alan, who has spent all morning in the *Styx* collecting the last three days' harvest of logs from the Gambier and Pasley anchors, will be bringing them in any minute.

During a brief lull, I ask how they will sell the boom.

"Through our log broker," Dick replies, leaning over the *Snark*'s gunwale, sticking his axe into one of the standing boomsticks to hold the boat still. "He'll try to find us a buyer who'll inspect it and get back to him with a price. Then it's a race between the buyer and the teredos." These, he explains, are sea worms that burrow into wood with their teeth and if left to their own devices could multiply and destroy a whole log boom. Even a few holes of damage can mean less payment.

Recalling tales of sailors from centuries ago who had to beach their vessels and paint the hulls with pitch, I mutter, "That explains the creosote pilings and docks. But how can you kill the worms once they get in the logs?"

"Store the booms in the Fraser River and its adjoining lakes. Freshwater's lethal to 'em. Father and I even tried blasting the critters with underwater explosives but it didn't work." And he removes the axe and drives to the other side of the grounds to where three logs are tied. As soon as I have looped their pickup lines over the stern cleat, he tows them slowly toward the temporary opening between two standing boomsticks. Inside the safety of the "corral" he shifts to idle, and I release them.

"How do they stop the log theft in the river and Howe Sound?"
I ask, thinking again of the miles of log booms lining these shores—
millions of dollars' worth of merchandise without a storekeeper or police.

"A few years ago," he explains, chaining the two sticks together
again, "the Ministry of Forests brought in a curfew. It's supposed to prevent salvors from working inside designated areas—log storage areas—
between dark until dawn. The Langdale ferry dock is inside one of those
lines … so are all those booms up toward Port Mellon and beyond, and
the Gambier bays."

"But you said, 'supposed' to prevent."

"The thieves?" he sneers. "If they see a boat approaching on their
radar, they set their tow adrift and take off until things quieten down. It
goes on all the time. Rules don't concern them!"

The approaching *Styx* is now within shouting distance. Alan slows
the revs and Dick drives up to the tug, while I grab its now slack towline
and hook it over the *Snark*'s stern cleat.

"Hey, Boss!" yells Alan as soon as we have tied the tows to the
standing boom. "I thought you said you had a collection over at that
West Bay tie-up."

"There were … twenty-one of 'em."

Alan bites his lip. "Well, they've gone."

"Nothing on the shore?"

His partner shakes his head. "Not a sign."

"I'd better go look," says Dick. "Jo, throw the towrope back to
Alan. He'll tie 'em up."

I do as he says.

Dick gathers the tools and ropes we have been using and stores
them ready for a trip. "We'll check the inlet first," he says.

"Good luck," Alan calls. "Don't forget I'm off to the Island
tomorrow."

Waving in acknowledgement, Dick wheels the *Snark* around and
we're away.

The first place he checks is the north side of the twin islands near
the ferry dock, then, taking note of the slight breeze from the west,
follows the Gambier cliffs and adjacent booming grounds northwards

before crossing Thornbrough Channel to where the other log storage grounds lie under the shadow of Mount Elphinstone. Like the lichen-covered walls of the great old cathedrals in Europe, steep granite cliffs thrust up on both sides of us. The water here is opaque, almost emerald, from the glacial silt suspended in the myriad rivers and creeks that tumble into Howe Sound ... So different from the dark torrents of Panama's tropical rain forests.

The *Snark* skims alongside several booming grounds and Dick checks some cliff tie-ups in the channel, but the logs attached to these are not his. An hour later we retrace our path, until we reach Grace Islands (or as he calls them, Twin Islands), but instead of turning to port and into the Gambier bays, he steers toward the ferry terminal at Horseshoe Bay.

Finding nothing there, he steers to port and follows the bluffs past White Cliff, around to Fisherman's Cove in West Vancouver. Then, just past a large bluff, he points to the collection of logs tied to an anchored buoy just inside Eagle Island. They're in full view of the fuel dock. And they have Dick's stamp on them.

"Any money on you?" he asks, shoving us away from the logs.

I hand over a two-dollar bill.

As we draw alongside the fuel dock, he leaps off and enters the office.

Minutes later he reappears, grim-faced. "The Forestry Department's seized them. The attendant says the man who tied them out there lives on an old forty-foot grey boat and looks like a hippy."

"Where is he?" I ask.

"He doesn't know. And the new boss at Gulf Log Salvage is out."

"That's the group that oversees the log salvors?"

"It's a three-way co-op. Ministry of Forests, logging companies, and the insurers."

"So you can't do a thing."

He frowns. "Not if they've been seized."

We have only just got inside the basement when Mr. Scott, the new Log Salvage office manager, phones with the news that the man in the grey boat has told him that not only do the logs have no LS stamps on them, an offence that could cost Dick his licence, but the word "stolen," had been used.

"But you stamped them. You always stamp them."

"Apparently they've employed this 'hippy' to spy on salvors in an attempt to cut down log theft. Well, he's either an ass or he's been smoking too much pot."

"You must be furious."

"I hate dealing with bureaucrats. But when they have me up against a wall, I fight back. I've told Scott I want to meet their representatives at Fisherman's Cove to prove my point."

The meeting is arranged for the following afternoon, and the pounding swells, a residual from a southeasterly storm we'd had the previous night, only worsen Dick's migraine. Soaked by the rough waters of Queen Charlotte Channel off White Cliff, we arrive at the Cove a few minutes late, relieved to see that Dick's seized logs, protected by Eagle Island, are still anchored there.

Thanks to the gas attendant's brief description of the Forestry-contracted boat, we find it moored to a nearby float. It's an ugly vessel with a grey-blue iron displacement hull about thirty-eight feet long and a cabin fitted with several portholes reminiscent of a small navy boat from the '40s.

"What's the point in having a slow boat like that to catch thieves?" mutters Dick.

While I stay in the *Snark*, he knocks at the cabin door and exchanges a few words with someone inside. I feel sorry for him. This environment is completely alien to him. How will he react?

"If you come with me, I'll show you the stamps," I hear him say. There's a slight tremor in his voice.

Mr. Scott is first of the three men to clamber down into our boat, finding an easy seat on the five-inch-wide gunwale. Even though his low centre of gravity helps his balance, it is obvious that he is used to boats. But the other two men, an RCMP officer from the log theft division, and the older man from the BC Ministry of Forests practically fall onto the engine cover and, in their frantic search for something to hold, end up curving their fingers under its air vents.

As Dick drives out to his logs, the two officials sit stiffly upright, staring apprehensively at the very slight side swell that now butts at the jet boat's side. The extra five-hundred pounds or so have lowered its normally low freeboard by another three inches. Under happier circumstances, I would feel sympathetic toward them. However, I suspect that Dick is not above enjoying himself a little as he sneaks an occasional glance to catch their uneasy reactions.

"There you are, gentlemen," he says, pointing to one of the stamps, clearly visible to us all. "And the rest … " He uses his axe to manipulate the logs so that the three men can see a stamp on every log, including five that have rolled over, and seven partly submerged low-floaters. The guests admit that every log does bear his stamp, LS 608.

The Forestry bureaucrat pauses. "Where's your stamp hammer?"

Dick pulls it out of the rope bin and hands it over.

Forestry studies the number on its face and turns to the RCMP officer. "See?" he says triumphantly, pointing to the raised eighth-inch-wide square border surrounding the number. "That's the problem. The edge is chipped."

"That's easy to fix," says Dick.

"And the number's intact," I point out.

Obviously ill at ease since he cannot see any evidence of theft, the young RCMP officer shrugs.

Their lack of response bodes ill. How will the Forestry official react to someone who refuses to be intimidated by wrongful accusations?

Back at the grey boat, we're politely invited aboard. The two officials relax as soon as they set foot on deck, and we follow them into the small, humid cabin.

The fuel dock attendant's impression of the boat owner had been pretty close to the mark. The granny glasses, pallid wax-like skin and foot-long braid of unwashed hair certainly brings the word "hippy" to my mind.

Dick greets him coolly and we all squeeze ourselves around a cluttered table and try to avoid looking at each other through the fog of cigarette smoke.

"Everything's stamped," states the Forestry man.

The hippy's vacant stare gradually changes to one of incredulity, then to frustration. "But I saw——"

"But you *didn't* see," Dick interrupts. He's controlling himself remarkably well, his anger as well as his nerves.

"We did notice that a bit of the stamp surround had chipped off," says Forestry, addressing the hippy. "Perhaps that misled you?" he suggests.

By now I'm getting angry too. He's obviously taken pity on the hippy. "But I saw the LS number imprinted on the log," I repeat. "It really is quite distinct."

The hippy boat owner glowers. The aroma of stale mussels and barnacles from our drying rain jackets together with the cigarette smoke, fuel oil, an unwashed body and some other kind of animal odour, makes for an unpleasant distraction.

Dick continues. "Don't forget we've had some rain. Those low-floats have sunk since I stamped them. And I guess you never noticed the twisted ropes, eh?" He's even handing the guy an excuse!

Hippy shrugs. "All I know is that someone reported they were stolen, and they could have been."

I feel Dick's thigh against mine. It's quivering, dangerously taut, ready for action. His right arm is pressed against the table, fist clenched, thumb on top, knuckles white. "Talk sense!" he retorts. "If I wanted to steal, I'd make it worthwhile. I'd steal big ones! High floaters. Not those dinky low-floats!"

"Dick," soothes Mr. Scott, "no one's accusing you of stealing. Everyone knows you're honest."

Then something quite bizarre happens. A brown capuchin monkey jumps down from the highest shelf onto the hippy's shoulder. Chattering loudly, it lands onto the table and snatches Forestry's pencil, leaps back to its shelf and scolds the group below. Upon discovering the pencil is inedible, it throws it back, hitting the official on the head.

Everyone laughs, except for the monkey's target who ignores the diversion, maintaining in a serious voice that since part of the stamp is missing, his department had every right to seize the logs. "However," he adds condescendingly, "since it was an unintentional omission on your part, you may regain possession of them."

"Will you be assisting us financially for extra fuel costs incurred?" asks Dick.

Forestry's eyes widen. "I really don't see how we can do that when it was your responsibility to make sure your stamp hammer was in good order."

I wonder if the Forestry man is aware of the fine line he's treading. For five tense seconds, silence hangs in the air along with the clouds of smoke. I break it with a few genuine choking coughs.

As we leave, Forestry barks, "Make sure you order a new stamp hammer."

Dick pushes *Snark* away from the grey boat. "There's nothing wrong with this one," he snarls, adding under his breath, "Nasty little jumped-up bureaucrat!"

"Fucking arsehole," I add quietly.

With his hand poised over the ignition key, Dick frowns, turns to me in mock surprise. "What did you say?"

"He's an arsehole. Even the monkey knows that. "

Turning into the channel with the logs behind us, I can tell that the swells have subsided a little.

"Just when you need the *Styx*!" I yell.

He shrugs. "Happens a lot," he shouts in my ear. "If I go to the city, there'll be a spill."

We return via Bowen Island's south end because it's closer to Tunstall Bay where we'll anchor the logs temporarily until Alan can tow them to Shelter Island. Although the southeasterly has abated, the swells are still averaging a couple of feet high with an occasional three-footer.

Almost at Cape Roger Curtis, Dick points in the direction of Worlcombe Island, the outermost island of the Pasley group. "What's that?"

"Large, reddish-brown and flat? Looks like the top of …"

"A boxcar?"

Deviating only slightly from our course we discover that it is a boxcar, about fifty feet long and ten feet wide, with only twelve inches showing above the water's surface.

He raises his foot off the accelerator. "It's very heavy. That's why it's barely moving up and down in the swells," he says. "Must've come off a railway barge."

"Resting on the sea floor?"

"Just about. But in another half-hour it'll be smashing up against the rocks. Let's anchor the logs first," he says, and continues toward Tunstall Bay.

With the logs secured, we speed back to the boxcar and circle it. Each corner has a metal eye at the top. I thread the long blue connector line through both eyes at one end—not easy with the boat bouncing in the swells and the heavy boxcar almost static—and we add two more fifty-foot lengths of three-quarter-inch diameter connector rope to it, hooking the extra-long towline onto the stern cleat.

"Worse than towing an iceberg," I complain.

"The long line'll keep it out of the jet wash. And if it sinks suddenly, we won't go down with it."

"It's probably still attached to its wheels."

He nods. "Must be full of plywood, or it would've sunk earlier."

At first it appears that we won't be towing it anywhere. Then it swings slowly out toward *Snark*'s stern and grudgingly begins to trail behind, the following swells giving it a slight boost.

However, Dick is aiming for Pasley. "Where are you going?" I ask.

"I'll beach it in one of the Pasley bays. I want to see what's inside."

During the hour-long tow, I ask him to show me how to tie his most useful knot, a bowline.

"There's a right and a wrong way," he says, retrieving a piece of pickup line. "If you do it wrong and put a strain on it, you'll have a heckuva time undoing it."

While I hold the wheel, he demonstrates a few times then hands me another spare piece of rope. As I start to warn him of my shortcoming, he cuts me off gently. "It's no big deal if you can't get it right away," he says.

He holds the wheel between his knees and this time I copy him six times, move for move, then practise almost non-stop until we're a few hundred feet off Pasley.

As he reduces speed to allow slack in the towline, I haul the two connector lines aboard and, with a little guidance from *Snark*'s bow, we allow the boxcar to drift under inertia until it grinds onto the beach. Dick attaches its rope to a tree on the shore.

"We'll check it on tomorrow's low tide," he says, shoving *Snark* off the beach.

By six the following morning the tide has dropped to a low of three feet, enough for the boxcar's door to be mostly out of water. The whole structure lies sufficiently at an angle that we can see that the wheels are no longer there. They must have fallen off the heavy metal frame underneath.

From the boat, Dick opens the door, displaying a stack of fir plywood layers.

"Someone's coming!" I warn.

He shuts the door and turns to where, further along the rocky beach, an older man clambers down and angles toward us. "Caretaker," mutters Dick and drives *Snark* against the beach to meet him.

After listening to Dick's explanation, the caretaker asks, "Gonna check inside?"

Dick nods. "That's what I was doing. It's packed tight with fir plywood."

The caretaker regards the boxcar with avaricious eyes. "I know where we can get a tidy sum for that little load … We could clear it out in no time."

Dick shrugs. "I've already reported it."

The man's face falls. "That's a shame," he mutters. "It'd be no skin off their noses because the insurance'd pay."

Out of earshot, I ask Dick if he had reported it. "No," he replies, "but it's an easy way out. I just don't like getting involved in that kind of thing."

Later in the day, I refuel *Snark* at the Boatworks so that Dick can continue the hard job of splicing pickup lines. Alan's also there, refuelling the *Styx* with diesel; he's been waiting for the tide to rise high enough to refloat the boxcar.

I hang the nozzle back on the gas pump, push past Walt Hendrickson's little tractor parked outside the office door and relay the amount of premium leaded gas I've just pumped.

He's sitting in a chair next to the counter, crutches propped beside him. "Tell Dick to keep an eye out for boxcars," he says. "According to the news, four of them fell off one of the Rivtow barges during the storm the other night. They think they've sunk to the bottom of the Strait."

"What's in them?"

"Didn't hear … And I've fixed his stamp hammer. It's in there," he says, pointing to the box on his tractor.

I grab it. "Thanks," I tell him. "That'll make him happy."

"It only needed a strip of stainless steel welding around its edge."

"That simple, eh?" I say, practising my Canadian.

"Sure was."

In spite of his useless legs—or perhaps because of them—Walt is a man of many abilities. His wartime job building planes at the Boeing Factory in Seattle has stood him in good stead. For a time he was responsible for playing and timing the music for skating competitions at the large ice rink in Vancouver. Since he and his wife, Inez, bought the Boatworks, he has single-handedly built a thirty-foot cabin cruiser as well as rebuilding another.

I store the hammer in the boat and drive back to our float. At the top of the beach steps I stop for a moment to watch Puss—half-asleep—under the five-foot-high fuschia that grows at the shore corner of our yard and the Boatworks'. Since Dick rescued her as a tiny kitten drowning in the harbour a few months earlier, she has grown into an expert fishercat and, alas, a bird hunter. Never satisfied with the daily fresh herring Dick brings her from the Boatworks' live-bait pond, she creeps down to the water's edge at night and uses her claws to hook sculpins or other little fish as they swim amongst the reeds. Once she brought in a duck, and another day it was a flying squirrel, or it might be a snake … But now, under the bush, her seemingly closed eyes tell a lie. A few inches from her head hovers a rufous hummingbird, its green jewel-like feathers glittering as its long beak probes each red-mauve trumpet for nectar. Without moving a whisker, Puss flashes her eyes open, then from her sphinx-like position she leaps up and seizes the tiny creature. As I try unsuccessfully to catch her, she runs through the open door of the basement.

"Grab the cat!" I yell at Dick, still splicing rope inside. "She's caught a hummingbird."

She stands between him and me, the bird in her mouth. He drops the wooden splicing fid and rope and springs up, catching the cat. As he forces Puss's jaws apart the bird flees through the doorway. I wonder how many do not escape.

As soon as I deliver Walt's messages, Dick phones the towing company. They will arrange for the plywood owners to call him around lunchtime the following day.

"If they think I'm going to let them have it for peanuts," Dick mutters, "they'd better think again."

So instead of our usual run up the inlet first thing the following morning, we make a detour to check on the boxcar that Alan had tied to our Shelter Island grounds the previous night. It is still floating peacefully beside the standing boom.

After finding a total of eleven logs around the Gambier bays and the Pasley islands, we return home for a couple of hours' sleep.

But when I awake around ten, I glance out of the kitchen window in time to see a large deep-sea tug pulling out from behind Shelter Island. Suspicious, I grab the binoculars and wait until the tug's tow appears from behind the island. It is the top of the brownish-red boxcar.

We dress hurriedly, jump into *Snark* and catch up with the tug as it passes old Mr. Corkum's dock on Keats Island. This tug is huge, three times the size of the local yarding tugs. Dick hoots the horn and waves to the captain who leaves his deckhand at the wheel.

"What can I do ya for?" he asks, holding onto the cabin door jamb.

Dick cuts the engine. "I salvaged that boxcar and I've not given permission for its release."

"I got orders from the company last night. They told me to collect it."

"The last I heard was yesterday, and they said they'd get back to me around midday."

"Sorry, but my orders were to pick it up ASAP." The captain's manner is polite but adamant. "I'll get 'em on the radiophone if you wanna wait."

"Please."

A few moments later he returns. "They said they'd tried to contact you a couple of hours ago but there was no reply."

"We were out working," Dick explains and courteously takes his leave. As soon as we're out of earshot, he shrugs. "Don't like it … but you can't argue with a tug that size."

Back at home, he calls the owners from the basement. I wait within earshot. But things do not sound good. He slams the phone down. "Six hundred dollars! They've offered six hundred! It's an insult. Our time alone's worth that, dammit!" And with the heel of his hand he slams a karate chop against a support post. The house shudders.

Following him upstairs, I point out, "And there's the plywood … But can you be so sure it's not water-damaged?"

"The sheets are so tightly bundled it would take a week to soak in. And the glue they use is waterproof. That plywood is worth a small fortune. Why else would they send a huge tug up here for it in such a hurry?"

"It could have been smashed to splinters on Worlcombe rocks!"

"That's exactly what I told them," he says, leafing through the local directory.

"What will you do?" I ask.

He picks up the kitchen phone. "Call the local marine insurance broker."

The conversation is brief.

"He agreed six hundred was ridiculously low," he tells me. "He'll do his best. It's typical," he mutters. "Large companies trying to take advantage of the little guys. No wonder people want to get back at them."

"Now you know how the cat felt about you taking her hummingbird!" I tell him.

He gives a wry smile. "She might forget. I won't."

I feel for him. He's had three rough days.

12
Fishing and Hunting

"Ready for a change of scenery?" Dick asks the following morning. He has just emerged from the basement stairs with a pale yellow fishing rod—reel attached—in one hand and a small rectangular aluminum box in the other. "I need something to take the bad taste out of my mouth." He's referring, of course, to the stamp hammer and plywood container episodes, only one of which would have been enough to cause a stomach ulcer.

"That's a strange-looking rod," I remark.

"It's my fly fishing rod. A 'Phantom Hollokona.' Split bamboo, made by Hardy. How'd you like to give it a try?"

An hour later we're driving the Citroën along the Wilson Creek logging road, and on the back seat are a couple of sandwiches and Dick's Hardy tackle. It is so warm that I am wearing running shoes and shorts.

"We're in Mission Creek valley," he points out.

I can't see a river or creek anywhere, just an extremely steep, dense tree-covered slope to our left. The road winds dramatically for a few hundred feet, then, to our right on its upper side, I catch sight of an old landslide. "I almost lost the Jackson's logging camp truck in that slide," he says. "I was working for them at the time."

"That's their house near the Wilson Creek booming ground, isn't it?"

He nods. "I lived with them for a time. Pop Jackson introduced me to poetry and classical music. String quartets actually. He had a collection of 78 rpm records."

"Unlike you, I came to string quartets late," I explain. "You'll have to educate me."

"Something to look forward to," he says, parking under some trees at the roadside.

Out of the car at last, there's a quietness, not even the song of a bird. Then gradually my ears catch the ceaseless shushing of the invisible river from far below. Beyond the lining of salmonberry bushes at the road's edge, the bank is so high and steep I can't imagine climbing down.

"Don't look so worried," he says, locking the car. "We're only parking here because I don't want passersby to know where we're fishing." Carrying the rod and tackle, he leads me northwards along the logging road for almost a mile before diving briefly into the salmonberry brush then re-emerging, only to repeat the manoeuvre thirty feet further on. "Follow me," he calls, beckoning.

"I should have worn jeans instead of shorts," I complain, trying to avoid the thorny stuff.

"It'll be easier in a bit … But don't touch these," he warns, pointing to an eight-foot-high plant with large maple-leaf-shaped leaves just over a foot wide. "Devil's club. *Oplopanax horridus.* If you accidentally tread on its stem, it might spring up and whack you in the face. See those poisonous spines?"

"Isn't there a safer way to get to the river?"

"Just trust me."

And that's exactly what I do even though he waits patiently and laughs at the way I struggle and curse my way over bouldery soil overgrown with wild blackberries, past old tree roots left behind from logging and the occasional devil's club. But it is really only a few minutes before we hit a stand of second-growth trees, trees almost ready for harvesting, and the way down is much easier. The sight of the water sparkling, winking at me from between the dark tree trunks makes me forget the brush, and I skid the rest of the way down, reaching the creek before Dick, who has to be mindful of the expensive rod and tackle.

Standing on the bank, I am taken aback by the wildness of the place. As the music of the water takes over, I allow my surroundings to come to me. The gentle breeze that caresses my limbs and face, the faint perfume of the warm moist air, and the myriad greens of vegetation that remind me of the tiny waterfalls set free by the melting snows on Elphinstone. The far side of the creek is bordered by brilliant emerald salmonberry bushes, and behind them on rocky banks, a wall of darker green stands solidly against a late summer sky.

Dick crouches over a tiny pool, creek water pouring from his cupped hands. "Come and taste!" he calls.

"It's cold!" I shout after a few sips.

"What do you expect from melted snow?" he yells back, spraying me with a handful of water. It must be the relative heat of the day that makes it feel like ice against my skin.

I retaliate by tipping some down the back of his neck, then sit cross-legged on the mossy bank. Alders and conifers dripping with ferns and festooned with beard-like lichens lean over the creek like tired old men, while amongst the moss-covered boulders, delicate ferns dance in the breeze, the movement of their overlapping fronds causing a moiré effect.

Impatient to see all around me, I wade into the cool shallows and gaze downstream to the south. Boulders upon boulders, silver-crowned in the noonday sun, compete for attention as they stand out starkly against the dark grey shadows of the ones behind.

Dick settles on a flat rock and assembles the rod and reel while I watch from behind. "This reel's a Hardy, too," he says, fixing it onto the rod. "A quality English make. This will never fall apart."

Like a priest performing a religious ritual, he slowly and purpose-fully threads the pale green line through the first and largest ferrule—the only one with a pink lining.

"Why is that ferrule different?" I ask.

"It's lined with a garnet ring—helps the line slip through," he ex-plains, passing the filament through the smaller rings all the way to the tip. "And this," he says, tying a much thinner transparent short piece of nylon onto the end of the green line with a special knot, "is called the leader." The noise and movement of rushing water at his feet seem to make his actions even slower and more circumscribed than they actually are.

Pulling the aluminum box from his pocket, he shows me the rows of flies that he has made with wool, feathers and other things to imitate insects and bugs. He has even used a few cat whiskers. I had not realized just how serious a fly fisherman he was.

"We'll try this," he said, choosing the smallest—a brown, yellow and red fly, knotting it delicately onto the leader before hooking it in the keeper ring near the reel. Then he hands the rod to me. "Follow me."

He leaps from rock to rock across the fast-flowing water in a way I would not even try to emulate. Then he waits at a deeper dark pool where there is current but no white water. "Fish habitat," he says. Wading slowly, I catch up. "The idea," he explains, "is to present the hook with just enough movement that the fish thinks it's a drowning fly."

"Can't I just dangle it?"

"Sure. Go ahead."

I clamber over to the edge of the pool, unhook the fly, pull out a couple of yards of line and let the fly sit on the water. Nothing happens.

"Jiggle it a bit," he suggests. "Make it look as if it's alive."

Immediately, the rod springs in my hand as if moved by an invisible force. I focus on the small fish tugging at the end. "I've got something! What do I do?" I shout.

"Reel it in! Grab the leader—just above the fish!" He takes the rod. "Go over there to the dry part of the creek. If it falls off, it can't swim away."

"Is it a trout?"

"A ten-inch-long cutthroat." He lays the rod on the ground, takes the fish in his right hand and the line in his left. Using his front teeth, he bites the brain-case sharply, just behind the eyes.

"Yuck! You're eating it alive?" I ask, horrified.

Laughing, he spits the taste out. "It's an old Scottish method. Nothing kills a small fish quicker."

"Hmm … I'd rather use a rock on its head."

"Okay, but hit hard or it'll suffer." He hands me the dead fish on the line. "Here, you remove the hook."

Not easy because the fish is so slimy.

Almost as soon as I drop the fly in the same pool, I catch another cutthroat, roughly the same size. In my excitement I pull the line out of the pool with a jerk and the fish flies up in the air swinging wildly on the end, falling off the hook and landing on the rocks behind me. I drop the rod and try to pick the fish up, but it slips out of my hands before wriggling and flipping its way back into the shallow, fast-moving water.

Dick laughs. "Let it go," he advises. "It's earned its freedom."

I have more control over the third fish and rest it on the dry part of the creek bed before finding a suitable rock to hit it with. But I make the mistake of crouching down to look more closely at the beautiful creature with its delicately coloured rainbow skin. I glance up at Dick. "I can't … It's like … murdering. It hasn't done anything to hurt me."

"You eat fish and meat. Someone else does the killing for you. Perhaps it's time you took that responsibility."

I stare at the gasping trout.

"It's suffering," he says. "Hit it right and it won't hurt."

Resisting the temptation to shut my eyes, I take a deep breath and aim at the head. Afterwards I turn my face away from the bloody trout with a deep feeling of despair and loss. Dick crouches beside me and puts his arm around my shoulders. "If it's killing for eating and the animal doesn't suffer," he tells me, wiping my tears with the dry heel of his hand, "you shouldn't feel badly."

I try to dismiss the trauma. "How many of these make a good meal?"

"I'll show you," he says, jumping up. Breaking a sixteen-inch-long fork of twigs from a nearby alder sapling, he removes most of one twig and threads the long end of the now hooked stick through the gills of the two fish so that they stop at the crook. "Here's your answer—when the stick's two-thirds full."

Although I use the rod most of the time, I insist that every so often he shows me how to cast properly. His graceful movements result in a bite every time. As the day wears on, it becomes easier and less traumatic to kill my catch, but I draw the line at using his "old Scottish method."

"Not bad for a beginner," he encourages while watching my first attempts at casting. Then I catch my hook on an alder branch. "Don't forget to look behind you!" he yells after the fact.

At first I have to be content with making short casts because, if I throw too much line out, it just forms a tangled mess at my feet. With a couple of hours' practice, I even improve my leaping from rock to rock, in spite of Dick's warning me not to take chances. "I don't want to have to carry you up the bank," he shouts after a near miss.

We work our way downriver to where the main channel of the creek tumbles ten feet into a pool about the size and depth of a large living room. Beside the waterfall stands a table-sized flattish rock, a perfect place for us to eat lunch.

Munching our sandwiches, we're almost surrounded by water. In the side channel behind the rock a brown water ouzel—a dipper—bobs up and down hunting for bugs, little silver globules of water running off its back whenever it surfaces. Large iridescent blue dragonflies and smaller red ones zoom noisily past, hovering above the pool as they search for mosquitoes. They are the dragonflies from my childhood storybooks, the ones that the fairies rode.

As I help to dismantle the rod after lunch, I hum carelessly, softly.

Dick slides the bamboo rod into its cotton case. "What's that you're singing?" he asks. "I know it."

"Schubert's 'Die Forelle.' The song about the trout."

He slaps his head. "Of course … He used it for a quintet movement, too."

It was written by a poet who stands in blissful peace watching a trout darting about in a clear brook. An angler on a nearby bridge also watches the trout, but as long as the water remains clear, the poet knows the fish will not be caught. When the angler deliberately muddies the water and catches the fish by unfair means, the poet is outraged.

"Whose side are you on—the poet's or the angler's?" I ask.

"The poet's, of course."

"But we fooled the trout today," I point out.

"Ah, but it's not the same as using salmon eggs and worms. That's cheating."

He keeps the fish, hands me the rod, and we turn to face upstream. "This way," he says, pointing right up a steep bank.

The exposed rocks and gravel keep sliding backwards as soon as we set foot on them, so that by the time we reach the brushy part near the top we are dripping with sweat.

"Only fifteen minutes to the car," he says. But as he turns onto the road he freezes, grips my arm and puts his forefinger on his lips. He points at a large, black fuzzy shape feeding off some roadside bushes not more than thirty feet away in the direction of the car. The bear turns its head, stares for a couple of seconds and begins to move toward us. Has she seen us? A snuffling from the other direction prompts us to look back along the road at two cubs, about twenty feet away, also ambling along toward us—and of course, toward her. Dick waves me back and points to the river. "Run!" he urges quietly, tearing a couple of fish off the twig and throwing them onto the road as a decoy before catching up with me. We skid back down.

"Along the creek?" I whisper loudly.

He nods.

"But black bears are afraid of humans!"

"She's got cubs! We were between them and her. She might have seen us!"

Adrenaline kicks in, and we begin the long scramble back up-stream along the far side, a slight advantage if the bear should decide to come charging down after us. Climbing up the slimy rocks at the side of the waterfall is the hardest part. "Careful!" Dick cautions quietly as he gives me a leg-up. In my hurry, my foot slips in between two rocks. "Bloody rocks," I curse, trying to keep my voice down as he climbs past to pull me up.

After following the creek for a while, I decide to hike along the far bank, thinking it might be easier on my twisted ankle.

"Not a good idea," he warns.

I should have listened. I trip over some ferns and, without thinking, grab a devil's club stem to steady myself.

"What have you done?" he calls from the creek after hearing my shrieks.

Cursing, I slide down the bank to the water and hold up my hand. "Devil's club thorns."

While I keep an eye out for bears coming up the creek, he removes five large yellowish-green spines from the palm of my right hand. "It'll be swollen for a day or two," he warns.

"I'll stick to the creek bed," I tell him. "Better the devil you know!"

He grins. "Not bad for a literal-minded Englishwoman."

I ignore him.

We climb the bank just below the parked Citroën, and as we approach the top, Dick goes ahead to clear the way, helping me up the gravel and over the slash in case I fall again. "I'm not taking any chances with you this time," he says. "Stick with me."

At the road he peers out of the bushes. "All clear," he whispers, taking the car keys out of his fishing vest. "You rest that ankle."

I lay our catch on a thick wad of old newspapers in the trunk. Exhausted, dusty and sweaty, we slump into our seats.

"Would she really have tried to kill us?" I ask as we drive off.

"Probably. Who knows? Depended on her mood."

That evening I am sitting at the kitchen table resting my bandaged ankle on a chair and soaking my hand in Epsom salts, when Dick, who's cleaning the trout in the sink, asks if I want a rod of my own.

"After all that excitement?"

"Fishing's usually a peaceful occupation," he explains. "I've been on some trips where things haven't turned out the way they should, but none of them included bears."

"Yes," I nod, "it would be nice to have my own rod."

Puss stands on her hind legs and stretches high up to the counter. But when Dick drops some morsels of fish guts in her saucer she races over to eat them.

That evening and the next, my partner breaks from his non-cooking role, dredging the fish in flour and frying them. With an accompaniment of buttered bread, the simple meal is hard to beat.

Although Dick expects me to take control of the kitchen, it isn't long before I find myself challenging his rather sexist ideas.

He accidentally knocks over a full mug of hot chocolate on the table and it runs over the edge and onto the floor. When I hand him a cloth to clean it up, he says quite calmly, "But it's your job."

Perplexed, I stare at him for a moment. "My job? Not if you spilled it."

"It is in my book," he explains calmly.

I have to get to the bottom of this. It doesn't seem to fit with his character as I know it. "I suppose your mother would have cleaned it up?" I ask.

"Sure she would."

"Well," I tell him in a surprised voice, "in my experience, anyone who spilled anything was expected to clean their own mess up."

He stares at me. He's obviously a little perplexed, too.

Trying to keep calm, I continue. "If I knocked over some engine oil on your basement floor, I'd never expect you to clean it up. I'd do it because it was my fault."

He says nothing, does nothing. His reaction has shocked me. It was not what I had expected of him and in a rational voice I tell him so. Without responding, he leaves the table and goes to work in the basement. I clean up the mess.

I needn't have worried. A few weeks later he spills some milk on

Puss inspects the catch of the day.

the kitchen floor. Before I can react, he grabs a floor cloth from under the sink and wipes it up.

"Oh, thanks," I murmur, trying not to make a big deal of it.

He grins. "You're welcome," he says in the same quiet tone.

Because of the increased local competition from smaller, more powerful log salvage boats, we are having the 289 engine replaced with a high performance, high compression Ford 351 HO, one that will turn up to 4,800 rpms to drive the three-stage Hamilton jet. It's being blueprinted, and that entails rebuilding it to the closest tolerances possible to improve reliability. At the same time Dick and I are rebuilding the jet unit in the basement, replacing the short-lived aluminum jet stators—fins that separate the impellors—with a set of custom-made stainless steel ones. These won't degrade in salt water like the stock aluminum ones. Not only is it a job I enjoy, it saves us a substantial amount of money. We have also discovered that if we buy a six-inch-long cutlass bearing, we can hacksaw and smooth the sawn edges to make three, two-inch bearings that suit our needs perfectly, an operation that will save us more than a hundred dollars. The only part I leave to Dick is some of the disassembling because it often requires brute strength coupled with specific tricks to separate parts that have been corroded together by sea water.

A couple of weeks after my first fishing trip, he is doing some of that grunt work while I nose around the far room in the basement, unearthing boxes of books: philosophy, theosophy, art, poetry, novels, science fiction, fantasy, ancient history, science, biology, cosmology and books of Greek and Roman classics, the kind that Oxford dons have studied. I also find other books on obscure subjects, including a 1923 copy of Havelock Ellis' *The Dance of Life*, which Dick has marked up in an uncharacteristically small hand. I leave the books and accost him beside the metalwork vise. "Have you read all those books in that room?"

He looks up from *Snark*'s frozen cutlass bearing and nods. "And some in the attic."

I turn my curious eyes into the more inaccessible workshop area with its old cupboards and boxes, mostly wooden ones darkened from age and use, boxes of ancient blacksmithing and metalworking tools, fibreglass, paints, oils, grease, wires, nails, boat parts, metal sleeves, bolts, screws, hardware of all kinds. I wonder if Bluebeard's last wife felt like this as she searched her husband's castle.

After snooping for another half an hour, I find a gun.

"It's my .22," Dick tells me when I ask him about it. "A Brno. Once in a while I use it to hunt grouse."

I laugh. "Grouse?" I echo, then, "Yuck!"

He gives me a quizzical stare. "How come?"

"When Gordon and I left Gib's that first week, he gave us some frozen grouse breasts. Neither of us liked them but I never told him. We thought the meat was bad ... off."

"I doubt it. Gib's very fussy about game. You must have the wrong idea about how grouse should taste."

Three days later, after stashing the Brno carefully in the trunk of the Citroën, Dick explains, "Andy sounded a bit gloomy on the phone last night. I think he's got itchy feet, so I promised to take him up the logging road the first decent Sunday. Want to come?"

"Grouse hunting?" I ask.

"Maybe," he says. "Besides, *Snark*'s engine won't be ready for at least another week."

We collect Andy from his house around the bluff and drive to Roberts Creek before turning onto a logging road. Dick stops to raise the Citroën's hydraulic ride height, so that the car can clear the large rocks and ridges that would hit the undersides of most vehicles. As we set off again, Andy nudges him from the back seat. "Hey! Look up there! A pack of dogs!"

Dick brakes, and we gaze curiously along the bank beside us at the yellowish-grey animals, one large one and five others about half the size. "Timber wolves. Mother and pups."

She stares at us for about ten seconds then bounces sprightly into the scrubby salal undergrowth with her family. Andy's mood has brightened already.

We travel four or five miles over the dusty gravel road, slowing down for potholes, until we emerge from the edge of the second-growth forest into an area of logging slash. Hiking in this terrain is not for beginners. The uneven ground is covered with all types of brambles, salal, ferns, fireweed, moss and some seedling alders, all of which might conceal old stumps, rotting tree trunks, rocks and mounds. It is the type of landscape that causes me to feel antagonistic toward it, as if it has deliberately designed itself to trip me up.

Dick parks, climbs out, checks his pockets for his clip and box of .22 "shorts" then pulls his gun from the trunk. "Why don't you two go for a hike further up the road ... as far as that ridge," he says, pointing, "while I spend an hour on my own."

Both of us understand the need for hunting without extraneous movement or noise and we know that Andy tends to be on the clumsy side. After arranging to meet at the car, Andy and I watch Dick wade into the dense slash while we continue walking along the boulder-strewn road at a reasonable speed. It is a relatively level area that follows a shoulder around the mountain, and although we cannot see the Strait, my companion is impressed with the wild scenery. A few moments into the hike, he stops to point at a patch of fireweed blossoms on the north side, one of many that have colonized after the relatively recent logging slash burn had cleared the ground.

"Yust look at this!" he says. "I mean to say, what more could you vant in a plant?" He pulls one of the flowers off the red main stalk and points to its four delicate and darker-veined pink lobed petals. Even the narrow sepals between them are coloured with a slightly deeper pink. And the whole flower is trumped with a group of pale stamens in the centre from which arises one startling long, four-lobed pink stigma. A single fireweed flower. He's right. It truly is a thing of beauty, particularly on its own, but most people look at them en mass and miss the point.

"And it's only a poor weed," I add.

He shakes his head. "Now yust think! That even if it is not a weed, then gardeners would grow it and try to change it to another colour." He turns and shrugs. "Ach! Vy is it that people vill never be satisfied with what they have?" There's even a tinge of anger in his voice.

Remembering what Dick had told me about fireweed, I explain that the Haida people had been satisfied, that they had used the fibres from the stem to make fishing nets and the fluff from the seeds to fill their pillows and mattresses, and they ate the pith in early spring. My response exasperates Andy even more, probably because I have limited it to the practical aspect.

"Vat I'm getting at," he continues irritably, "is this: vy do people want more in life?"

"I don't," I tell him.

"Ah, you've found vhat you want ... or you think you have," he says, with a touch of envy, or perhaps cynicism. "I haven't."

"What are you looking for?"

"Well, I might vant to live in a warmer place. Somewhere like Honolulu. Start a garage there."

"You could. Your daughter's left home."

"My vife doesn't vant to leave Gibsons ..."

So that's why he's cranky. Dick and I always had the feeling that Andy has been marking time with her. Particularly when he occasionally reminds us that he has never shirked the responsibilities of their shotgun marriage in Holland before they emigrated. I think he wishes she shared his love of classical music.

"Maybe I'll go, spend a year there on my own," he says, "but I believe that once a man and voman have married, they should stick it out."

Knowing how Andy likes to argue, I do not remind him of his comment about my failing first marriage, and he soon returns to the subject of our surroundings. "Yust look at those branches!" he enthuses. "Have you ever seen anything so green, so vonderful?"

"Then why would you want to leave?" I demand.

"Ach ... because there's something more in life. I *know* there is."

"Then you'll have to find out for yourself."

Back at the car, there's no sign of Dick. Half an hour later he appears at the roadside, sweaty, dirty, and covered in fireweed fluff. Without a single grouse.

Andy grins. "The great hunter returns. Skunked, eh?" He almost sounds happy at Dick's misfortune.

"It's probably too early in the day," Dick reasons. "They like to feed at dusk."

He decides to take a different route home. About halfway down the mountain, he steps on the brakes—gently—obviously trying not to skid. "Quiet!" he orders. "Don't move."

Andy and I are puzzled.

Very slowly, smoothly, he climbs out of the car, slinks back to the trunk, pulls out the gun and quietly lowers the trunk lid. In the rear view mirror I see him loading the clip, feel the Citroën's self-levelling hydraulics adjusting as he rests on the roof to aim at something in front of us.

That's when I see—about forty feet away—a log lying alongside the road, on top of which are perched six grouse. Andy sees them, too. Obviously changing his mind about his shooting position, Dick creeps toward the roadside so that the log is exactly end-on to him. He aims at the row of grouse on the log, but he is still dissatisfied with his shooting angle. At last he crouches, aims and fires.

Two grouse fall at once. Instantly he shoots again. A third bird flutters and falls. The other three fly off, clucking noisily.

"Man! Vhat a shot!" yells Andy.

We both climb out of the car and follow the mighty hunter to pick up his game. We're amazed. One shot has gone clean through a bird's head to kill the bird perched next to it, too. Instantly. Two with one shot. The third bird lies dead, also from a head wound.

I'm so surprised by the situation that the tears I had expected never materialize. "What kind are they?" I ask.

He checks their plumage. "They're not a blue grouse, nor a willow grouse either. I'd say they're a cross between the two." Then he tells us how he remembers, as a child, the family bantams escaping to breed with the local willows.

As soon as he's stashed the game in the trunk, I ask if I can try my own hand at target practice. He shows me the basics then pins an old gas receipt on a nearby tree trunk.

I line up the gun's crosshairs with the paper, try to keep it steady … hold my breath. Shoot. The .22 short hits the paper. Not just the paper, but the centre of the paper. I'm so overjoyed I ignore Andy's shout of "Beginner's luck!" Five more shots, four paper hits. But I don't know how I would have made out if it had been a live bird. At the moment it is just a challenge and I am enjoying myself.

Tasting the stew of three fresh grouse in red wine I soon realize the so-called "bad" flavour in Gib's bird was actually the normal grouse taste—reminding me of a perverted mountain blueberry, their favourite diet. Now viewed in this light, I admit to Dick that grouse is one of my favourite meats.

Before the colder weather sets in, we employ Frank Fritsch to build our fireplace. A master stonemason originally from Germany, now living on Gambier Island, he leaves home every morning in his little outboard to cross the busy channel to Hopkins Landing wharf where he keeps his old truck. His expertise means that he's able to follow Dick's rather idiosyncratic plans, constructing the fireplace against the centre of the outside wall but angled toward the south end of the long room. As soon as it's finished, it looks like a great grey monolith with a large arched hole. Since neither of us can stand that for very long, we steal a spare morning, take the second ferry of the day and drive down Fraser Street in Vancouver to check out the tombstone manufacturers' raw materials. I feel rather foolish standing inside the first shop we visit listening to my companion explain what we're looking for.

The owner takes us out to his yard littered with gravestones and slabs of various colours and sizes, and shows us a huge jade boulder from way up the Fraser River valley that someone no longer wants. Dick and I nudge each other and exchange excited glances. "I think that'll be out of our league," Dick tells him.

"But it's not gem quality," explains the store owner. "That's why it's here." Then he adds that he's just ordered a huge computerized rock-sawing machine from Switzerland, and would welcome a chance to try it out. "If you send me the design you want, I'll give you a deal."

We shake hands and leave a deposit. The only downside is the fact that the computerized machine has not yet left Switzerland.

13

Seal Songs

The phone rings. After a short conversation Dick shouts up the stairs, "I've got a rush float job to do, and Alan's repainting the *Styx*' hull. Want to come along?"

It turns out that a Vancouver resident who owns a summer place on one of the Pasley islands has a sinking float that has been badly damaged by a recent overzealous westerly. It needs repairing urgently so that his family can access their house during the last few days of summer. That means towing it to Shelter Island where Dick can utilize material from three older floats he has stored there. Having worked with his father for some years on government dock installations, he is an expert float and ramp builder, and the extra money is very welcome.

Avoiding a group of annoyed mallards feeding on the algae growing on the Boatworks' dock, I ease *Snark* past the floatplane tied to the government dock and steer out of the harbour. It is at the beacon where today's westerlies draw attention to themselves, their wind-whipped whitecaps now blowing in off the Strait. Bouncing and pounding, we cross Shoal Channel and I cut between Salmon Rock and Keats Island, taking the same route that had scared me only a few months ago. Half-expecting a scraping crunch, I pass through it slowly, gazing fearfully at the rocks below.

"You're doing fine," Dick encourages. "Water fools the eye. Those rocks aren't as close as they look."

Even though I remembered the illusion from my physics courses, I still prefer to proceed with caution. "What's our draft … eight inches?" I ask.

"If we're planing" he replies. "Fourteen if we're stationary."

Since the rocks under the hull appear closer to our planing draft, the fact that we don't hit them proves how drastically the water distorts images. However, the width of the passage either side of us is no problem because I am familiar with it at low tide.

So far, Dick is happy with the new Ford 351 engine. That, coupled with the renovated jet, gives the *Snark* a top speed of fifty knots, but of course we rarely hit that because high revs wear engines out.

The damaged float is attached to one of the smallest islands in the group, an island with only one house on it. Dick leaps off *Snark*, raises the articulated ramp and counterweight, then detaches the float from its anchor chains. He also removes a wheel from the end of the ramp because its bearing needs replacing.

"Remember how to tie a bowline?" he asks. "I need one of those connector ropes tied onto the float."

Having only practised that knot once since he had taught me the previous week, I am caught off guard. To diffuse the situation I try to imagine I'm watching his hands rather than my own, as if he were demonstrating again. I had been struck by the graceful flowing movements of his arms, particularly how he had used his right hand to make two moves simultaneously at the start of the operation while holding the other part of the rope in his left. Recalling how everything seemed to fall naturally into place after that one crucial movement, I am so intent on the hand ballet that within three seconds I am astounded to find the finished product in my own hands.

"You've been practising."

"Not as much as I should have."

"No shoulds," he says. "And while we're out here, I may as well take a quick run round the islands. We'll anchor this temporarily in one of the bays. Want to come … or would you rather sit on the float? You might see a seal or two."

I choose the float.

He anchors it inside a small island bay that's sheltered from the westerly. There's more than enough room for me to lie full length on its sound planks.

The air temperature is perfect, similar to the light breeze I had felt as the *Canadian Star* passed the Azores, but the sun is not as strong. I sit cross-legged, breathing deeply through my nose until I am surprised to find myself humming a scale, a sustained warm-up exercise used by opera singers before embarking on the more florid ones. The previous week I had unpacked some of my old music in the spare room in the basement and had run through a few songs, including the Britten arrangement of "Waly Waly." But until then, I had not sung since I had left the Old Country where I'd studied piano, trumpet and voice at college in Liverpool. I had even taken three singing exams including the final grade of the Associated Board of the Royal Schools of Music, but my decent marks were certainly not justified by any diligence on my part. Neither did I practise for most of my numerous choral performances.

Now, with only the company of a few quacking ducks and a pair of squawking black oystercatchers searching for food on the nearby rocks, I try a few arpeggios, then progress to some vocalises. My voice seems quieter than it used to be. Is it because I have not sung for so long? Or is the sea stealing the sound? Using the diaphragm properly for support, I'm able to project a little more and, during some florid passages, I discover that at least the high notes are still there.

A movement in the water catches my eye, and a silvery-grey seal's head emerges twenty yards away between the float and the rocky promontory on my right. Pretending to ignore it, I continue singing, and the animal dives.

But the seal reawakens memories of my grandmother's living room in Bognor where she and I—aged six—had listened to the sweeping *Hebrides* overture on her wireless. Not only had she asked me if I could hear wave music, she told me there were seals frolicking in the sea too. And when I was older she told me about her dream to become an opera singer, dashed when her youthful marriage and consequent pregnancy put an end to her free vocal lessons. One of the pieces of sheet music she had given to me before she died was a Scottish song known as "The Boatmen of the Forth," praising the fishermen who brave all weathers to bring their sea harvest to the townsfolk. The melody has an unusually wide range and each verse ends with a strikingly evocative yodel-like call of the oyster-seller lassies, "Caller Oo–oo!" repeated three times but with a slightly different tune. When Dick had played Jean Redpath's recording the previous week, I had to restrain myself from singing along.

It is a good time to try it again out here with the seal, which has now resurfaced, and so with no one around, I sing freely and from the heart, lingering on certain word sounds to convey their meaning. Lacking accompaniment, I do what I wish with it, singing without bar lines, using pauses as I see fit. As I end the final verse holding the three false yodels long and loud, it begets an unaccustomed feeling of inner power and control. I think I'm beginning to understand what unaccompanied folk singing is all about, particularly that while rhythm is intrinsic to the song, it has to be subservient to the context. Just as the sea's swells are repetitive but slightly irregular, a musical performer will know instinctively where to use rubato and accelerando.

Why has this taken so long to understand? What has allowed me to delve more deeply into myself for artistic expression? Could it be my new partner's way of presenting life to me, teaching me through the sea?

Gazing out toward the distant islands, I had forgotten my solitary listener. Now resurfaced only a few feet away from the float, it stares questioningly at me with its limpid—almost human—dark eyes. Another seal joins it, followed seconds later by two or three more. Within a minute, about twenty or more heads—silvery mottled with black or brown—poke up around the float, and I repeat the yodel call with my own variations of trills, short arpeggios, both staccato and legato—for the seals' entertainment and, of course, my own. They actually give the impression that they are listening.

What would these mournful-eyed animals like next? An old exam piece, the slow, beautiful "Porgi Amor" from Mozart's *Marriage of Figaro* comes to mind. Sung by a woman who is afraid she has lost her husband's love, it seems to echo their expressions. I almost stop singing when two adult seals clamber onto the adjacent rocky promontory thirty feet away. They preen themselves and stretch out lazily in the sun like a pair of overweight tourists on a Waikiki beach.

"How about some Handel?" I ask them. When they ignore me, I turn to serenade the bobbing heads beside the float.

But it seems that "Let the Bright Seraphim," the brilliant aria from Samson that I used to sing as an exercise, is not particularly to their liking because they keep their heads under the water longer than above it. Suspecting they'd prefer a lullaby, I begin Gershwin's "Summertime." The two Waikiki tourists sway their heads from side to side, almost in time with the slow-paced tune. One scratches behind its ear with a flipper then rolls easily onto its side for the second verse. The sixteen adult-sized swimmers and bobbers certainly appear to be listening attentively, so are their pups, little silver snuffly creatures that remind me of human babies.

But as I begin the last word, "By-y-y ..." on a slow descending scale at the end of the song, *Snark* roars around the corner with a tier of logs. The two fat sybarites dive off the rocks and flop into the water to sink out of sight along with the others.

Dick shuts the engine off and pulls the float's anchor rope over the stern cleat. "What the heck were those seals doing?" he asks.

"Listening."

"To what?"

"Me, singing."

"How come you've never sung to me?"

I shrug. "I'd rather not. You're used to hearing the best."

"That's nothing to do with it. I'd never compare your singing with anyone else's. It's your voice, and that's all I care about." Giving me a sideways glance he adds, "See if they'll come to 'Waly waly.'"

"How do you know I can sing that?" I ask, taken aback.

He sits on the gunwale with a guilty curl at the corner of his lips. "You were singing it in the basement the other day."

I blush. "I'm out of practice."

He just tells me to keep practising.

That evening he plays me an old recording of John McCormack singing "Dan nan Ro'n" or "The Song of the Seals," supposedly sung by the selkies. He explains that a well-known Scottish singer was able to draw a crowd of seals to her when she sang it by the water's edge.

A sea maid sings on yonder reef
The spell bound seals draw near
A lilt that lures beyond belief
Mortals enchanted hear

He lifts the tone arm off the record. "You've heard of the selkies?"

"From the Orkneys and Hebrides? The people who climbed out of their seal skins so they could pretend to be human and marry a local?"

He nods, sliding the old shellac record into its cardboard sleeve. "Some of those families still believe they're related to the dark and hairy selkies."

I laugh. "A handy excuse for producing a darker baby when the locals are all fair-skinned."

He agrees. "I believe there were quite a few dark-haired seafarers sowing their wild oats on those islands …"

The thought of having a child scares me. I am reminded of the time near the end of my first marriage when I thought Gordon might settle down to a more responsible existence if he had a child to focus on and I shudder when I think how close I came to making such a stupid mistake.

"Do you want children?" I ask.

"Don't mind one way or the other," he replies casually. "Why? Got your eye on a selkie?"

Glancing at his dark hair and summer tan, I can't help smiling. But I'm compelled to add, "I just don't think I'd be a good mother."

He shrugs. "Don't let it bother you. There's plenty of time."

About a week after this, Dick receives a phone call from Maryanne West, a waterfront-dweller who lives on Gower Point, asking a "great favour." There is a large dead sea lion on her beach, and her dog insists on rolling itself amongst the decomposing flesh whenever he leaves the house. Apparently the corpse has lain there for some time, but since the highest tide has been a couple of inches lower each day, there is no chance of it being floated out to sea any time soon, and certainly not before the bacteria have had their way with it. So she wonders if Dick can use the *Snark* to refloat it.

"How about a backhoe?" I ask him.

"That beach isn't accessible from the road. It's at the bottom of a high cliff. Besides," he explains, "she's already tried the Conservation Officer, the Fisheries people and the regional district. None of 'em want anything to do with it."

In the basement he picks up a bundle of old, frayed, three-quarter-inch-diameter rope, grabs his long-wristed thick rubber gloves, then climbs into his waders.

I can tell we're closing in on Mrs. West's beach as the unmistakable nauseating stink of rotten meat drifts out to greet us on the light westerly.

"Phiew!" I yell. "No wonder she wants it moved!"

On a bouldery beach twenty feet above the water line lies a huge, bloated, grey-brown mass, and for a split second, with my wind-watered eyes, I am fooled into thinking there is some remaining life in it. But it's only Mrs. West's boxer rolling ecstatically in the foulness.

One lone California sea lion sits in the middle of this group of Steller sea lions.

Dick turns the engine off and allows the *Snark* to drift up against the shore. "It's a Steller," he says, "about fifteen hundred pounds. I'll do the dirty work, and you can pull it off."

He dons his rubber gloves and picks up the old rope, while I shift to the driver's seat.

"A sad sight," I mutter.

"Not for fishermen … Take it easy to start," he advises. "Don't want the rope to slip off or cut the hide."

Trying ineffectually to keep downwind of the sea lion, Dick ties the rope around a back flipper, curving it along the body, around the head and knotting it around a front flipper. The dog watches closely, barking constantly. Perhaps he knows we're about to remove his stinky toy.

"Hey, pooch!" Dick shouts before running back to collect the pulling chain, the other end of which I've already looped over the stern cleat. He pushes the *Snark* back into the water then hooks the chain onto the rope-parcelled cadaver. Standing to one side, he motions for me to go ahead.

Bearing in mind the carcass might even weigh as much as a ton, I accelerate more gradually than I would have done for a log, so that the line will not suddenly snap tight. I wait until it pulls taut before increasing the revs to 4,300. That's when the blubbery mass starts slipping, wobbling, over the rocks and down the beach. The dog, tail between its legs and ears flattened behind its head, snarls and watches in horror and fear as the dead becomes alive. But as the corpulent body slides further toward the sea, the dog's demeanour changes to that of a vanquishing hero. Barking savagely, it chases the monster all the way into the water.

Once Dick is aboard, we tow the floating remains about a mile out into the Strait before releasing it.

Three days later, Mrs. West drops in with a carton of chocolate ice cream. "Did you hear that a sea lion's body has turned up on a Davis Bay beach?" she asks. "They're having a problem finding anyone to dispose of it."

We all laugh.

I'm glad we hadn't stamped it with a log salvage number.

Occasionally we take in Vancouver Chamber Music concerts and opera performances. Thanks to a late ferry sailing that leaves Horseshoe Bay half an hour before midnight we can still make the daylight rounds the following morning. But sleep catch-up afterwards is a must.

And of course we continue, with Andy, to visit Gib for our Wednesday music evenings. Gordon no longer shows up there. Rumour in this small community has it that his social life has become even more scattered and we never see each other let alone communicate.

That fall, he files for divorce, citing Dick as co-respondent. When the RCMP officer drives down to the house in early December and hands me the official form, I wish the doorstep would swallow me up. So this must be how it feels to be a scarlet woman. And in spite of Dick reasoning with me, explaining that he is the one who should feel the shame because he's the one being cited, it makes no difference. Then he quotes Dickens' character, Mr. Bumble: "The law is a ass—a idiot." He says we should be celebrating the fact that the whole nasty business will be over in six months.

Then I ask Dick what he thinks about the rest of Mr. Bumble's comment: "If that's the eye of the law, the law is a bachelor; and the worst I wish the law is that his eye may be opened by experience—by experience."

"But he meant a young bachelor," Dick reasons. "Surely you don't think I'm lacking in experience after keeping my eye on you for two and a half years?"

14

The Hammonds' Christmas

Since I seem to be turning into a Canadian by osmosis, and since neither of us are religious, I'm wondering how we will be celebrating our first Christmas together. However, it is a given that we will be eating our celebratory meal with Dick's parents.

One early afternoon about a week before the big day, he drives me in the *Snark* through the Salmon Rock shortcut until, just off Keats' southern shore, he turns the ignition off and allows the boat to drift. To my surprise, he removes his chest waders—essential in winter weather— and trades them for running shoes. He throws a coil of three-eighths-diameter rope over his shoulders then, from under the bow, brings out a small axe that has its single blade protected by a hand-made leather sheath, a sure sign it has been kept sharpened and oiled.

"Let me off here," he says. "I'll call you to pick me up."

I glance at the almost bare beach. "Where are the logs?" I ask, knowing full well that what he is carrying has nothing to do with pulling logs off a beach.

"You'll see," he replies mysteriously.

I have learned to appreciate his trait of springing surprises on me. He really gets a kick out of teasing my insatiable curiosity.

He leaps off the bow onto the gravel and pushes the *Snark* back into the water until it's afloat. I stick the pike pole down into the sea floor below and hang on to keep the boat stationary.

Bounding into the ferns and salal brush, Dick vanishes amongst the head-high greenery. Moments later, I hear a Tarzan-like yodel from

the swaying summit of a forty-foot-high fir tree, and there he is, clinging on like some bizarre male Christmas tree angel, waving at me. He
disappears down amongst the branches, but it isn't until I hear the sound
of chopping that I understand what he is up to. Within seconds his arm
appears, lowering a length of treetop to the ground at the end of a rope.
After pushing noisily through the brush, he emerges near the water's
edge with his harvest behind him. "Okay!" he shouts, waving me in.

He lays it on the engine cover.

"I thought you didn't believe in Christmas," I say.

"I don't," he replies. Then in one continuous movement he pushes
Snark off the beach and leaps onto the bow. "Pagans used trees for their
solstice celebrations long before the Christians."

He stows the rope and tells me to hang onto the tree. "Now we
have to find one for my parents and another for the Hendricksons next door."

One at a time he drags the treetops up the cement beach steps. Leaving
ours on the grass, we tie his parents' tree to the Citroën's roof.

"My mother will complain that it's too big," he warns, "and
Father will tell her off for complaining."

"Sounds as if they have a ritual of their own," I mutter.

Sure enough, on hearing our car draw up, Lil marches out of the
house and exits their back gate. "Watch this!" Dick whispers.

"Dick!" she howls. "For heaven's sake, why on earth do you have
to cut such a big one? Don't you ever learn?"

Hal, following her, protests, "Good heavens, woman! Can't you
just be grateful that you've got a tree?" I can hear the resignation in
his voice.

As I help Dick undo the rope, we sneak a grin and nudge each other.

"I suppose he's cut a huge one for himself, too," Lil says to me.
"Don't let him get away with it next year. And keep on at him about
finishing the living room."

"Mother," Dick addresses her a little sharply, "mind your man-
ners! This Christmas will be special for Jo and me."

Religion or no, he's right. Even this early I feel an unaccustomed
relief that there will be no complications to disrupt our day.

But she turns abruptly, purposefully, to him. Does she have something up her sleeve? "I hope that means that you won't be going out to work on Christmas Day," she says in a combative tone.

My future husband bristles. "Of *course* I'm going out."

"Dick!" she wails in frustration.

Hal has obviously heard this second complaint before. "Mom," he says, "leave the poor man alone."

From this point on, I know that my future mother-in-law will never win any of the arguments she has with her only child. And somehow I know that he will always take my side against her.

"I don't mind him going out," I tell her. "The boom men get careless at Christmas and that means more logs for us. Besides, there'll be no competition."

"Surely you won't be going, too?" she asks me.

"I wouldn't miss it."

"Well, good for you ..." she says, segueing into, "By the way, I've left a box of extra tree ornaments and lights in your basement."

I thank her and say they'll be useful.

As we drive away, I tell Dick I found the visit entertaining.

"I should have warned you about her other perennial complaint," he says.

"Working on Christmas Day? I was prepared for it."

"So was she ... but I think she hoped you'd be on her side."

It's quarter after seven early Christmas Day and still dark, but I turn the kitchen light off and slide the window open a crack, allowing a refreshing draft to blow against my face. It's a southerly wind that is sliding up the little draw on the south side of Keats, occasionally forcing its way over the island, across the channel and into the harbour. But having found itself trapped inside the bowl, all it can manage are a few surface ripples shimmering under the Boatworks' office lights.

Twenty minutes later we are aboard the *Snark* and passing the government dock, but instead of turning to port as usual, we veer south into the dark Strait, almost into the path of a slow oncoming tug. The three round white lights displayed in a vertical line above its wheelhouse indicate it is engaged in a tow over two hundred yards astern, and I know it is pulling a log boom because I can see the four telltale kerosene-fuelled hurricane lamps that have been hung on iron posts at the boom's fore and aft corners. The waves are quite rough here in front of Gospel Rock where Keats no longer acts as a windbreak, some swells rising, perhaps, to three feet. But now as the gusts hit my face, I suspect that the southerly is changing to a westerly.

Dick steps on the accelerator, obviously intending to circle the boom, but when the skipper flashes a searchlight at him, he steers for the tug's open window and pulls alongside.

"Dropped a few off Gower," the skipper hollers.

"Where were you when the wind came up?" Dick yells back.

"Roberts Creek. Trying to make the tide. Westerly'll help us now."

Dick acknowledges him with a wave, and using the hand-held searchlight that plugs into the dash, we drive the *Snark* along the side of the boom, inspecting it until we come to a broken tailstick on its south side. Each end dangles uselessly in the water and the section's two side-sticks hold nothing between them. All the logs from that section have already drifted out.

Drawing on experience, Dick uses his combined knowledge of the tug's approximate speed, the changing wind's behaviour, and that of the tide during the last couple of hours to figure out where most of the logs should be found. The brightening dawn makes the job easier, and over the following two and a half hours we gather thirty-three good-sized fir, most of them about to go ashore off rocky Gower Point beach. Fortunately, only four are aground. Working that particular shallow shore in a wind of that direction and velocity is dangerous. Dick had told me that, a few years before I met him, a similar wind and wave combination in that area had thrown his boat upside down on top of him after he'd gone ashore for a log. He had been fortunate that one of his competitors working nearby had been able to use his own boat to right the hull.

By the time we have collected the logs, the tug and boom are well on their way to Long Bay. Knowing that the slow-towing *Snark* will never catch up to it, Dick decides to continue on to Shelter Island and tie the logs at the storage ground before speeding to the tug to advise the skipper of our find. But when we catch up to him, we learn that he is in a hurry for his Christmas dinner. He says his boss will be contacting us to arrange for the spill logs to be towed to the damaged boom later, perhaps in a couple of days.

"And how long before we're paid?" I ask Dick as we wave our goodbyes.

"Several months, maybe," he tells me. "We'll be lucky to get what we've asked for. BC Log Spill Co-op are supposed to negotiate for us, but their hands are tied by the insurance companies and the log owners."

Finally understanding the difference between logs gathered directly from a specific spill like this morning's and those we find on our daily rounds, I remark, "I don't know why you beachcombers don't unite and fight the buggers."

He laughs and shakes his head. "They're far too independent, and the companies know it."

"Then why do you keep working?" I demand.

He idles the *Snark*'s engine past the log boom so that he can reply to my burst of questions. "It's one of the few jobs today that fulfills man's inherent nature as a hunter-gatherer."

"So you think every man should be a hunter-gatherer, do you?"

"Some more than others," he says. "You know how I hate bureaucracy. At least I'm my own boss."

"But what about the days you come home with nothing? What if the gas bills aren't covered?"

"Then I have to try harder. I like challenges and I'm not going to let things like foul weather and the competition get the better of me." And he depresses the accelerator and aims for the harbour, bright in the winter sunshine …

We hear our basement phone ringing even as we climb the beach steps after tying up the *Snark*.

"Mother," mutters Dick, opening the door for me.

It is. "Where on earth have you been?" she demands. "When are you coming over?"

I hand the phone to Dick who appeases her with a "Happy Christmas," and the promise that we will be over as soon as we have changed our clothes. It isn't until he says, "Let's get the presents into the car," that I realize his parents have an established ritual of opening them at their place first thing after breakfast. In fact I now learn that "Christmas presents shall not be opened until Christmas morning" is the Hammonds' rule. No wonder his mother has been trying to phone us.

Another surprise is the size of the large mound of gifts under the tree, most of them in neat, well-wrapped boxes alongside Patches, Hal's large calico cat. Lil urges us to settle down and orders her husband to hand the parcels out. Most of the boxes contain work clothes, gloves, thick socks and sweatshirts. Then she hands out an envelope filled with two fifty-dollar bills and five twenties to each of us. I'm suitably impressed because to me that is a lot of money. And as I'm fumbling with the bills, she reaches behind her large easy chair and brings out three more presents. "Be careful with the boxes," she says. "We'll reuse them next year." Dick's and mine contain identical navy-blue parkas, almost too good to wear in an oily work boat. She has also bought Hal a down vest, green on one side, red on the other.

My mother-in-law is in her element. Christmas Day is obviously her domain and it suits me fine. Her voice is loud, bursting with energy, her speech heavily weighted with inflection. I have never seen her so vivacious before. Since she holds the purse strings and Hal refuses to shop, she has carte blanche to buy the presents she wants and to disperse the money the way she wishes. Like her, I have also been raised in relative poverty and I can't help showing that I am suitably impressed with her—their—generosity. This must be the only day in the year when she wields so much power, including that in her kitchen. She is happy, too, when Dick and I bring in his parents' present from the car, a colour TV to replace their old black and white one.

Only Dick and I exchange gifts that have little practicality. During our previous visit to Vancouver we had separated to shop secretly for each other in the Persian Arts shop. The store's Armenian owner, a romantic old man who gets a kick out of oiling the wheels of love, always greets us with a knowing smile when we visit. Dick's gift to me is an antique Scottish cameo brooch, and for him, in keeping with his strong affinity for dragons, I have chosen a Japanese antique: an ivory netsuke, a carving of a dragon around an egg.

"Isn't that a good Christmas tree?" says Hal after unwrapping his down vest and carefully folding the paper along with the cardboard boxes. He has obviously plugged a couple of branches into the trunk where it needed filling out.

"But it didn't need to be that big," my mother-in-law reminds us. True to form, she will not let sleeping dogs lie.

Hal points out, "Well, I know many folk who'd be only too happy to get it."

Dick and I wink at each other. Poor woman, instead of two against one, it's going to be three.

As we leave, Lil orders us to return in good time for the celebratory meal, three o'clock on the dot. During the short drive home, Dick tells me that this is the only day of the year his parents break their sacrosanct rule of eating their dinner at five p.m. precisely. "Years ago, if Father and I happened to be working on a log spill shortly before supper time, he'd look at his watch and drop everything so that he could get home for five. It would make me so mad!"

I tell him I'm glad he's not a stickler for mealtimes.

The aroma wafting out of Lil's kitchen window as we wander in from the car just before three is so rich, so dense, that it is almost edible. My ravenous appetite must be a result of the morning's boat work.

Lil's jovial voice is even louder than it had been earlier, and there's an empty wine glass by the sink, but she has everything under control. Immediately she calls, "Hal, time to carve!" Her husband, who's been quietly talking to Dick in the living room, takes the floor in front of the large kitchen table. Whenever he wields tools, his body language amazes me, and now is no exception. As he sharpens the knife on an ancient steel, his arms barely move and his motions are quick and economical. There is absolute conviction in the way he stands ready to make his first masterful slice, and when he does sink the knife into the meat it might as well have been butter. Again and again he demonstrates his ability, while his son watches, undoubtedly with a bit of envy.

"I'm impressed with your carving," I tell my future father-in-law.

"I've had a lot of practice in my lifetime," he explains. "You know, what with all the game I've had to skin and dress. And living on the farm at Wilson Creek, we were never hungry even though other folks in the city might've been."

During the meal he tells us about the days when almost every country man and most women owned a gun and knew how to use it and how, just before Christmas, turkey shoots were popular events around Vancouver Island and the Lower Mainland of BC. A competitor would pay twenty-five cents a shot, and a bull's eye would net a turkey. He then tells us that he was eventually barred from entering because he would win every time. "Would you believe," he adds, "someone even wrote a newspaper article about it!"

Lil rises from her chair, rummages in one of her kitchen drawers and brings me a ragged bit of yellowed newspaper. "Gun bags too many birds. Barred from turkey shoot!" is the headline followed by a brief description.

As soon as we have finished eating, Lil insists on clearing the dishes away and washing them because, she says, "I can't relax knowing there's all this mess." Leaving us women to clean up, the two men disappear into the living room.

By the time we join them, Hal, resting on the recliner with his cat sprawled over his midriff, is in the middle of one of his stories.

"If I'd known you were going to tell stories," I complain, "I wouldn't have let you out of the kitchen."

"Well," he says, "it doesn't really matter if you missed the first part. All you need to know is that I was about twenty-five years old at the time and I'd been hunting alone for a coupla days … on the mountains up one of the inlets. Late fall it was, and it had started to get dark so I was beginning to feel quite chilly. It had been pouring—you know, that rain with drops about two feet long—but the sky had just cleared and I knew there'd be a frost because I was pretty high up. I lit a good fire to cook my meal on … and after I'd eaten, I spread the hot ashes over where I was going to sleep, letting them cool off a little. Then I cut down some boughs and lay them thickly over the ashes before unrolling my sleeping bag over the lot."

"Didn't it burn?" I ask.

"No, not at all. It worked out fine. Kept me warm all night.

Anyway, the next morning I got me a mountain goat … But it was when I was sitting quietly near the top of the mountain afterwards that I got to thinking …" He pauses, and I sense that he is about to tell us something important. "I looked at the inlet a long way down below me … then I looked all around at the mountains in the distance as far as I could see … By that time the clouds had disappeared. There was not a sign of people or houses. Not a single soul." He talks slowly, almost meditatively so that his vowels have a flow—an inner force that emerges from somewhere deep inside his mind—and in spite of his slow delivery I find myself waiting patiently, entranced with the view that he is presenting to me. "I just sat there listening to the wind in the trees on the shoulder below … and all of a sudden I felt so alone." Again he pauses, nods his head slightly as if agreeing with himself. But I don't want him to hurry, I want—perhaps as he does—to linger awhile in this desolate place. And when he continues, his voice is quieter, lower, and it feels right. "It was at that moment I knew I had to have a companion for the rest of my life. I knew then that a man is not meant to be alone. He is meant to spend his life with someone …"

I press my knee against my new partner sitting beside me and he reciprocates with a gentle, protracted nudge of his powerful thigh.

"So it wasn't long after that that you met Lil?" I ask Hal.

He nods. "She was only fifteen, but I told her I'd wait for her until she was twenty-one. And I did."

Unlike some other previous Christmases, my first Christmas with the Hammonds has definitely been a happy ritual. And I have discovered that my future father-in-law is an exceptional storyteller.

15

Sammy's Advice

Japanese
Fishing Float

One morning we enter the harbour after delivering a summer visitor's float to Keats Island to find a well-maintained dark blue tug tied to the Boatworks' fuel dock. Painted on its hull are some LS numbers and on its stern the name *Vulture*.

Dick nods toward it. "Sam's boat," he says, "Sam Lamont from Pender Harbour. He and his first wife used to play cards with my parents."

"He must be the one you lent money to so he could buy his first salvage boat."

"That's him. He'll be visiting the Hendricksons."

Rather than interrupt Sam's visit with our neighbours, Dick waits for him to drop in on us. Half an hour later there's a loud knock at the door.

Whatever the black-haired, stocky little fifty-year-old man in front of me lacks in height is more than compensated for by the animation in his shockingly blue, long-lashed eyes. Not only does he have double-thick lashes, he has a layer of double-thick fur on his shirtless body. It is so dense that it puts me in mind of the selkie, the seal people. I try not to stare at the fascinating sight, but it is rather attractive.

"C-come in," I stammer.

From the way he marches into our house I know that whatever job he takes on will be done fast and efficiently. He's just not the dithering kind. His compact five feet two inches—and that is my highest estimation—will not hamper him in the least. In fact, his low centre of gravity will be an advantage on the deck of a rolling boat.

"So you're his missus?" he asks.

Without explaining the reason, I apologize for not introducing myself.

"You know we tried for years to find him a woman, but he was too damn picky."

Dick emerges from the bathroom and grips one of Sam's hairy shoulders. "What's wrong with being picky?"

Sam's eyes spark like firecrackers as he grins from ear to ear. "Nothing," he says. "Nothing at all. Just as long as you take the advice from one who knows: Don't tie the legal knot."

As Dick ignores the comment and points him toward a chair in the living room, Sam stares up at the renovated ceiling. "So you're starting work on it at last, are you?"

"When I get time," Dick replies.

"Yes, well ... if you decide to have kids you can forget that."

Dick throws his hairy friend a cushion to stuff behind him. "Where's Ann?"

"Pender Harbour. As a matter of fact we're wondering if you'd like to come for supper tonight. I'm on my way back from Vancouver, so I should be home by then."

Dick and I exchange glances. He must know what I'm thinking.

"So you're going to Pender Harbour in the *Vulture*?" I ask Sam.

Right away Dick adds, "How'd you like to take my deckhand with you?" I knew he had read my mind.

"Excellent idea," Sam replies. "Give me a few minutes to refuel."

And it is arranged that Dick will drive up by car and we will all meet at the Lamonts' house in Garden Bay.

On our own, I ask Dick, "What's his problem with 'tying the knot'?"

"A bad marriage, a wife who didn't like boats. Now he's found the right partner, he doesn't want to ruin the relationship by getting married."

"Hmm."

"No, not 'hmm'!" he says a little sternly. "You know my views on that."

Down at the Boatworks' dock, Sam hands me aboard the tug. I am amazed at the matching upholstery, fridge, freezer, stove, double bunk downstairs, and toilet and shower, nothing like Alan's oily, utilitarian *Styx*. "This is like a home," I exclaim.

"That's what it is," he says, starting the engine. "We spend a lot of time in her, working spills when and where we're needed."

"Dick just works the local spills."

"Because he's a homebody."

Obviously Sam is not. Perhaps that was another reason his first marriage failed.

The *Vulture*'s diesel engine is at least twice as noisy as the *Snark*'s gas engine, so loud that we can barely hear ourselves talk over it, and I am annoyed that I didn't think to bring my ear protectors. Since I am only familiar with the Gulf shore as far as Davis Bay, I wait until we reach that point to sit outside on the bow where it is a lot quieter.

As we follow the coastline northwest from Sechelt, it is inevitable that the row of waterfront dwellings with their backdrop of evergreen forests should evoke memories of my first few months in Canada three and a half years earlier. And when, from the *Vulture*'s bow, I spot the little cedar cabin with the Emily Carr tree beside it, a strange mixture of hope and depression returns, feelings I now overlay with the undiscovered promise of the log salvor who had worked the same beach during the storm surge. Then I turn toward the Vancouver Island mountains and gaze at them as I had done that miserable icy November morning. Instead of being a mistake, emigrating had been the solution, but certainly not the one I had expected. After all, how can someone search for something they have never experienced?

Sam's yell from the *Vulture*'s window snaps me back to the idyllic present. "Gotta check a tow in here!" As we enter Smuggler's Cove northwest of Halfmoon Bay, I clamber off the bow and make my way around to the cabin door.

"Didja know that rum-runners used this place during prohibition?" he asks.

I didn't. Satisfied that his seventeen logs are still anchored securely, he steers to starboard and accelerates.

As we dock at Sam and Ann's float in Garden Bay shortly after six, my ears are ringing loudly. "Phantom sound," Sam explains, assuring me it will stop soon.

Climbing over *Vulture*'s gunwale, I spot a couple of pink jellyfish in the water, but under the ramp that leads up to the seawall there's a huge pulsating mass of them. "Do they sting?" I ask.

"A bit," says Sam, "but they won't kill you. Just make sure you're wearing gloves when you pull in the ropes."

Lying around the yard are perhaps forty or fifty glass balls—green, blue, brown, amethyst and black. The largest, almost two feet in diameter, the smallest a few inches, and various sizes in between. Each has a flattened blob of glass on it, so I assume they're hand-blown.

I pick up a large green one with rigid rope-work fitted tightly about it. "Where did you get these?" I ask.

"The Charlottes. We take the *Vulture* up there each summer," he explains.

Ann is at the door to greet me. She appears to be a perfect match for Sam, the same height, expressive but paler blue eyes than his, and cheekbones that remind me of Katharine Hepburn's. I can tell from the way she moves that, like him, she's not the dithering kind either, but then there's no room for ditherers in log salvage.

I hold the ball up to the evening sun.

"They're fishing net floats," she says with an impeccable BBC English accent. "The ocean currents carry them from Japan."

As I hold it in my hands I wonder if the Japanese artisan who made it ever imagined that his sealed breath—his *spiritus*—would find its way in this glass sphere to the other side of the ocean. Even more remarkable is its survival in the *Vulture* while sailing the infamous rough seas between the Queen Charlotte Islands and Vancouver Island. And to think that one careless movement would now set that glassblower's breath free …

Ann has prepared venison stew. "Sam shot the deer," she tells us.

After exchanging a hunting story or two with our hosts, Dick mentions he's recently bought me a fibreglass fly fishing rod.

"Remember our last trip up the Tzoonie?" Sam asks him.

"You mean when you caught that big salmon?"

"What happened?" I demand.

Sam grins shamefacedly. "Dick'll tell you when I'm not around."

On the drive home I ask for Sam's fishing story. It must have been one of the times Dick had referred to earlier when he'd mentioned that some of his fishing trips had ended badly.

"It's nothing really," Dick begins. "He'd bought one of those cheap reels without a brake and ratchet. Then he caught the first fish—a large salmon—and left it hanging in the shade. I worked ahead of him, downriver, spending a minute at each pool."

"Didn't he mind you going ahead, stirring everything up?"

"No. There were so many fish that it didn't make any difference to his chances ... Anyway, first I saw his hat floating by. Then bobbing up and down just behind it was his head. Should've heard the spluttering and swearing!"

"Can he swim?"

"Like a fish ... He'd accidentally slipped down a gravel bank into the deepest part of the river. Then, just after he'd crawled out with his rod, his hook—he hadn't seen it was dangling—got caught on a low

Our wedding day, June 28, 1971.

bush. The whole line had pulled off the reel before he'd realized it. Temper? You can say that again! He was so mad he broke all his tackle into little pieces, swearing and throwing them, one by one, into the forest as far away as he could."

"At least he'd caught the biggest fish."

"That was the worst part. It wasn't in the shade anymore. Shrivelled and sunburned and covered with blowfly eggs. If he hadn't been a man, he would have cried."

In spite of Sam's advice, Dick and I are spliced at the end of June. The new glass-covered Robson Street law courts are fully booked for that month's weddings, so we are married by a retired minister in his house on Fraser Street, with Dick's parents as our witnesses. At the top of the Blue Horizon on Robson Street for our celebratory meal afterwards, we are placed at a corner table that overlooks the sea. As a glittering English Bay reflects the late afternoon glow onto our faces I know that the sea is our witness, too.

The most interesting wedding present is from Sam and Ann. It is the glassblower's green fishing float.

Shortly after our marriage, I apply for Canadian citizenship. Even though I didn't need to pass an exam to obtain it, my citizenship certificate makes me feel like a real Canadian at last. But I am still missing another licence, a log salvage licence. And so, since I have not been found guilty of any offence under Section 381 of the Criminal Code, I apply for one, enclosing my money, boat registration, and new citizenship certificate. A month later I'm issued with a stamp hammer with my own LS licence number in relief.

As if proof that important events often happen in groups, the gravestone manufacturer phones that same month with the news that the jade fireplace facing is ready. Within a week, the local tile setter, another European master—from Denmark—installs them. Now the facing just needs framing in wood, and a wooden mantelpiece set over it. But I find myself wondering when my new husband will find time to do this job now added to the long list of others in the living room. A year or two, perhaps?

16

Fall Adventures

A fall southeasterly has been blowing all night, and the water between Gambier and the ferry slip has a peculiar type of wind-ruffled surface that makes it difficult to see pieces of driftwood less than a couple of inches high floating on it. Larger swells, at least three feet high, are out here, too, some of them rolling between the main island and the little twin islands. Since the ferry has just sailed past, there will surely be an extra-large swell or two amongst them.

Whenever Dick is driving, it takes a while for me to get used to riding these "pounders." We have to brace ourselves for the landings, particularly if we're travelling fast. But if I am at the controls, the slams never seem as violent. I suppose it is because I am operating the accelerator as well as the wheel and can anticipate the crashes a split second before the passenger.

This morning, as he steers just east of the tiny Grace islands, I prepare myself for one higher-than-average swell. The length of time we spend in the air on our descent certainly bears my assessment out, but I am not prepared for the sickening shock as the hull smashes down onto something solid. We're almost thrown out.

Neck, back and tailbone jar. Head aches. Neck hurts. Has the boat split? Can't be a rock because there are none here. "WHAT?" I yell.

"Deadhead!" shouts Dick. He cuts the engine and we drift, automatically pivoting to face the opposite way. But there is no deadhead to be seen … at first. Then, in the following trough, the cut end of log projects barely an eighth of an inch above the surface for one second, only to be completely covered by the following swell. It does not rise. It remains invisible until the next trough reaches it. No wonder we hadn't seen it. It is one of those frequent "expect the unexpected" happenings that seem to plague us. But this particularly critical incident could only happen to a boat once in perhaps a half a million trips.

"How's your neck?" he asks.

I shrug. "How's yours?"

"Could be better."

The water slowly seeps into the narrow longitudinal hull depression near our feet where the push-pull cables and wiring pass to the engine and the jet.

"We should be able to make it back with the bilge pump," he says. "I guess you know what happened?"

"The deadhead was resting on the sea floor."

"Yep. No give. Same as landing on a huge rock from the top of the swell."

The Hendricksons have a smaller boat ways designed to pull a speedboat inside their workshop, and it is here that the *Snark* spends the following two or three weeks. Since fibreglass resin has to be applied to bone-dry material, even with four heat lamps underneath, it takes several days for the severely damaged hull to dry out. We cannot afford to take the time to make the best repair—on an upturned hull—because that would entail removing engine, jet and fittings. Poor Dick. As if he hadn't suffered enough already, the fibreglassing chemicals cause a prolonged migraine.

A spell of warm October weather moves in, and it coincides with some atypical behaviour from Dick. He's planning something, but rather than spoil the surprise, I feign indifference. He has unearthed an old monochrome timber-cruising map of Nelson Island and I catch him showing it to his father, questioning him about various areas. None of the places they talk of have any relevance to me so the names don't stay in my mind. The following day I notice that a foot-square chunk has been cut out of the map. Around the same time I overhear him asking Alan if he can borrow his 7.5 hp Mercury outboard engine and fuel tank. That afternoon he phones Tyee Air, asking about chartering a plane to Bruce Lake.

"Where's Bruce Lake?" I ask. My ability to feign has its limits.

"Nelson Island. Where my father grew up."

"What's the plane for?"

"How would you fancy a couple of days up there?"

I'm speechless. My partner never takes days off.

He continues. "The weather's been so calm this week and there haven't been many logs about, so …"

"But …"

"Don't worry. When I go on a fishing trip I don't believe in roughing it. You'll see. I'll book the plane for the day after tomorrow."

Amazingly the weather holds, and we drive the loaded Citröen to Al Campbell's Tyee seaplane float in Porpoise Bay, Sechelt. I have merely organized the food in a freezer chest, while Dick has packed the outboard and tank, a very sharp axe, his custom-made Randall knife, our fly rods and tackle, some big spikes, rope, and, of course, our sleeping bags and a tarpaulin. When I had broached the subject of a non-existent tent the previous day, he had snickered and insisted it would not rain, and when I reminded him that this was mid-October, he shook his head and sighed, "Oh, ye of little faith!"

The pilot helps us load. "We'll take the Beaver," he explains, leading us to the larger ochre-painted plane at the end of the float. "The lake's too short for the Cessna. Not enough power."

The flight only lasts fifteen minutes. As we circle over the little four-armed lake with its three miniscule islands, I can't help but ask the pilot if he's landed there before.

He nods. "Sure."

Dick, who has flown in small planes to his various timber cruising jobs, obviously believes him. He points to our destination—the northwest arm. There is not a sign of a house within miles.

We skim the treetops and the lonely lake arises to greet us with alarming speed. The engine sputters, the plane's pontoons slap onto the calm water and we slow down. We have landed on the longest stretch in the south arm, probably no more than half a mile in length.

After taxiing around islands and bays to the bay of our choice, our pilot helps us unload.

"See you in four days—weather permitting," he yells with a grin as we push the plane off.

The blaring growls of the accelerating Beaver echo all around the lake. As it takes off, it passes each little arm, which grabs the sound, reverberating it until a chorus of echoing echoes are produced inside the whole basin. The stunning sonic effect takes at least twelve dramatic seconds to fade.

But it is the ensuing silence that shocks me. I feel an absurd sense of abandonment. For a few seconds I panic. We have suddenly moved into another world and another time. What if the plane never returns? There are only four things that matter now: light, water, food and warmth. My mind even fantasizes that I, we, could be killed here and no one would know for ages. I quickly add a fifth need: protection.

Dick's voice returns me to semi-reality. "Well," he says, "I'd better get to work."

We carry the food and sleeping bags twenty feet or so up the gentle bank and unroll the tarp under a tree at the edge of the second-growth fir and hemlock forest. From here we can see across the arm to part of the rim of low hills that surround us.

Dick takes his axe, spikes and rope and marches off, leaving me on the tarp with the food and a book.

Within three hours he has built a small raft, roughly twelve feet by four, mostly of small diameter logs cut from cedars, some of which he has found floating against the shore. He has also felled a couple of young cedars of similar diameter. I can tell from his movements and the fact that there is debris stuck on his sweaty back that he must be exhausted. By five o'clock he has the outboard fixed on the end of the craft. After taking it out for a short spin he ties it onto a low bush. "No tides to bother us here," he says with a satisfied smile. He is totally at ease here.

"Too late for fishing?" I ask.

"It's suppertime. Campfire time."

"Need help?"

"No thanks," he says, "but it's nice of you to ask."

He has always taken pride in his fire building abilities. Like his fly fishing preparations, he treats the operation with a kind of artistic delicacy. He balances dry sticks meticulously on top of each other with the optimum space between them so that his structure will not collapse but will burn fiercely enough to ignite the larger, damper wood on top. He usually laughs disparagingly at my own fire building methods, accusing me of being too impatient. And then I explain that I don't mind if my fires fail to catch first time because I can always try again. Besides, I enjoy taking my chances, pushing the envelope. Sometimes we are both surprised at my success. His attitude must be the result of him being raised by a father who made sure he learned the correct way—the survivalist's way—from day one. And as I watch him now beside Bruce Lake, it strikes me that this same careful mindset is responsible for his beautifully handcrafted woodwork in the bedroom.

He had suggested I buy steaks for our first outdoor supper, explaining that they are the perfect food for fishing trips. So beef tenderloin it is, accompanied by potato salad and lettuce. We open a bottle of Rothschild Mouton Cadet Bordeaux 1970, our recent bargain wine discovery. Afterwards we lie by the fire's embers and stare up at the stars.

I think of Dick's father who, as a boy, must have done the same thing in the same place, perhaps sixty or seventy years earlier. At this moment, in the quiet dark night when one's imagination tends to run wild, I have no problem leaping back in time. Hardly anything here has changed.

"What was Hal like as a father?" I ask.

Dick hesitates. As far as I am concerned it is a loaded question, and he will not gloss over his reply. "When I was very young? Not that great … I don't think he could empathize with the way a young child thinks and acts."

"I suppose you can thank his mother for that," I mutter. Dick had told me how the old Mrs. Hammond's stiff and stern manner had left an impression on him as a young boy.

"Maybe. But I couldn't have asked for a fairer, more predictable parent. We've always trusted each other. He is the most honest man I've ever known."

"I'll bet he'd never react irrationally like your mother."

"No," he agrees. "He was very consistent." He grips my hand. "But if we have children," he says, "I'll remember what he lacked."

"What was that?"

"A closeness. He never read to me, didn't play with me. I think it was because he was always working so hard. Just never had the time."

Before we turn in, I wonder aloud why there aren't any mosquitoes.

"They don't like these cool nights," he explains.

And as we climb into our sleeping bags I understand why the hateful insects have not appeared. I even have to put my clothes on again because my cheap sleeping bag is almost useless against the cold. If I had shown it to my guide first, he would never have approved. But the new experience of sleeping under the trees instead of a tent makes up for the discomfort.

Dawn awakens me. While it hovers tardily between darkness and light, the clash between the lake's surface and air temperature casts a sheet of vapour over the water. I can't stop staring at its luminous presence spread a few feet below us as it glides strangely about, sometimes breaking apart to dance slowly in swirls then blending to reform the amorphous layer. As the sky above the treed hill brightens, the mist glows, radiates with more intensity, and by the time the sun peers over the rise, the shroud has vanished. But the silence remains.

Dick leaps out of his sleeping bag and runs down to the shore. He stands there for more than a full minute, nude, motionless, hands on waist, staring out at the lake and then at his new raft. But there's nothing statue-like about him. He is too full of life for that. So striking is his body against the placid early morning water, I quickly take a photo of my man in his element.

He hears the click, turns, grins and chases after me.

We fish for the whole day with no luck. We keep trying different flies, some of them homemade. Each of us feels a couple of fish bites but that is all. Even when we try fishing from different parts of the lake neither of us is successful.

"I can't understand it," Dick mutters as evening approaches.

"Father said it was full of trout."

"Years ago," I add.

He nods. "Could be that there aren't any mosquitoes or flies to attract them to the surface."

The following day he steers the raft around one of the little islands and between a slightly larger one toward the south. At the end of the lake he ties up to a huge bank of partly rotten, mossy logs that have sunk into the lake bottom.

"An old dock?" I ask.

"I'm pretty sure it's the old camp cookhouse float Father told me about."

"Is that why you were showing him that old map?"

He nods.

The only antique he finds in the mud is a half-buried rusty stove, but no old bottles or tools.

After breakfast on the final day at Bruce Lake, he suggests we search for the remains of his paternal grandparents' house in Hidden Basin. "There's a creek that goes from the lake to where their house was," he tells me. "But who knows if the trail's still there. It's probably grown over after all these years."

"How far is the house from the lake?"

He shrugs. "Two miles, maybe."

We pack up camp and secure the raft near the entrance of Bruce Creek. It is very dark under the tree cover, and if there ever was a trail beside the creek, it is now non-existent. The going is very slow with plantations of devil's club and various types of brush, and far too many boulders. Even Dick is frustrated by our progress—my fault, but he'd never admit it—so that after about an hour he looks at his watch and says, "Guess we should have done this the first day. We only have another couple of hours." Then, as we turn to hike back, he adds reluctantly, "We'll come another time."

At our camp, we tie up the raft and remove the outboard and almost-empty gas tank. And we wait.

An hour after the pilot had arranged to pick us up we hear the sound of the Beaver's engine. We even hear the multitude of echoes as it lands in the lake, but when there's no sign of it after another five minutes, I begin to worry. It starts up again, taxis somewhere, stops, starts again then taxis to another place. Ten more minutes pass.

"I hope he's not broken down," I mutter.

"Lost is more like it," suggests Dick.

During the silences we shout, but I don't think the pilot can hear us through the bluffs and trees, and even if he can, there's no way he would be able to tell where our voices are coming from. What if he takes off without us?

The Beaver's echoey starts and stops continue for another ten minutes until at last we spot it approaching from behind one of the islands. We wave a towel and the plane makes a beeline for us. As we wade out to guide it closer to shore, we see that the pilot is a different man from the one who had dropped us off.

"They told me you were at the other end of the lake," he explains.

In spite of Dick's efforts, Bruce Lake would yield no fish.

17

Monsters and Ignoramuses

My father-in-law, Hal, has found himself another boat. Actually, Dick and I had found it drifting out in the Gulf the previous winter. Six months after reporting it to the RCMP and with no one claiming ownership, the old sixteen-foot lapstrake becomes our property. It needs several new strakes and a complete recaulking. On any dry day that we visit my in-laws, Hal will be working on it in their back garden. If it is raining, the boat will be covered by a waterproof tarp. As a thirteen-year-old who had never attended school, my father-in-law had been the major source of income for his mother's large family [author's note: see *Tales from Hidden Basin* by Dick Hammond, Harbour Publishing], working at various jobs and eventually at age nineteen, boatbuilding in Andy Linton's shop near Vancouver's Stanley Park, and later at Wallace Ship-yards in North Vancouver. Even to me it is evident that he is an expert boat builder.

He is one of those people who accomplishes a lot while appearing to expend the minimum of effort. I watched him digging in our garden one day, his slow and powerful actions producing consistently straight, even rows. And when I returned from shopping an hour later, he had moved an amazing amount of soil.

His boat renovation consists mostly of scraping, cleaning and caulking, all meticulous, painstaking labour. When I ask him what he's using to fill the gaps between the planks, he explains, "Oakum. It's got the best hemp strands. They're presoaked in a special oily tar from some kind of tree."

For the rebuilt boat's propulsion, Dick buys him a tried and true Briggs and Stratton inboard motor with matched prop and shaft. Hal is ready to go fishing again.

Later that week, Dick and I finish our morning rounds with a pass along Gower Point when we spot Hal beckoning us from his "new" boat.

"Any luck?" Dick asks him.

"Depends what you call luck," Hal replies ruefully. "I've got something pretty heavy on the end of my line."

"A seal?" I ask.

Hal shakes his head. "It doesn't move like one. More like some kind of large fish. And I don't particularly want to cut the line."

Dick persuades his father to let us tow him into the harbour to beach whatever it is that's hanging on. Alongside our chain of floats at last, Hal ties his boat twenty feet from the shore and gradually reels in the line, while Dick and I watch from the nearest float. As the line becomes more resistant, Dick transfers to his father's boat to help.

"By golly!" Hal yells suddenly in that booming voice of his.

Dick crouches, bends over the water and grabs the line. "Jo! Get the extra-large landing net and the empty garbage bin—the big plastic one. Quick!"

Fifty seconds later I am back, and there on the float is the biggest octopus I've seen, bigger than one I'd seen at San Diego's Sea World during my emigration trip. It's alive, but lazy. Lying beside it is a seventeen-pound ling cod a little the worse for wear.

"Told you I had a fish," my father-in-law insists, a mischievous grin on his face.

"You mean the octopus had the fish," I point out.

He laughs. "I *still* have it."

With Hal's landing net and the super-sized one, together with an oar, we manage—with great difficulty—to persuade, manoeuvre and scare the recalcitrant octopus into hiding inside the large garbage bin. It barely fits.

Dick turns to go up to the house. "Be back in a minute," he calls. When he returns, he tells us, "The Vancouver Aquarium wants it. I've ordered a plane to take the three of us."

"I hope you don't expect me to go up in one of them things," says his father.

"No," says Dick. "I'm counting the octopus."

A fifteen-minute sea plane trip and a five-minute taxi ride takes us to the Vancouver Aquarium in Stanley Park where the staff welcome their new resident with open arms.

That same month Dick drags out the old, untippable ten-footer he had used while beachcombing with his father. After a week of sanding the hull and patching with fibreglass and resin under the hot sun, I decide that fixing boats is not my favourite occupation. I stick with it, finishing the hull with three coats of azure marine enamel before clamping a twenty-horse Mercury on the stern. The best part, however, is painting my log salvage licence for display: LS 1820, black numbers on two white boards, one for each side of the boat. Since the hull is far too small for a towpost installation, I thread a six-foot length of rope through a pulley assembly and fasten each rope end to the two stern handles. Now I can connect a pickup line to it if I find a log to tow. It's far from ideal, but if the *Snark* is unavailable and I spot a merchantable log floating off the harbour beacon, it's adequate.

One day Dick calls through the basement door after finishing an oil change in the *Snark*. "D'ya feel like doing a little job in *Snark* while I work on the boom?"

"That depends," I tell him, peering from the other side of the furnace after checking the washing machine. Double rinses, even double washes, are important with work clothes that have been soiled with engine oil, WD 40 or molybdenum bearing grease, never mind the stinking juice of dead and decomposing barnacles or teredos.

He looks a little concerned. "Depends on what?"

"On what we're going to eat tonight."

"Yesterday's leftovers will be just fine," he says with his customary lack of concern about what I cook. He invariably approves whatever I put on his plate.

I knew before I married him that he was one of those men who had grown up believing strongly in the idea that married couples should have their own roles. "It simplifies things," he had said, before explaining that his own hunter-gathering job was basically fulfilling his ideal. "Not that the roles couldn't be reversed under certain conditions," he continued after I had put forward my own case. Although I had been educated in a government-funded grammar school for girls, we students had been tested, interviewed and selected at age eleven for a further seven years of schooling that was expected to lead to a college or university education. The idea was that we would fulfill ourselves by working at a "proper" job, rather than having to find work as a mere secretary or, even worse, by falling into the dreaded marriage and baby trap. Indeed, most of us teenaged girls would look down our noses at those who left school to get married and have babies. "Foster the Inborn Light" was our school motto, but I never discovered what my inborn light was, and the visiting careers woman who pushed me into teaching certainly hadn't.

Since living with my new partner, I have discovered that, like him, I prefer going with the flow, following the seasons, rather than society's trends. I don't mind that he is a recluse, partly because I know he won't drag me to a pub or Legion as my first husband had done. As an autodidact with his brain filled with history, philosophy, literature, music, science and art, he is better educated than I, even with my post secondary education. He also has an incredible memory. Much of his practical wisdom he gleaned from his father who mentored with Charlie, a sea-wanderer and survivor from a coastal First Nations' band that had been decimated in the late 1800s, and occasionally I see Charlie's idiosyncratic philosophy emerging in Dick's decisions. But as long as things run relatively smoothly, I don't care who cooks the food and when, as long as it tastes good. And it doesn't matter if I have to leave the washing up in order to go towing, nor does it bother me that there might be a bit of dust on the dressing table or some salt spray on our windows. Log salvage comes first. There's a late fourteenth-century proverb that applies to our job almost every day: "Time and Tide wait for no one."

So as Dick tips the basket of clothes into the machine, explaining, "I need those two big float logs on Hopkins beach. The tide should almost be up to them by now," I'm ready and willing.

He always needs high-floating cedars—not necessarily of commercial grade—for his float construction or renovation jobs. Even old notched, high-floating logs with iron drift bolts left in them from wrecked floats can be used. The timbers from river floats in particular are ideal; the wood is usually sound because the wood-boring teredo worms cannot survive in fresh water.

The particular beach I am about to "work" lies between the harbour and the ferry slip. Today's conditions are perfect—calm water, high tide, and no wind. The first log I have to collect lies behind another—a non-commercial log and heavy cull already partly submerged. Rather than pull the cull, I decide to leave it. I drive the *Snark* against the pebbly shore and choke the float log, using a roll, and wade back to the boat.

The first pull is not strong enough to drag it completely over the cull, and it teeters dramatically for a few seconds before crashing back to its original position. I reverse the boat until it is almost aground but faces out to sea, ready to pull again from a different angle. Clear of the beach, I floor *Snark*'s accelerator until the rev counter hits 4,500 rpms. The log jumps up into the air, over the other, and splashes into the water, one end resting on boulders. A few more rpms and I pull it out a couple of hundred feet before dogging and anchoring it.

I'm returning for the other log about fifty feet further along the beach when an older man steps off his veranda, strides along his cement seawall and climbs down toward me. Sensing something in the man's body language that reminds me of my stepfather in attack mode, I steel myself against an automatic inclination to run.

"What authority do you have to pick up these logs?" he demands.

I choke the end of the log, stand and face him. "I'm a licensed log salvor."

"A woman? You're kidding," he says derisively. "You're destroying this beach."

"Do you work for the Forestry?"

"Irregardless, you can't touch these logs." His misuse of the English language makes his imperious tone sound even more ridiculous. "They're on my property."

I adjust the hook and chain. "They're below the high-tide line and I have salvage rights."

"We'll see about that," he snaps and sits on the float log.

"Would you please get out of the way?"

He doesn't move an inch.

"I can't guarantee what might happen when I start pulling," I warn as I push the boat off the beach and climb into it.

His face flushes and he springs to his feet. "I'm calling the RCMP—now!" he booms. "And the Forestry. You've got no bloody right!" Muttering something about "a crazy woman," he climbs onto the wall and marches back to his veranda.

"Go ahead!" I shout, and he disappears quickly into his house.

Nearly all the local waterfront residents know that they have no rights to anything below the high-water mark unless they own a water lease, which is extremely difficult to obtain. Even if the man wanted to use beach logs for firewood, he would have to obtain a permit from the Forestry department who would send someone down to inspect them because they do not want people cutting up merchantable wood.

I pull the float log he had been sitting on. I can't wait to watch this idiot being made to feel a fool, so I take my time and even pull four smaller cull logs for firewood. By this time two constables have arrived, trudging through the yard to where I am holding the boat off the beach. What on earth has this fool told them?

"Good afternoon. Is this your boat?" asks one.

"It's my husband's, but I have my own log salvage licence," I explain, rummaging around in my pocket until I find the plastic container. "Here."

The policemen study the little card, nod, and return it to me.

Meanwhile, the idiot marches eagerly out of his house and points to my anchored tow. "She took them off my property. She has no right to them," he barks to the constables.

"Where exactly did you find these logs?" asks one officer.

I point to where they'd been lying, and both constables walk over to inspect the depressions in the wet sand and gravel.

"I see no problem at all, sir," one of them tells him. "Since they're well below the highest tide line on this public beach, they're salvageable by those who have a current log salvage licence—which this lady possesses."

The idiot's face begins to change colour again and his voice rises in pitch. "But … but they've been here ever since I've lived here. Any fool can see they've been protecting the beach. And there's clams and oysters on this beach."

"How long have you lived here, sir?" asks the more junior policeman.

"A couple of years."

By now I've been standing far too long in the water in my running shoes and shorts. "Look, I've been trying to catch the high tide and it's already started to go out."

The sergeant nods and addresses the idiot. "There's nothing I can do, sir. This is all quite legal." Turning to me, he says, "Sorry you've been bothered. Carry on." He and his colleague hike back to the road.

But the man hasn't finished. As I push off the beach he yells across the water, "I'm writing to my MLA … and to the Minister of Forests!"

He is probably still muttering as I tow the logs across Shoal Channel to our Shelter Island storage grounds.

I shut the engine off and drift toward Dick on the standing boom. "What on earth kept you?" he shouts. "I thought you'd had an accident!" He glances at my tow. "Why all the firewood?"

"I was just asserting my salvor's rights," I explain before telling my story.

"Good for you," he says. "I usually pretend I'm deaf. Gets 'em so mad."

I decide to try that next time. It should be a lot easier.

18

The Big Squamish Log Spill

The Secret Weapon

Just before bedtime on a clear, moonless January night I step outside the back door to drop an empty milk carton into the garbage bin. But instead of returning to the warmth of the house, I am drawn to linger. There is a strange ambience out here, a feeling of mystery. Curious as to how and what the something is, I shut the door behind me and wander down to the log stump by the creek. The air is still, and it is cold, but not excessively so—perhaps five or six degrees above freezing. The little waterfall from the trout pond trickles softly into the creek, which itself barely whispers a sound as it nears its salty destination. A furry creature rubs against my leg. Puss must have heard me from her favourite fishing ground in the harbour reeds, fifteen feet away.

A skyward glance is not enough. I'm spellbound. Not even from the deck of the *Canadian Star* have I seen so many stars with such clarity, such depth and variation. They pulsate with a vibrant luminescence, singing with light instead of sound, calling to me in their own shimmering tones to join them. I want to embrace them all…

But the cold motionless air brings me to my senses, and I start to shiver. During my few minutes outside, the temperature has plunged dramatically. Followed by the cat, I retreat indoors.

In the middle of the night I am awakened by some strange sounds, clangs, bumps, rattlings from the harbour. A wind howls about the house and the attic creaks, always when I least expect it.

"Are you asleep?" I whisper.

"Yep."

Obviously I don't believe him. "What are those noises?"

He lays his heavy arm over me. "A Squamish …" Within five seconds, he is snoring.

In the eighteen months I have been living in Gibsons Harbour, I cannot remember a storm sounding quite like this. The gusts last longer than usual, and our forced-air furnace hasn't shut itself off once. Had last night's mysterious atmosphere been caused somehow by the approach of this strange wind?

It is still dark around seven-thirty when our mental alarm clocks wake us. But seconds later as I slide the south-facing kitchen window open, a blast of frigid wind shocks me even more awake. Judging by the waves breaking against Keats, it is a northeasterly, but it is even stranger than I thought; it can turn corners. I slam the pane shut and stare at the drunken swaying of the harbour lights. There must be some large swells outside to stir the floats about like that.

"Not nice working weather," Dick mutters, pulling a sweatshirt over his head.

"We should stay home," I suggest.

"That's not an option," he states. "I'm concerned about our own boom, never mind anyone else's. It's vulnerable in this wind. If the anchors let go, everything will be blown straight out into the Gulf."

I mix a pan of porridge on the stove. "What *is* a Squamish?"

"A high pressure area from the Arctic that blows over the mountains toward a low pressure in the Pacific. Ours exits the Squamish River valley, but its direction can vary within a few degrees."

"We didn't have one last year, did we?"

"Nothing of consequence."

The temperature has plummeted. There's no doubt about it. It is now several degrees below freezing and we dress accordingly, donning some foam-insulated, bright-red rubber gloves called Red Flambé.

Our floats bounce as we make our way precariously down to the *Snark* trying to avoid the ice where the waves have slopped over the planks. There is no sign of the resident wild geese or mallards. They're probably sheltering behind the Boatworks' large shed or perhaps in someone's yard.

On the end float at last, Dick turns to me. "You don't have to come, you know."

I ignore him.

Just outside the harbour we're hit by a series of vicious icy blasts that gain in strength the further we travel across the channel to our grounds. Turning my face cautiously to the northeast, I see a lemon-clear dawn rising behind the mountain range, and beneath that, myriad whitecaps chasing out from the inlet, riding toward us on an angry, navy sea. Past the Langdale ferry dock they charge before tearing out through the gap and into the Gulf. If it wasn't for Soames Point acting like a breakwater between the ferry slip and Gibsons, the rough waters inside the harbour would be even more destructive.

Swells break against the port side of *Snark*'s hull and sweep up the windshield before being blown over us and into the boat. Only our constant pounding keeps the ice from sticking to the smooth surface on top of the bow. Meanwhile, the wind numbs my cheeks against pain as the eye-stinging spray slaps my face. We both try unsuccessfully to adjust the wool balaclavas under our Helly Hansen jacket hoods so that only our eyes are exposed; this type of headgear is quite unsuitable for such weather. We need only a gap for our eyes, not for our whole face. While I've already experienced winter speed boating, this is the first time I have tried it in a temperature of minus twelve Celsius with the two additional wind chill factors of a boat speeding into a powerful Arctic outflow.

Shelter Island, viewed from the northeast, no longer suits its name. Dick nudges me. "Not good!"

It takes a moment to see through my salt-stung eyes what he's referring to, that nothing is as it should be, not only on the shores of Shelter Island, but also inside Keats Island's Plumper Cove opposite. Hundreds of logs and boomsticks have been caught in the northeast-facing bays and coves and are being thrown by the five- or six-foot swells against the rocks along with useless pieces of driftwood. Numerous fresh logs have also been trapped against the exposed side of our standing boom, forcing it into a concave shape rather than its usual rectangular one.

Dick points up the inlet in the direction of Thornbrough Channel. "All the booming grounds must've let go!" he yells against the wind.

"Corkum's dock'll be wrecked."

Old Corkum, the year-round inhabitant of an old farmhouse a mile further along Keats' northeast shore across from the Langdale ferry slip, also owns a hundred-yard-long dock built on pilings.

"First things first," Dick shouts, and we start picking up the fresh logs that are putting so much pressure on our storage grounds. Gathering logs with frozen ropes and thick gloves is not easy. At one point I slide on the ice that has formed on the fibreglassed floorboards and bang my knee. Dick is very solicitous, but this is not the time for an accident and I'm annoyed with myself.

"Alan coming?" I yell.

He shrugs between axe strokes.

Working in this cold weather, I now discover why Helly Hansen, the Norwegian outfitter, is famous. Their waterproof gear—unlike the rope we're handling—does not stiffen or freeze solid, and I'm thankful that I can still crouch in this sub-zero temperature, bend my elbows and move relatively freely. Speed and ease of movement in this job is essential.

At last we have about fifty or sixty logs gathered and tied to the Shelter Island dock pilings to the lee of our grounds.

The *Snark* idling off Soames Point in a Squamish wind.

"Home!" Dick hollers.

Although we haven't even started searching elsewhere, I know better than to question him.

Around nine we follow a forty-foot commercial fish boat into Gibsons Harbour. Reminding me of the *Flying Dutchman's* ghost ship, it plunges through the swells, layers of ice hanging from wherever the sea has hit it above the water line. Rows of long icicles hang from the gunwales and every rail and beam.

Back in the basement we warm our hands under the laundry tap and tell each other that the agonizing pain it causes is a sign that we don't have frostbite.

Dick phones his partner and learns that he has already left home. "I'll check Corkum's dock right away," he tells me. "You tell Alan where I've gone."

"Don't you need me out there?"

"He and I will work together," he says, half out the door. "It's better that way."

"I'll give him a sandwich for you!" I call after him.

It is barely wrapped by the time I hear Alan moving about downstairs. He nods as I deliver Dick's message and hand him the sandwich. "One of my mates phoned," he says. "All hell's broken loose out there. Logs all over the Sound. No one was ready for this."

"I guess they've closed the area."

"You betcha!" he says, then slams the door.

A closed area means that only veteran log salvors approved by the BC Log Spill Association can work in Howe Sound. Because they are known as well-equipped experts in the field, Dick and Alan are already approved.

I squint through binoculars out the kitchen window against the bright winter sun. Close to the other commercial vessels near the harbour entrance lies the ghost ship, three men standing aloft smashing the ice off. The waves are still forcing themselves through the dense parallel rows of pilings under the government dock and pier. Inside the harbour the foam-streaked water is unusually turbulent, hurling floats against their restraining pilings and pounding large chunks of driftwood onto the beach in exposed parts of the bay. Waves ram boats against floats or each other, and boat owners who have neglected to install rubber boat fenders or tires are surely going to regret it. The cacophony of squeaks and thumps from wood chafing wood, metal scraping wood, wire rigging clanging and twanging incessantly against metal masts, are all clearly audible through our closed windows. Nothing is still.

The phone rings. It's Mr. Corkum, the retired school principal who owns the farm. "Is Dick there?"

"I'm sorry, he's out in the—"

"Are you expecting him back soon?"

"I know what you're—"

"It's urgent," he almost shouts, speaking abnormally fast for someone in his late eighties. "There are hundreds of logs crashing against my dock. It's falling apart."

"Dick knows," I tell him calmly. "He and his partner are taking care of it right now. There are logs all over Howe Sound."

This understandably irate old man obviously cares little about the state of the Sound this morning. He has his house and his acreage, much of it thickly forested, his orchard, his prize dahlias—now in boxes in the basement—and his ten beef cattle. During the winter he closes off the rest of the old house and lives, hermit-like, in the kitchen with the oil stove and a large TV set that can only receive two stations. For almost thirty years Dick and kindly Hal have been doing odd jobs for him, but whenever they are done, he has always told them, "You will get your reward in heaven." And even though they never believed his promises of heavenly reward, they have continued, out of the goodness of their hearts, to help him. All this in spite of the common knowledge that he owns much of forested Keats Island as well as a couple of streets of real estate in Vancouver.

At least, I think, his dock repair will be paid for by someone's insurance—eventually. And I commiserate a little with him.

There is no sign of Alan or Dick for the rest of the day. It is at times like these that I wish Dick had a radiophone. But he has always refused, explaining that he does not want to be bothered by people behind office desks telling him what to do. His mindset reminds me somewhat of Horatio Nelson's when he put his telescope up to his blind eye … except, as I have pointed out to him, that Nelson did own a telescope to check out the horizon with his good eye if he really needed to.

The moment I hear the growl of the *Snark*'s reversing engine and see its distinctive bowlight pattern draw up to the fuel dock, I run a hot bath. Minutes later Dick strides, shivering, into the kitchen. With his oversized waders and his Helly Hansen jacket hood partly covering his cold-reddened face, he makes me think of Frankenstein.

"Can't undo the string," he says, dried cracked lips barely moving. "Frozen."

As soon as I've loosened it, he takes his gloves off and runs his hands under the warm tap. His moans and agonized expression demonstrate his suffering. "Well," he says at last, "I'm luckier than some. One of the deckhands was frostbitten so badly they had to fly him to hospital."

I ask him how many boats were working.

"About twelve," he says. "The Fraser River hot shots have come up—the ones who work the spills. They'll be sleeping at the Port Mellon hotel."

"Were you the only man working from an open jet boat?"

He nods. "It can go where the others can't."

Presuming this means he's taking chances by going where others won't, I only say, "I've run a bath for you."

He kisses me with icy lips. "You're a wonderful woman."

I lay a plank of wood across the bath so he can eat his beef stew and still warm himself up. "Wonder what your mother would say if she could see you eating like this!" I joke.

He grins at the thought of getting away with such a thing. "She'd tell us we're crazy …"

I sit on the bathroom floor and ask about the state of Corkum's dock.

"Sagging badly. About a third of his pilings have broken. At least three spans are gone. The logs were jammed against the windward side, and the waves were throwing others against it." And he describes how another salvor brought a chain of boomsticks from somewhere, how they tied one end of the chain to the lee-side shore-end of the dock and the other end to the towpost of a salvor's tug—also on the lee side but further away from the shore—allowing the chained logs to form a U-shape on the water's surface. Working together in their respective boats, Alan and Dick had to dislodge most of the spill logs from the pilings, manoeuvre them under the dock, and nose them into the floating U. "We call it a bag boom," Dick explains, "because when it's full, we draw the ends together to close it."

"That bit about you dislodging logs sounds pretty dangerous."

"Only if you don't know what you're doing. You have to look ahead, make split-second judgments, jump onto the logs if you have to."

I shiver at the idea. "I'll bet you were the only one to do that, right?"

He shrugs. "Someone has to."

I decide I would rather not know the risks he's taking out there in such unpredictable situations. We have no workmen's compensation and no life insurance. But as he sits there naked with the bright bathroom lights defining his glistening body's perfectly proportioned muscles, I feel a sudden surge of admiration for the honest way he makes his living. Out on the water he is always striving, using his physical and mental prowess to the limit. While it is only now that I realize he is the first and only man I have ever admired, it is also the first time in my life that I have ever regarded—and appreciated—any male from a physical aspect. As far as masculine bodies have been concerned, it's as if I have always had blinkers over my eyes, even when I first met Dick at Gib's house ... And instantly my very first memory—also from beside a bath—flashes, lingers, the first time I had seen my adulterous father after he had returned, muddied, from the Normandy invasion. When my mother found me staring at him in the bath—the first nude male I'd seen—she had angrily snatched me away. What a contrast to the man now in front of me. My father never had such muscles. Neither did he have such strength of mind.

"What are you thinking?" Dick asks.

Wondering why my appreciation of the male form has suddenly

blossomed, I smile a little bashfully. "Great muscles!"

He laughs easily. "It's all that fighting with logs."

After informing him that the Arctic outflow gales are expected to continue for at least a week, I ask why he doesn't want me to help him in the *Snark*.

"It's just not practical in this wind in such a small boat. I'm set up to work with Alan. Besides," he adds, "I have my own rhythm and—" He gazes silently at me for a moment, then strokes my hair with his wet hands. "Don't look so hurt."

"I just want to help."

"But you are," he assures me, "far more than you realize. I'll need you to get a new starter tomorrow. I've got a spare for now but …"

Even after eighteen months of log salvage I know that nothing mechanical lasts long around salt water. A new replacement part can be faulty from day one, or it may have been fabricated in such a way it will no longer be compatible with the rest of the engine, something that may not become evident immediately. And using a part in a seagoing work boat, particularly in a marinized car engine like the *Snark*'s, will usually void a manufacturer's warranty.

Around seven that same evening, we both dress warmly and take flashlights, the spare starter and tools down to the boat. Constant swells make engine tinkering even more difficult than usual. "If this keeps up, we'll be getting sea sick," I complain.

While we have no problem removing the defective starter's bolts with our gloves on, sensitive fingertips are essential to start the nuts on the long bolts' threads while installing the new ones. Also, it is positioned down under the engine in an unbelievably cramped place so hard to reach that even with the flashlight we can barely see it. We take it in turns, doing what we can until our bare hands turn numb and we're forced to warm them under our armpits before trying again. Both of us fumble a few times, losing—then retrieving—nuts from the oily bilge.

Finally I hold the flashlight while Dick inspects the engine for loose oil, water, and electrical fittings, then checks points, spark plugs, and the oil and water-cooling system levels. I ask him what's in the milk container next to the engine.

"Fresh water," he explains. "It won't freeze in there." There's also a spare pair of insulated Red Flambé gloves next to it.

At last he closes the engine cover, pumps the jet bearing with moly grease, then cleans the salt off the battery terminals. "I think that's everything," he mutters and we head for warmth.

As he lays the malfunctioning starter on the kitchen table, he reminds me to buy a new one, not a rebuild.

I ask him how they go about collecting the thousands of logs that have escaped. "Surely you don't have to stamp LS numbers on them all?"

"Not these spill logs," he says. "We have to round them all up as fast and efficiently as possible—that's where the bag booms are useful— no matter which grounds they've come from and regardless of loggers' stamps. Sorting comes later."

"What about payment?"

He shrugs. "Could be a combination of piece-work and hourly rates, or some kind of average to be worked out later by the insurance companies. Either way it won't be for months, and of course they'll cheat us every way they can."

"I still don't see why log salvors can't form a union."

"Men like that? They'd never agree about anything!"

Having spent the second day of the spill working around the shores of Gambier Island and Port Mellon, he arrives home in much the same state as the first. But the *Snark* hasn't fared so well. One of its gunwale lights has been smashed, but more alarming, the alternator has given up, keeping Dick on tenterhooks wondering if the charge in the battery would last long enough to bring him and the boat home safely. "It's not easy crashing through the swells in the dark with all that debris around," he says.

I am sure he is playing it down for my benefit. What would have happened if the battery had died? He has no radio, and there would have been very little traffic in Howe Sound in these weather conditions, particularly at night.

I set his spaghetti Bolognese in front of him across the bath plank and sit on the floor as I had the night before. "Do you have a spare alternator?"

"Yep. But you'd better get another, also a spare set of points for the distributor."

On the evening of the third day I'm helping with an oil change in the dark when I confess to him that during that afternoon I had suddenly been hit with an unusual feeling of depression. I add, "I shouldn't even be telling you this after what you've been going through."

He pokes a screwdriver into the can of oil and carefully, in the rocking boat, pours the oil into the reservoir. "Don't worry about it," he advises. "This wind affects a lot of people like that, particularly if it keeps up. It's the positively charged ions and high pressure." He adds that since he's always working hard during such times, he suspects he's immune to it.

We haven't been in the house more than a few minutes when the phone rings. I pick it up and a man on a radiophone asks for Dick.

After a short conversation, Dick replaces the phone and turns to me. "How'd you like to help us tomorrow? Breakfast provided."

I nod enthusiastically. "Where? Who?"

"Sam. Didn't you recognize his voice? We'll be working the south end of Anvil Island with him and Ann."

"I didn't know they were working this spill."

"Forgot to tell you. They joined us a couple of days ago after finishing another off Nanaimo."

Alan, it appears, will be working with the others, closer to Squamish. Apparently the bulk of the spill work should be completed within one more day, and the Howe Sound area will then be declared open to other salvors.

In the middle of the night we are both rudely awakened by what sounds like a single, very loud gunshot. Both of us get up and wander around the house until Dick finds the cause. The antique sideboard in our kitchen now has a quarter-inch-wide split the full length of its four-foot-long surface.

"No wonder we both have cracked lips," I mutter, much relieved that it's only the ultra-dry Arctic air and not an armed robber. Never-theless, the adrenaline rush and the annoyance of the damage keeps me awake for another hour. Not Dick. He's so tired he falls asleep immediately.

As I leave the warmth of the basement the following morning, the malevolent wind is ready. It rushes out of the darkness and lays its icy blade flat against my face, warning me there is plenty more to come. Down in the *Snark*, Dick suggests I might want to experience driving the boat under these conditions.

By the time we reach the ferry slip, the lingering stars that have been resisting the glow behind the mountains have vanished. A wave breaks over the bow and drenches us, rudely reminding me to pay atten-tion, to slow down as I drive into each approaching swell. I try to take my foot off the throttle as the *Snark*'s flattish hull reaches a crest so that the jet intake grill won't suck in air as the boat falls—partly airborne—belly-flopping into the trough. Only when the grill lies in the water will the jet function properly, and only then will there be any point in accelerating. As it is, we barely manage twelve knots in these seas.

Ploughing northwards through the narrower Latona Passage between Woolridge Island and Gambier's precipitous Mount Liddell, we are forced to slow down even more. The gusts have suddenly increased to at least sixty knots.

"Wind's stronger!" Dick shouts. "Venturi effect!"

The swells we're heading into are now almost six feet high, and their foaming crests blow into the boat even before we've passed through them. Balancing on one foot while controlling the throttle with the other in the bucking, jarring boat is exhausting, and although tools, chains, rope bins and other moveable objects have been wedged in their places, they still manage to jump and crash. Dick nudges me and points at the steep slopes to port.

I reduce speed and stare, shocked, at a mile-long, hundred-yard-wide swath of devastation that extends along the forested mountainside. Every single treetop has been sheared off about a third of the way down, leaving jagged white ends.

"Wind damage!" he yells. "Second-growth fir! Sap's frozen!"

Further on we pass a high waterfall, silenced by the Arctic air. The white ice sculpture hangs against the granite cliff like a trapped troll, its icicle-tipped feet clinging to an overhanging rock twenty feet above the roiling sea. It must have been there for days because the winter sun never shines on this north-facing slope. Compelled to gaze at the icy prisoner, I'm seized by an inexplicable sadness, a kind of misplaced empathy. But there's no time to dwell on why.

"To starboard!" yells Dick.

I turn the wheel and face the northwest to where the snows on the higher mountains in the distant Squamish River valley are already a pink-gold, but the mountain ridges to the east remain stark and black. We have yet to see this morning's sun.

The icy blast is now hitting the stern of our small boat, and while it's easier to ride with the swells rather than against them, the *Snark* still thumps disconcertingly into their troughs.

"Swells are closer," I shout.

"Freshwater from the glaciers," yells Dick. "Freshwater's lighter. Wind carries it higher."

Ten minutes later he draws my attention to Daybreak Point on the southern tip of Anvil Island where the dark-blue *Vulture* is anchored inside a protected bay. As I slide the *Snark* alongside her rubber bumpers, Sam's compact, jacketed figure bursts out of the cabin door and he grabs our gunwale before I can hand him the tie-up rope. "Good to see ya! C'mon, get inside!"

Within seconds we're sitting at the table surrounded by the tantalizing aroma of bacon.

"Just in time for sunrise," welcomes Ann, pointing to the dark ridge of the steep 5,700-foot-high Coast range to the east.

Above it, the sky has already ripened from pale primrose to a deep daffodil, which intensifies by the second until a red-gold disc explodes above the peak with such fiery brilliance that its rays set everything ablaze … and I can't help recalling the Panama sunrise after my night vigil on the freighter *Canadian Star*'s monkey island as we passed through Gatun Lake. The shrieks of an exotic bird that had startled me out of my short doze set the brilliant scene so indelibly that I have never forgotten it, and on this frigid morning, the two sunrises become superimposed on my mind. The tropical scene with its lush, multi-hued leaves so clearly defined by the early sun's startling brightness should have taken first place even without the flashy bird that had welcomed me to my new world. But in the end, the present vision, this dramatic display of fire, ice, wind, water, mountain and sea, surpasses and is without parallel. I'm swayed, too, by more recent and powerful memories: of cool sea mists brushing my skin, wisps of moisture drifting, vanishing into thin air above the forests, the spicy perfume of rock mosses drying in summer heat, bullets of cold winter rain beating against my face, indolent ravens circling on a warm updraft, and a hot summer hour stolen on a secluded island beach when the two of us had thrown off our clothes and under the high tide to become as one with the sea … Today's sunrise owns a mystery that now means more to me than the rain-muddied waters and unchanging seasons of Panama. I grip my partner's hand under the table and blame my teared eyes on the cold wind.

The incongruous perfume of freshly baked bread wafts around us. It must have been masked earlier by the frying bacon. "Baking bread in this weather?" I ask.

"We had to," Ann explains, lifting two loaves from the small oven. "No time to shop. We just tore over here from the Nanaimo spill. But it was so cold in the boat that we had to raise the dough directly in front of the heater."

"Which is next to the toilet!" Sam adds.

Ann hands us our omelets and starts slicing the hot bread. "Go ahead," she orders. "I'll join you in a minute."

The warm, gently rocking boat has a soporific effect and rather than going out to fight the sea and the cold I feel more like returning to bed …

But once in the *Snark* again, I'm ready. Even though the wind has dropped very slightly, the swells have not. The Lamonts work the rocky beach several hundred feet away from the area we have chosen.

Before Dick—clad in chest waders—goes ashore, he delivers his instructions slowly and clearly. "When I beckon you," he says, "come in stern first so that you can drive out again straight through the oncoming breakers. NEVER get yourself side-on against the shore or you'll be swamped."

From where we stand in the idling boat, the waves pounding the rocks appear twice as high as the *Snark's* freeboard. I yank my hood back and pull the balaclava completely down around my neck so that I'll have a clear view of Dick's hand signals.

Leaving the other end of the long pulling line looped on the *Snark's* stern cleat, he picks up its chain end. At slow speed, using short bursts of throttle, I steer in a semicircle as close to the rocks as I dare, then turn the stern to shore. With the boat now facing outward, I have to fight to keep from being smashed onto the boulders and yet allow Dick to land. The wind, the current, the swells, the breakers, the biting cold, the rocks, driftwood, the noise … even the *Snark* seems against me. Fighting the tossing craft so that Dick can jump off safely, I manage to catch the odd word: "Hard over!" … "No reverse!" … "Ease throttle!" … Then I give up listening because I'm too busy concentrating on what I'm doing. I don't need reverse because the wind and waves are already pushing the *Snark* backwards, and by keeping the engine in a fast idle forward I can maintain an approximate position. But I have to turn constantly to check ahead for waves, behind me to see how close I am to the beach, and all around and beneath for rocks. I daren't even blink while adjusting wheel and throttle. Immediately I discover how easy it is to make a mistake while facing the oncoming swells. While assuming I was going forward, it was only when I glanced behind at the shore that I realized I had actually been going backwards. The waves either side of me had given a false sense of forward movement.

The moment *Snark* is correctly positioned—between swells—Dick vaults into the pounding surf with the pulling chain. Once he's clear of the jet's nozzle, I step on the throttle and plunge straight into a large oncoming breaker. It curls over the bow, slides up the windshield, over me and inside the boat. Gasping from the icy shock, I steer away from the beach. It takes the automatic bilge pump almost thirty seconds to clear the water at my feet.

Once more I take the weather's onslaught personally, and a long-buried anger surfaces to help me fight, to act faster while steering the boat under these dangerous conditions.

I have to keep *Snark* close enough to the beach so that the pulling line—still looped over the stern cleat—has enough slack in it to allow me to manoeuvre. Using short bursts of throttle, I stay out of the breakers and wait until Dick has hooked the chain around the first log. He raises his right hand and twists his wrist in the air. Accelerating at right angles to the beach I pull the first log—a fir peeler. No problem. I tow it into deeper water and anchor it.

Dick wades out into the water ready to collect the chain from the stern. We repeat the procedure for the second log, but the first pull only moves it a few inches. I steer in a semicircle and try again in different directions until it's afloat so that I can tie it to the temporary anchor. Within an hour, we have collected eight fir peelers.

Around the corner in a little cove also filled with beached peelers, the sea is calmer. But there's a problem of a different kind lurking under the water: Algae-covered boulders. The reason they're difficult to see depends on my angle of view because they're either in the shade and seem to be the same colour as the reflected trees, or they're masked by the silver-mirrored sky. Even when viewed from above, these damn boulders are not really where they appear to be. Most of the time as Dick wades out to take the chain from me he points to them. But sometimes he doesn't.

The fourth log in this bay lies at an awkward angle and I have decided—privately—that if I pull it at the angle he has indicated, I will hit some submerged rocks. Sure that he cannot see what I can see, I choose another course. But it is only after I've committed myself—with the boat at full throttle—that I discover the reason for his choice: yet another submerged rock immediately ahead.

Clenching my jaw, I yank the steering wheel hard over while automatically releasing the accelerator. The *Snark* hits the outer edge of the rock with a mean scrape. From the feel of it I suspect that the new gouge in the reinforced part of the hull is only shallow, but my relief at having cleverly avoided the rock's highest point is short-lived. Dick briefly covers his face with his hands.

After finishing work in the cove, I collect Dick from the beach and we tie the two tows together, anchoring them inside the cove for protection. Still feeling devastated by my mistake, I wait for him to berate me. But he doesn't … yet.

Around the next corner, the breaking swells look almost the same size as those on the first beach. "If you don't feel up to this," he says, "we'll leave it to Sam."

I shake my head. "I'm fine."

An hour later, with the third tow collected and anchored, I drive the *Snark* toward Dick, who is waiting for me to pick him up. He's standing on a fairly flat beach composed of small boulders averaging just four inches high.

But as I steer the boat to face out from the beach, a rogue gust blows it against the shore—starboard side on. I had not given enough throttle as I steered left. The hull has caught on the submerged rocks.

Dick's voice echoes in my head, Never get the boat side on to the beach!

The *Snark*, now vulnerable to the sea's onslaught, teeters sideways. It's buffetted onshore.

Dick's right there. "NEUTRAL!" he yells.

No point in revving the engine until the jet grill and nozzle are totally under water. Like the waves, thoughts hit me thick and fast. I'm petrified. It is my fault and I can do nothing. I can't win with this sea! Breakers crash repeatedly over the seat and engine cover as Dick tries frantically to push the stern off the beach. But I must fight, use my buried fury. Turning the wheel hard over to port, I wait, the gear still in neutral … As an extra large swell hits the beach, raising the water level around the hull, my partner is ready. At the wave's highest point he heaves, strains, and turns the two-ton boat. Without letting up, he gives an almighty push against the stern on the backsurge until the hull is completely afloat with the bow facing out. With a final shove he bellows, "HIT IT!" and hauls himself aboard.

With a scream of rage I thrust the gear forward and depress the accelerator. *Snark* is free.

Exhausted, I'm immune to the icy battering of yet another head-on wave. Fifty yards further along the beach, I point to a lone log bouncing end-on to a very steep rocky beach. This is not a good place, even for him, to venture in this wind.

"Leave it?" I ask.

He shakes his head and burrows quickly under the bow, bringing out a menacing, long-handled iron implement the size of a large hammer. A sharpened pike-pole point has been welded onto the end of the hammer's striking surface and a thirty-foot coil of rope fastened to the top of the handle. He instructs me to loop the far end of the rope over the stern cleat.

With the instrument beside him, he accelerates toward the plunging log, and so fast that I can't figure out how he manoeuvres *Snark*, slams the spike-hammer deeply a few inches from the cut end, and he's out of there before the next swell catches us. After pulling the log through the breakers, he dogs it and adds it to the tow offshore.

"Secret invention," he yells. "I've used it a hundred times this week!"

As soon as we've had lunch and warmed ourselves in the *Vulture*, the four of us spend most of the afternoon working the beaches below the Squamish Highway. By the time darkness falls, we already have the day's logs on a long towline, ready for the *Vulture* to tow to the nearest sorting grounds several miles away. Dick and I wave goodbye to the Lamonts and set off southwards.

Dick volunteers to drive home. Wedged between a large coil of connector line, a rope bucket and an extra floater jacket, I allow my mind to drift as he aims for Daybreak Point and then to Brigade Bay on Gambier's northeast shore before following the large seas southward to Halkett Point.

We travel without lights, partly because the powerful beams cannot project through such high swells and partly because their reflection hinders vision. Besides, our eyes adjust to the darkness sufficiently that we can always see a certain amount, and our familiarity with the environment helps our minds supply some of the missing information. Dark land masses are no more than gaping cutouts in the starred sky, while alongside the boat, white-foamed, ghostly rollers glow eerily in the blackness. Is it an illusion, a reflection of the stars, or some kind of winter phosphorescence? As the frigid wind blows the top off the swells, the foam curls, rolls over and slides downward into the trough where its white-crusted claws scrabble and hesitate for an instant before back-tracking slightly as the swell ahead begins to mount. With uncanny control over the boat, Dick surfs in tandem with the waves, and I sense that he, I, the *Snark* and the sea have finally settled our differences to become as one. Our motion is rhythmical, but while—like my own pulse—its intervals are never exactly even, it is predictable, and I am comforted by its inevitability.

After a while the engine's surging roar and the rushing sounds of wind and waves blur into a background of indistinct noise. Trying to ignore my icy feet, I lean back against the engine cover and stare up at the brilliant stars. In contrast to the turmoil below, they seem immoveable, permanent. As I focus on a group of them, it seems that each star is suspended on its own invisible thread from an infinite point—a thread of a different length from the others—so that they appear three-dimensionally in space. Then in my mind, note by shimmering note, I hear the bell-like celeste playing a phrase from Holst's *Planets* suite. Drifting down from the night, the melody echoes around, evolving into chords and arpeggios that join other instruments until the whole sky is ablaze with sound. The last thing I remember seeing is the black cutout of Grace Islands ...

Later that evening I apologize about the boulder episode. I feel particularly guilty about this because the *Snark* is not insured. "I didn't think you'd seen the rocks that I'd seen ..." I begin before he disarms me with his smile.

"I knew exactly what was going through that head of yours, but I saw the ones you couldn't. You just have to trust me ... Anyway, it's not important. What you did today more than compensated for a little scrape."

The following morning he rises before me. But instead of turning on the light, he climbs back into bed. "Jo? Go back to sleep," he whispers.

"You sick?"

"There's six inches of snow."

"Okay, boss."

I lie back and listen to the sound of our breathing.

19

Jim and Hidden Basin

"Can you smell cigarette smoke?" I ask Dick during breakfast.

He nods. "Must be Jim using the basement phone. I've already asked him not to smoke in the house."

Jim, a friend of Alan's, is owner of the *Coho Charter*, a white and sky-blue thirty-two-foot fish boat built without the fishing gear, so that inside it's rather like a roomy cruiser.

"He's been mooring to our float quite a lot recently," I point out.

"I don't think he's quite decided where he wants to stay. He's a liveaboard."

And over the following weeks, like the proverbial camel who finagles his cold body into his master's tent, Jim makes our boat dock his yard, tying his floating home between it and the *Styx*—rafting—so that Alan has to access his own boat by climbing across the *Coho Charter*'s deck. It's a practice that encourages the two friends to share a smoke, a cup of coffee, and a bit of gossip.

Rather like Bluto, Jim is dark-haired and he's large, and even if he is lacking muscles like Dick's I wouldn't want to tangle with him. But I soon learn that he is a gentle sort, preferring to spend his leisure behind his arborite galley table with a cigarette, a mug of coffee, and maybe a glass or two of rum and coke. He is about Dick's age, and although he seldom talks about himself, male gossip leads me to believe that he is living in hope that one day his ideal woman will come aboard. More recently, a couple of locals have whispered that he has taken a shine to someone else's unhappily married wife—with children attached—and is prepared to wait almost indefinitely for her to make a decision. My mother-in-law informs me that Jim is a builder by trade, who five years previously had helped build their new house behind Gibsons' bluff. These days, however, he prefers to make his money from a bit of fishing or by towing other salvors' logs.

One day after hearing him dial the basement phone, I ask Dick, "How come you don't charge him moorage?"

"Remember the drunks at last year's salmon derby?" he says, replacing the milk carton in the fridge. "The ones who started a campfire on our float?"

Recalling the young men in three pleasure boats who had blatantly ignored our PRIVATE FLOAT sign by tying up to our dock then setting a fire on the float's planks, I understand what Dick is getting at. If we hadn't seen the flames from our living room, the story might have been quite different.

"I don't think that would have happened if Jim had been there," he points out.

So Jim stays—rent-free. Eventually he gets the message about not smoking in the basement, and even joins Alan, Dick and me for a few bottle-hunting trips in the mountain forests on our searches for hidden treasures at old logging camps.

One morning, Jim drops in to use the phone when Dick's father, Hal—splicing ropes in the basement—is telling us stories of his fascinating childhood in Hidden Basin on Nelson Island.

"Why don't I take you guys up there?" Jim offers.

Dick and I glance at each other. We still haven't had the time to repeat the Bruce Lake trip we had taken the previous year. "Sounds good to me," he tells Jim.

Jim takes out his pack of cigarettes but, like Alan, he knows better than to light one in here. "Any time's okay with me, as long as there isn't a strong westerly."

Having seen the *Coho Charter*'s wide beam and flattish hull exposed on the boat ways, I agree with Jim's stipulation. But Hal politely refuses the invitation, pointing out that his travelling days are over. Perhaps he doesn't want to be reminded of his lost youth.

On a sunny day the following week, we return from our early morning rounds and join Alan and Jim aboard the *Coho Charter*. It reeks, as always, of coffee, stove oil and cigarette smoke.

Once we've passed Gower Point, Jim sets course for the almost invisible grey-blue tip of Thormanby Island. "Help yourselves to coffee," he yells. "Mugs in the sink, cream's by the stove."

Oh yes, I remind myself, these real Canadians—one of whom I have now officially become—call evaporated milk "cream."

I try his opaque, black brew, adding a bit of "cream," and I'm hooked. "What kind of coffee?" I ask Jim.

He turns away from the console. "Too strong?"

"It's perfect."

Alan explains the secret. "You have to boil it and let it sit … for ages."

Dick, however, refuses it, and the three of us accuse him of being a wimp. But he laughs, tells us that it's worse than drinking battery acid and warns us that our stomachs will rot out.

When the cigarette smoke starts watering my eyes, I grab a life preserver to sit on and climb the ladder onto the roof. With two wide fibreglass-backed benches and a three-foot-high dodger—the fibreglass screen in the front to deflect the wind—it is well set up for enjoying the scenery. Much of the journey follows the identical route I had taken with Sam in *Vulture* the previous summer, but this trip will probably take half the time because the gas-powered *Coho Charter* is lighter and has a faster planing hull.

Jim has picked a good day. The Gulf of Georgia is unusually quiescent. In spite of the cloudless sky, the prevailing summer westerlies from the Pacific high pressure area have so far not materialized.

For miles around, the sea is glowing, ethereally luminous, strikingly paler than the clear sky above. Like a giant sheet of opaque glass, it gives the illusion of lacking depth. But where the bow cuts through it, pushing the water aside to set waves in motion, it appears as a liquid and something not to be walked on. Sitting up here, removed from the engine's roar, I imagine I am floating in that half-liquid half-gaseous medium, the strange vapour that had surrounded me in the most vivid of my boat dreams, the swirling mist from the transformed sailors that had displaced the sea. But I feel no fear, no chill, on this placid morning. My frustrating boat dreams are long gone. Instead, the surreal ocean now buoys me up, carrying me and my partner aloft.

This is a quest for his family, not mine. I never did find satisfaction from rediscovering my father. No connection, just sadness, a feeling of having missed something that should have been part of me. My mother had closed her mind to him and he had closed his mind to me. While I was lucky enough to have been a part of my grandpa's life, Dick had never even met his paternal grandfather, Jack. Perhaps he has a couple of buried stones to uncover. Perhaps Hal's stories have prompted him to search for something. Still, after those few days Dick and I had spent on Bruce Lake, the closest thing to a honeymoon, my own curiosity is at last more than a little piqued.

As we pass between Thormanby Island and Smuggler's Cove, I suddenly feel the gentle firmness of Dick's hand on my shoulder. "This is more like it," he says, cozying beside me. "There's a limit to my tolerance for stinky cabins."

Thanks to Jim's remarkably efficient muffler, it is quiet enough up here to hold a normal conversation. "Why did Grandfather Jack settle on Nelson Island?" I ask.

"He moved there from Texada." He points over the port side of the bow to a couple of fairly big islands. "That's Texada ... the largest one."

"What made him move?"

"No one knows ... But he never was one for a settled life," explains Dick. "Remember me telling you how his freight schooner idea failed? After that he'd take the occasional job with his surveyor and timber-cruising brother-in-law, Eustace Smith ... That's how Jack discovered Hidden Basin. He knew there were some trees ready to log, and it looked like a good place to homestead, so ..."

"What year was that?"

"Must've been 1902 or 1903. He built a big raft out of salvaged logs. Then he loaded his wife, children, livestock and possessions onto it and had an acquaintance tow them northwards twenty miles across

Malaspina Strait. A few hours out, the old one-cylinder gas engine quit.
They were unlucky. A fog came up and they drifted out there for a
couple of days and nights."

"Wife and kids on the raft? That's a bit cruel."

"Not in those days. They'd fixed up a tent. And the logs they'd
used to build the raft would be considered huge by today's standards. It
floated well above the water."

"I hope he had a compass."

Dick nods. "He'd chosen to leave Texada in the spring because he
knew that the currents and tides would help them. Good thinking on his
part because even in the fog and without the engine they landed on the
beach near the entrance to Hidden Basin. He knew exactly where they
were from the type of rocks on the beach."

"Is this true?"

"The whole family, including Father, knew the story like the back
of their hands. Four of my aunts told it independently. Besides," he
adds, "my dour old grandmother, May, would not have approved of
embellishments."

"Did you know her very well?"

"Enough to be rather scared of her. I often wonder what had gone
on between her and Jack …" He pauses awhile.

There's something he's not telling me. "Such as?"

"He left the family to go to New Zealand when Father was thirteen. Mostly for health reasons. He returned two years later, but of
course, things had changed, and his wife had no more time for him. I
had the impression she'd found someone else … Anyway, he left again,
never to return. He'd painted quite a few pictures, sent them to her, but
Father told me she burned them all."

So Jack had escaped on a ship, like me. "How did the family survive without him?"

"He had to grow up in a hurry. No time for school. I think I told
you, he was building boats in Vancouver when he was nineteen. But
before that he found various jobs to support his mother and his siblings.
The government released him from war duty for that reason. He worked
for the granite quarry on the northwest corner of the island where the

old Vancouver Courthouse lions came from. He'd ferry fresh water to Hardy Island, assist the quarry blacksmith." Then he turns to me, a glint in his eyes. "Now the smith was a fascinating character. Kept to himself, ate by himself. I'm sure he was a Zoroastrian."

"A fire worshipper."

"Very much so. He'd talk about it to Father."

"What sort of things?"

"He'd sound as if he was talking to himself, then he'd say to Father something like, 'From Fire we come, boy, and to Fire we go!'" Dick gazes into the distance toward Nelson Island. "One of these days I'll write those stories out."

"Why not now?"

He shakes his head. "Hate writing longhand. I can't type."

"Neither can I," I tell him. "Only would-be secretaries learned to type at my school."

Instead of entering Pender Harbour, Jim keeps going, past forests with the occasional summer cabin, past Irvine's Landing, past the inviting half-mile-wide slash of Agamemnon Channel that takes off to the northeast, separating Nelson Island from the Sechelt Peninsula. I climb down and check Jim's chart, loosely rolled and available on the table. After another two miles of thickly forested Nelson Island coastline and the promontory of Cape Cockburn, we see what Jack might have seen if it hadn't been for the fog: a long V-shaped bay—Billings Bay—and at its head a narrow gap with a tiny treed island in the centre. Jim steers toward it. Whitewater gushes out, falling from both sides of the little island. Navigation through either channel is impossible. Not even *Snark* could have made it into Hidden Basin at this moment. But behind the guard island a tantalizing blue lagoon beckons.

"Oh, no," Jim groans. "Never thought of the goddamn tide."

Nobody had. On top of that, it is a summer tide, with a large height differential and a long runout.

I turn to Dick. "Surely they didn't live on the other side of this waterfall?"

"You can only get in and out on the right-hand side of that little island when the tide's a certain height." He shrugs. "It doesn't matter.

Their house is long gone. Nothing in there will be as it was in Father's day."

Although we have again failed to visit the place, I get the feeling he is just as glad not to have seen it. I suspect it is because he's afraid he might see a stranger living there.

Jim turns the *Coho Charter* away and continues, as planned, to take us clockwise around the whole of Nelson Island. When he shows us an ancient petroglyph painted by the Sechelt Nation on one of the rocks, I wonder what Jack had made of it.

Shortly after the trip, I can't help noticing that Dick is spending more time than usual in the basement splicing ropes with his father, questioning him, listening to his stories about his youth. If the weather is warm, the pair of them sit outside on the low cement wall, and Jim, coffee mug in hand, comes ashore to listen, his cigarette smoke drifting upwards.

While the Nelson Island trip anchors itself into my memory as unfinished business, I too, find myself listening to my father-in-law's stories about his childhood there. But because they are so different from those of my own youth, I don't empathize—at first. However, over the course of a few months and without realizing it, I am seduced by Hal's unhurried telling of them, his facial expressions, the way he suddenly halts mid-sentence to present an important fact or to add an aside in a totally different voice, only to resume the story seamlessly. And as the strands from several of these tales become spliced into some of my own distressing childhood memories, the happiness and enchantment from his young life overrides mine, convincing me that family life can be rewarding. Unwittingly he causes me to rethink the idea of motherhood.

When I learn that I'm pregnant several months later, I vow never to belittle, beat, or distrust our child. Dick has his own ideas about child rearing, too. Like mine, they're deeply chiselled by personal experience. I look forward to parenthood as an interesting experiment and make sure I read up on the basics ahead of time. A friend of ours, a world-famous pathology professor, offers some useful advice: "Disciplining children simply comes down to protecting oneself and the child."

But nothing prepares me for the role of mother to a colicky baby.

20

Loud Voices and Towing with Baby

Our daughter, Patricia, is born at the end of September 1973.

She establishes her status on her first night home from the hospital. At two a.m., as soon as she stirs in the borrowed carrycot beside our bed, I take her out into the living room to avoid disturbing Dick who has to rise before the sun. I feed her, change her diaper, bundle and burp her as I have been taught and gently lay her back in her carrycot. But she gives me a hostile stare, takes a deep breath, and starts screaming or crying—as a new mother, I cannot decide which. I pick her up and try the feeding ritual again but the result is just the same. What have I done wrong? Was it something connected with my pregnancy?

An hour later she is still howling. Exasperated, I snatch the pile of magazines from the coffee table and throw them across the room. "What can I do? I don't know what else I CAN do!" I yell, pacing around. "WHAT DO YOU WANT?"

Dick blunders into the room with a half-dazed, half-shocked expression. "What's going on?"

Tears of frustration run down my face. "What the hell can I do?" I cry. "I've tried everything. Nothing works. I'm so tired and she won't shut up! I'm no good as a mother!"

He walks over to the carrycot and begins to stroke Patricia on her back as if she were a cat. Immediately her crying slows then quietens. His persistence pays off as she slowly falls asleep, probably because she has tired herself out.

Dick joins me on the chesterfield and holds me close. "She's only trying to sound like *Snark*," he explains. "After all, that's what she's been hearing for the past nine months."

He does have a point. I had continued to work until a week before she was born—although my dogging abilities had been somewhat limited after the eighth month of pregnancy.

The doctor mutters something about colic and advises me to drink a bottle of stout with supper. But it has no effect on Patricia, and I am not consoled by the comments from some of my friends—"Surely you wouldn't want a cabbage baby? It's the noisy ones who have the brains," and, "She'll soon get over it."

A week later, deciding to test her reaction to the sound of the *Snark*'s engine, I bundle her up and take her—crying—with us into the boat, wedging the borrowed waterproof English carrycot under the flat bow. She is already asleep by the time we've left the harbour and stays that way for the rest of the trip.

While for obvious reasons I no longer go out on morning rounds, I still volunteer for towing jobs.

During lunch one January afternoon, after I warn Dick of the latest weather forecast—the possibility of Arctic outflow winds expected the following day—he gives a frustrated sigh. "That's annoying," he complains. "I was counting on Alan collecting my island tows but he won't be back from working upcoast until tomorrow evening." He is recovering from one of his four-day migraines and had been intending to catch up on some sleep that afternoon, so I offer to collect the logs with the *Snark*, taking Patricia with me.

"Do you think that's a good idea?" He sounds unusually cautious. "You two out there alone in a little boat while the *Styx* is away? Jim's ashore, too."

"You're a fine one to talk. Look at the chances you take."

"That's quite another kettle of fish. I'm responsible for both of you—"

"But it's beautiful out there. It's perfect for towing."

"Okay, if you really want to. I'll put the alarm on."

"Don't be like your mother," I add for insurance.

I dress the four-month-old Patricia warmly and bundle her, screaming as usual, into the hooded carrycot. I cover it with the waterproof canopy then wedge it amidst the anchors and piles of rope under the bow in front of my feet.

"See you in a couple of hours," says Dick as he pushes me away from the float. It's 2:10, the weather is cool and clear and the sea is calm.

Patricia's protests stop even before I'm past the harbour beacon. Off Preston Island I spot a couple of floating hemlock logs and leave them anchored in the bay where I'd sung to the seals. Almost an hour has passed by the time I reach my favourite tie-up on the west shore of Pasley, a rope tied to the trunk of a picturesque overhanging arbutus tree growing out of a wide crack in the rock bluff. In the afternoon at this time of year the tree appears at its most beautiful, its red arching boughs mirrored in the still, clear water below. Reflected afternoon light from the low winter sun dances on the bluff and the undersides of the broad evergreen leaves. I turn off the engine and tie the *Snark* to the neatly arranged tow of seven logs—two of them wide and heavy low-floaters— lying there. With the water softly lapping against the bluff, it's a perfect place to feed Patricia, now awakened by the quiet.

The golden reflections flicker upwards against my face like hundreds of little flames, and even though it is late January, there's just enough hint of warmth in the sun's rays to remind me that spring is not far off. A couple of hundred feet away, a flock of squawking surf scoters slap their wings on the water as a mating ritual, occasionally stopping to feed.

Enjoying the solitude and a brief respite from housework, I sit there with Patricia at my breast, procrastinating for a minute or two before reminding myself that winter sunsets are early, and like the surf scoters I'd better get on with the job at hand. With the carrycot back under the bow and the logs behind us, I set off along the burnished path of the setting sun.

As I turn my head to check on the tow, I spot a shiny buff-brown head on the water's surface about forty feet from the side of the boat. It's the same shape as a seal's head but three times as big. The reddish-brown humped body that follows slides under the water. Apart from its large size, there's a snake-like smoothness about its movement that disturbs me, a menacing inevitability rather like that of an advancing tank. It is a Steller sea lion, obviously out on a foraging trip. Remembering them from my first boat ride with Dick, I wonder how I could have felt so little fear at the time. Since then, I had read of two accounts of sea lion attacks on small boats in Pacific coastal waters. Seconds later, a splash, a hissing snarl, and there it is again, staring at me a few feet from starboard. Judging from its size, it must be a male, possibly weighing around two thousand pounds. Heavier than the *Snark*. It dives fiercely then shoots up on the port side, whooping and snarling with its bared teeth. Perhaps it thinks we are poaching its food supply.

I am not prepared for the turbulence from its next dive. The boat rocks violently. If the beast chose to surface directly underneath us it could easily capsize *Snark*.

Here we are, out in the middle of a group of islands in mid-winter with no other vessel in sight. Should we be knocked into the sea at this time of year, the pair of us would only survive ten minutes before succumbing to hypothermia. I put one of the two life jackets on—ten minutes are better than none. How can I protect Patricia, now asleep? I slide the carrycot out so that I can grab Dick's heavy spike-hammer, placing it beside me.

Suddenly, with a great snort, the sea lion rears again a few feet ahead of us, displaying its massive neck and forequarters for a second before diving. In desperation, I shove the gear into reverse and gun the engine loudly, simultaneously pressing the horn button before throwing the towline off the cleat. Then with the horn blaring, I circle the tow twice at top speed before cutting the engine, stopping about two or three hundred yards from the logs.

Waiting to see if the animal reappears, I loosen my lifejacket, pick up Patricia and slip her inside my Helly Hansen. Frightened by the loud horn, she is crying hysterically, and I speak comfortingly to her—and myself.

A few minutes later, a telltale swirl a few hundred feet further away from the drifting tow leads me to think that my scare tactics have worked. But even after collecting my logs, I can't relax. The fading light adds to my anxiety and I keep checking behind the boat every twenty seconds or so. Lulled by the engine's steady surge, Patricia falls asleep again and I replace her in her bed under the bow.

I keep asking myself if I have been catastrophizing. Would the sea lion really have tried to jump into the boat or tip it over? Or has motherhood given me an extra dose of the concept of danger? Have I been reading danger into a situation that didn't warrant concern?

Continually distracted by these thoughts, I automatically steer the *Snark* toward the short-cut between Salmon Rock and Keats Island.

Halfway through it, I suddenly realize that while the engine is grinding away, the *Snark* is going nowhere. Glancing back in the dusky light I notice that a couple of the wide tow of logs are floating higher in the water than before. No, they're not floating. The two largest and heaviest logs are absolutely still. Not a sign of rocking motion. They must have caught on the submerged reef in the passage. We've used the channel many times with the jet boat—even at fairly low tides—but never with a tow of heavy logs. Damn! I should have taken the longer route outside the small island.

I try pulling from different angles, but the narrow passage gives little leeway for manoeuvering. The tow is well and truly stuck. I shut the engine off and curse myself for not paying attention. Then I begin to panic. Stuck helplessly in the *Snark* with darkness falling makes me think yet again of the day my mother remarried, the day I had met Mr. Sisman, the man trapped with his floppy legs. But only now does it strike me that his legs hadn't been totally useless. They were perfect for holding the willow baskets he was weaving.

Calmer after my seemingly disconnected thoughts, I see that the rocks beside me are dry above the water, which means that the tide is rising ... unless—and this is my main concern—it is now at its peak. I have to be patient.

Using a little ridge on the rock above the water line as a reference, I'm relieved to learn that the tide is still rising. Every few moments I aim the hand-held searchlight at the logs to check if they are afloat. Not only has darkness fallen, the air temperature has dropped sharply. Twice I rev the engine, peeping at Patricia after each pull, but she never stirs.

Neither does *Snark*. On the third try, the logs slide grudgingly off their rocky shelf.

Free at last, I turn starboard around Keats' western promontory and gasp as a blast of frigid northeasterly wind hits my face. The shockingly familiar sensation prompts me to gaze up at the newly darkened sky. Resplendent in its own three-dimensional space of the universe, each star asserts its presence. The Arctic outflow has beaten the forecasters—and me.

The *Snark* strains against the current pouring out of the inlet along with the dreaded wind. In the bow light's powerful beam, relentless armies of foam-crested waves charge toward us. Although they are barely a foot and a half high, their size will soon change as the wind increases.

Dragging its heavy tow, the boat churns slowly alongside the shore. Then, without warning, the engine gives an ominous metallic death-rattle and expires. For one brief moment, I actually feel sick. Why do bad things so often come in clusters? What else could go wrong?

My mind starts to race. Restarting the engine will probably cause even more damage.

I throw out the boat anchor, and while the logs continue to drift toward me under their inertia, I halve the length of the towline so that they won't hit the rocks.

Save the battery! I shut the running lights off. The last thing I need is for the bilge pump to quit. My partner has a saying: "Check the simple things first." As I grope around in the rope bin for the flashlight, Patricia protests.

"Please, Patricia, not right now," I beg. *Blast you, Dick. Why the hell didn't you install a radiophone?*

I lift the engine cover and check the hot block and its attachments, but the flashlight shows nothing cracked, broken or disconnected. The distributor seems fine. The battery terminals are clean and tight. The damage has to be internal and terminal. From the clatter as the engine quit—an unforgettable noise I've heard once before—I'm almost sure it's a broken piston. I can do absolutely nothing about it. So much for a blueprinted high-performance engine.

Where is Dick? When will he send someone to search for us? Since this is Friday evening, it's more than likely the water taxi is out on a job. And there had been no sign of Jim on the *Coho Charter* when I left.

Patricia screams and the wind howls. The noise of waves crashing onto the rocks a couple of hundred feet away makes me question the anchor's holding power. By shining the hand-held searchlight onto the shore for a few moments to check our position, I confirm my fears; the combined weight of logs and boat are dragging the anchor. We will either be thrown against the rocks or blown out into the Strait. I have to separate the *Snark* from our tow.

From under the bow I grab another anchor and tie the end of its rope into the towline loop straining on the cleat. Gripping the loop, I try to pull it off. But the logs are keeping the rope so taut that it's impossible to lift it over the seven-inch projection on the side closest to me, the piece of metal that prevents the loop from jumping off when the boat reverses. The flashlight rolls off the engine cover and goes out. I pick it up and twist the base, holding my breath until the light comes on again. This time I wedge it inside a coil of rope with the beam aimed at the stern cleat.

Tears of frustration and fury mix with the cold sea spray on my face. "You bastard!" I shout, struggling again with the loop. "I'll bloody well get you off if it kills me!" But the pressure of the current and wind against the logs is more than a match for *my* strength. If I cut it free, we would lose the logs out in the Strait and they'd end up on Vancouver Island. How would my husband react if he was limited by muscles like mine? Of course ... he'd take it as a challenge.

I point the flashlight at the cleat and along the towline. Once in a while as a larger wave passes along the tow and hits the logs, the line slackens, but only for a half a second before jerking taut again. Dick has told me that waves sometimes come in groups of fives or sevens, the last one often slightly higher and longer than the others. Keeping the beam aimed at the sea behind the jet guard, I watch and wait, wondering if the wind has been blowing long enough to establish a reliable pattern. There is an irregular one of sorts; the largest wave most likely to be the seventh. Using this new information, I grip the flashlight between my knees, tie an extra anchor line to the towline loop and grasp the loop with both hands, ready for the next slack. But before I have time to pull the rope and slide it up and off, it snaps tight again, trapping the tip of one of my oversize gloves between the loop and the cleat. What if it had been a finger?

Ignoring the plaintive cries from under the bow, I wait once more for the critical moment. This time—again the seventh wave—I'm ready. Snatching the rope forcefully toward me I yank the loop up and off the cleat and anchor line. As the anchor sinks, most of the towline submerges, demonstrating the powerful current. But the logs hold.

Relieved, I sit facing the windshield and shine the flashlight onto the oncoming swells. They are now averaging three feet, but within a couple of minutes a larger wave breaks over the bow and windshield, deluging me with icy water. Occasionally the wind gusts from the side too, lifting the wave crests and throwing a barrage of heavy spray across the gunwales into the boat. It is during these moments that I am comforted by the gurgle of the automatic bilge pump.

I pull Patricia from her carrycot. As the bitter wind hits her face, she gasps and stops crying. With my back to the windshield I unzip my spray-soaked jacket and start to feed her. But she's distressed. She struggles and fusses, then refuses to feed altogether. Even when I talk to her, she will not relax. Obviously hungry, she is still convinced this is not the time nor the place for a meal. Another wave curls over the windshield, spilling about half a cupful of frigid sea onto her upturned face and neck. Incensed, she screams. I pull out a small towel from the carrycot, dry her and bundle her back under the bow.

Straightening up, I catch a glimpse of a lighted window in the McQueen's house further up the hill. I had forgotten about Rob, the church camp caretaker who lives there year-round with his family. He also looks after the summer cottages. There's a slight chance he could be out gathering firewood from his shed, even emptying the garbage. Since his house is away from the noisy shore, he might hear if I call. I cup my hands and shout, "H-E-LP!" And after a deeper breath, "H-E-L-L-LP!"

With the life jacket ready beside me I try again, supporting my voice like an opera singer, prolonging the vowels and using vibrato to project the most ear-piercing sound possible. And every few seconds I wave the flashlight at the lighted house.

Then, close to the window, a flash answers. And in reply to mine, another.

Almost ten minutes pass before a bouncing light approaches and something bangs against the *Snark*. A dark figure leans over the gunwale and aims a beam at me. "Broke down, eh?" Rob shouts.

Yelling against the wind, I start to explain.

"It's okay!" he interrupts. "Dick just phoned, asked if I'd heard the boat. I went out to check. Never expected to hear an opera singer—"

"Where is he?"

"Gone to get Jim. I told him I was going to row out. Wanna come back with me?"

I glance at his tiny rowboat. "Thanks. We'll manage till they get here."

He lets go of the *Snark* and fights his way back to Keats' dock. Waiting impatiently facing the stern, my thoughts oscillate between anger and relief, but in the end I blame everything on Dick for not having a radiophone.

Fifteen minutes later, the *Coho Charter*'s bright lights charge toward me, catching great billows of hissing, glistening spray each side of its bow as the wide hull plunges up and down in the swells. Jim draws alongside the crippled *Snark* while Dick stands at the gunwale ready to take Patricia in the carrycot.

"Where the hell have you been?" I yell.

"Later!" he bellows.

After he's placed the carrycot safely inside the cabin, I point my flashlight at the logs, porpoising in and out of the swells. "Tow's anchored!"

"Here!" he shouts, grabbing my hand as Jim holds the *Charter* against the wind, allowing me to climb aboard. After hooking the *Snark*'s bow line with his pike pole, Dick slips it over the *Charter*'s towpost and raises the boat anchor. Jim allows the *Charter* to idle backwards a few feet, holding it steady until Dick can hook the log anchor up with a pike pole. With logs and jet boat on the towpost, he enters the cabin and gives the go-ahead for Jim to start towing to Shelter Island.

"Had a hard time, eh?" Jim asks me.

"You can say that again."

"Hell of a tide against this shore," he mutters. "Lucky you weren't blown out into the Gulf."

"We're lucky to be alive," I grunt. After changing Patricia's diaper and settling her again, I join the two men at the console.

Jim points to the fixed wooden basket behind the table. "Get some rum down ya," he orders.

I thank him, explaining that I have never felt more like taking a drink than I do at this moment. Adding a few ounces of coke helps the rum's effects and after a couple of minutes I am forced to relax my frown muscles.

"So what happened to you?" I ask Dick.

"No, you first," he counters.

I drain my drink, and while the *Coho Charter* bucks its way to our storage grounds, I tell my story.

After hearing it, Dick raises his eyebrows with a "told-you-so" expression. "Remember how I didn't want you to go? And you wouldn't take me seriously. No, you had to find things out for yourself."

"How did I know the weather forecast was rubbish? Anyway, why didn't you come looking earlier?"

"I didn't mean to sleep that long and I'm sorry. The alarm didn't go off."

I must have underestimated how sleep-deprived he had been. However, I'm not going to let him put the blame totally on me. "None of this would have happened if we had a radiophone on the boat," I insist, unsuccessfully trying to keep the emotion out of my voice.

He puts an arm around my shoulder. "You have no idea how worried I was. But I knew you'd cope. And you did. I keep telling you you're always underestimating yourself."

I place my mug in the beverage holder, unzip his Helly Hansen jacket, slide my ice-cold hands under his sweatshirt and warm them on his bare midriff.

With Jim watching, he doesn't dare flinch.

21

The Move

Gibsons is a small village no more. By spring 1974, its growth has given the town council reason to build a sewage system and they have sent a letter informing us harbour residents of plans to lay large sewage pipes and cover them with a promenade. Since the construction will be between our yard and the sea, we will technically cease to be living on waterfront property. It will affect us more than most because the new promenade will be blocked by the Boatworks' dock and their two sets of ways, and unless the promenaders turn to retrace their steps, they will be tempted to access the main road above us through our property.

"Don't like it," grumbles Dick. "We'll have strangers and dogs wandering up through our yard. Things will be stolen off the float and boats ..."

"Puss won't like it either," I add, "and think of the dog poop."

Even though we can't do anything about it, the trout in our pond think otherwise. Two days after receiving the council letter, I spot two of the fish flip-flopping down the creek bed where it flows over the muddy eelgrass bed at low tide. They must have leaped over the dam. As I cradle them in my arms and start walking back to the pond, Dick calls out from the kitchen window, "Let em go! They must've had a letter from the council, too!"

After gently depositing them into the harbour, I traipse back to the window to ask the fishing expert, "Won't the salt water kill them?"

"No," he explains. "Their bodies adjust."

I hope that they will survive.

Returning from a rare early morning towing job later that same week, I find myself steering the *Snark* past the breakwater into the midst of a shimmering, seething mass. As far as I can see, every square inch of this usually peaceful harbour is alive. Slowing the *Snark* to a barely manoeuvrable speed, I aim for our float, turn the key off and lean over the gunwale. Groups of small glistening fish curve and arc gracefully around the pilings and under the floats, occasionally surfacing to form little swirls that flicker and shine in the sun. Then that particular group will stop, turn about and move on. They're so dense one could almost walk across the bay on their backs. All the local sea birds, ducks, geese, mergansers, seem to be getting in on the action, too.

The sudden engine silence—or perhaps the squawk of birds— awakens Patricia under the bow and she starts to cry. But I cannot move. This sight mesmerizes me in the same way as falling snow. What kind of fish? What are they doing? They remind me of lemmings, but they don't seem to be going anywhere.

At last my stomach reminds me I'm overdue for breakfast, and I carry Patricia up our chain of floats. On the shore float I'm distracted again, this time by Puss standing awkwardly ten feet away amongst the eelgrass in an inch of water. She hooks a wriggling fish and starts to chomp on it.

Dick meets me at the basement door. "They're herring," he tells me. "They've come in here to spawn. Father was just over. He says it's the best year he's seen in ages."

"What makes the fish glisten like that?" I ask.

Of course, he knows. "It's the guanine crystals in their cells."

Later that afternoon we take a small-diameter fishnet down to the *Snark* and, dipping it alongside the noisy, flapping seabirds, fill a bucket with herring. That's when Dick points out the thick, brown masses of tiny eggs stuck to the eelgrass, pilings and practically everything that floats. "They'll hatch in about ten days," he tells me, "if nothing eats them."

"Well," I point out, referring to the proposed beach promenade that will soon replace our eelgrass bed, "if their offspring ever return to spawn here, they'll be in for a nasty surprise."

Dick shakes his head. "Fortunately they're not like salmon. They don't return to their birthplace to spawn."

Not only have the escaped trout presaged the town council's plans, they must have told the herring to have a last kick at the can, too.

It's around this time that Jim realizes that his Heart's Desire will never choose him over her husband and children. He has sold the *Coho Charter* and has moved to Queen Charlotte Islands to start a fish-and-chip café.

Dick's partner, Alan, has also left Gibsons. Realizing that there are fewer logs to be found each morning and fearing the eventual demise of log salvage, he has moved to Vancouver Island with wife and family, taking the *Styx* to go handlogging with one of Sam Lamont's sons. Since then, we've been using the *Snark* as a dual purpose boat, but on occasions when we have a particularly large log accumulation on the tie-up anchors, we'll hire Tom Penfold and his tug, the *Gambier Scout*.

A week after the trout breakout, I'm feeding five-month-old Patricia in the living room when I hear four sharp knocks at the back door. The dot-dot-dot-dash rhythm catches my attention because it's the same as the "Fate" motif that opens Beethoven's Fifth Symphony.

Adjusting my clothes, I carry Patricia to the back door. As I open it, I'm conscious of having to raise my eyes a good ten inches higher than I normally do when I greet a visitor. The man in front of me is also so broad that there's hardly any light between him and the door frame. He's carrying a black briefcase, sometimes a Jehovah Witness' trademark.

"Mrs. Hammond?" he asks.

He can't be a Witness. They seldom address householders by name. Suspecting he might be looking for my mother-in-law, I respond with a cool, "Mrs. Richard Hammond."

"That's de one. I am Olaf Klassen. I wonder if I can haf a word vit you and your husbant. I am a defeloper and I haf sometink to say what you may be interested in."

After shaking his bear-sized hand, I find myself staring at his unusual features. The winter sun reflecting off our beige lino seems to accentuate his pale green eyes and the unblemished, almond-coloured skin lying taut across high, wide cheekbones. And yet his greying brown curly hair suggests he's in his mid-forties. The fine nose, flared nostrils and his accent make me think he's from the Baltic area. But a developer? At least he's not a salesman.

"Please come in."

Ducking under the door lintel, he has to enter slightly sideways. "It's a nice place vhat you haf here," he says, staring out at the harbour. "Vhat a view."

Dick emerges from refilling his jet bearing grease pump in the basement. Dark grey molybdenum grease glistens on his hands and arms, and splotches of it decorate his already oily work jeans.

"Good mornink, Mr. Hammond ... Ah, a man vhat vorks hard, after my own heart ... I am Olaf Klassen and I have a proposition. About property exchange."

Dick points to one of the chairs at the kitchen table. "Please take a seat while I clean my hands."

The stranger sits and opens his briefcase on the table. "Like I say to your vife, I haf dis idea ..." He pulls out some blueprints and unrolls them. "I am interested in profidink a good hotel in dis harbour. See here," he says, pointing to the top drawing. "I haf already made a model of this to show in de Bank of Montreal so people can see it. I mean, I belief in being honest and lettink everyone see my idea. Dat's de trouble with defelopers. Dey never tell everytink." He pauses. "I vould like to build on dis place and next door property."

"But we don't want to sell," Dick says. "We need this place for my work. The water lease is—"

Olaf interrupts. "But like I say, I haf a proposition for you. I own a summer cottage and three acres vaterfront just cupla' miles avay, and for dis place here, I can gif you one acre of dem."

For the following four seconds the only sounds are the squawks of seagulls on our roof.

"Supposing we take you up on your offer. What about a house?" asks Dick.

"Ve could arrange sometink. But first, come vid me to see de property."

I wrap Patricia warmly and Olaf drives the three of us halfway to the ferry landing before turning down a short dirt road that ends a couple of hundred feet from the sea. After parking, he takes us past a small rancher—his family's summer place—and shows us one acre of south-facing, gently sloping grassland leading to a gravel beach with a promontory to its left. A row of poplars and four high fir trees grow on the property as well as two large arbutus trees and a quarter-acre patch of blackberry bushes.

"Vy don't you go to de beach?" suggests Olaf. "I haf someting to do in de cottage ... I follow you later."

The low bank waterfront is grass down to the high-tide line. To the east rises the snow-covered Coast range, Keats Island and our Shelter Island storage grounds are a mile to the south, and to the west there's a view through the Gap of the Gulf of Georgia and Vancouver Island.

Dick shakes his head. "Can't believe it," he says. "I've had my eye on this piece of land for years. I didn't even know it was available."

"You've never said anything about moving before."

"There's been no reason to—until now." He sticks a grass stem in his mouth. "How would you feel about living here?"

"I'd like it, but it won't be as convenient for work. When I first came here, I missed the city ..."

"... And now you don't even want to live in a town," he finishes.

"Strange how a person can change."

"Vell, vhat you tink?" asks Olaf, catching up with us. "You could haf your house moved here or build anodder."

"We couldn't afford to do that," said Dick.

Olaf shrugs. "Vell, I mean to say, I vould pay for dose tings."

"And would my father be allowed permanent moorage at the dock?"

"I vill arrange for dat. Certainly."

"We'd need to anchor our boat year-round ... and we'd have to row out to it," Dick points out as we wander back to the developer's car. "We'll have to think about it. Do you have the deed, property plans and proof that there are no easements?"

Olaf opens the passenger door for me. "No problem. I bring dem to you. Like I say, I vant to do dis as soon as possible. It can vork out goot."

Dick and I spend the rest of the day going about our business as usual. When by the end of supper he still hasn't mentioned the subject of the move, I broach it.

"Developers are all fancy plans and talk," he replies. "I don't even want to think about it."

I take the hint. But that night I can't sleep and I am still awake when Patricia starts fussing at two a.m. As I feed her in the dimly lit, still unfinished, living room, Dick walks in and plonks himself down beside me.

"Can't sleep either?" I ask.

He shakes his head and leans back against the cushions. "I hate planning for things that are beyond my control. It's like tempting fate."

I remember how he had wanted to hold off buying baby clothes and furniture until the two weeks before Patricia's due date, but his attitude didn't prevent me from buying a few items from the Eaton's catalogue. "Would you build a new house?" I ask, turning Patricia to the other breast.

"I'd move this one. Two years of spare time went into rebuilding the bedroom. Can't replace those rare plywoods now." He gives a sigh.

I sympathize. "There's the fireplace too," I say.

He nods. "You'd rather build, wouldn't you? But I could fix this house to look like new." He's beginning to sound more enthusiastic.

I can't forget the time I moved in with him and discovered how it felt to live for the first time in a permanent, stable, loving home. Perhaps it is just as well that my partner has never had enough time to finish the living room. The plans are certainly finalized in his mind. Sure, this is just a house, but it already holds four years of very special memories for us.

"Are you asleep?" he whispers.

"I was thinking … You're right. Let's move it—if the deal goes through."

The three of us return to the bedroom and I lay Patricia in her crib beside our bed.

"It's not just sentiment," he says quietly so as not to disturb her. "What if Olaf starts building a new house for us and can't afford to finish it? You know how these things always cost at least twice as much in the end."

I agree.

"I'd feel safer doing it this way," he whispers. "Can't explain why."

Dick's admission that he's acting partly on intuition surprises me. But for some reason it makes me feel better about going along with his decision.

We obtain estimates from two house-moving companies. As expected, both tell us that we'll have to build a new basement under the house on the new lot.

In mid-April, Olaf brings the deed, plans, and other pertinent information about the property. We sign agreements, exchange deeds, and choose Nickel Bros House Moving Ltd.

Since we'll have to barge the house from shore to shore, we'll need one of the highest tides of the year. Murray Nickel suggests that mid-summer's day would be just perfect, but that only gives us two months to prepare. "There's one thing I have to warn you about," he adds. "We can't guarantee the chimney or the fireplace. Our insurance won't cover that."

"No problem," Dick assures him. "I'll deal with it."

I hope he knows what he's getting into.

With a month to go, we accompany Olaf to our new property to discuss the house placement. As we leave the car, he informs us, "I haf two retired men from de old country in Estonia. Cabinet makers, dey are, but dey vork goot. Dey vill build de basement."

As Olaf walks on ahead of us toward the water, I ask Dick, "What about asking them to finish the living room?"

"I'd rather not. They wouldn't know what I want and I won't have time to explain things."

Stopping on the grassy slope about ten feet from the high-tide mark, Olaf turns to face us. "You vant de house near de vater? Yes? Tovards de midday sun?"

We measure thirty feet back from the highest logs and hammer some stakes in the ground.

"The seawall should be extra strong," Dick insists. "Logs and storms can do a lot of damage." Then he points at the neighbours' yard on our right. "It should be two feet higher than theirs. After a few days of southeasterlies the tides surge higher."

"As you say," Olaf agrees. "I haf here my Caterpillar tractor. I can do dese tings like de excavations. Leave it to me. Like I say, it vill work out goot."

"And I'll take care of towing the barge," Dick tells him.

"You don't haf to do dat. The tugs can do de towing."

But Dick insists.

The next most pressing item is to remove the accumulation of fifty years of logging tools, mechanic's tools, engine and boat parts from the basement. We hire a friend, Len Wray, the owner of the local moving company, to pack and store it in his warehouse.

With six days left, Dick strings a thick wire cable around the outside of the chimney, through the wall on each side of it, across the living room, the hall, the bathroom and around a timber outside its window before pulling it back inside the house to join the two ends with a tightly-cinched come-along. In spite of the red flag he's tied to this neck-high trap, I anticipate several run-ins with it over the next few weeks, particularly first thing in the morning before my brain has reached full throttle.

Olaf eyes the contraption with admiration. "I haf the engineering degree. Dis ting vill vork good." He turns to me. "Your husband has good ideas for strange problems."

But later that day after hearing a couple of my choice swearwords, Dick warns me, "You'd better get used to it. It'll be there for two or three months until the new basement's finished."

During the final two days before the move, the weather becomes almost unbearably hot, but it doesn't slow the workmen down. I'm outside with my camera as they break holes in the top of the concrete basement wall and use a crane to slide massive I-beams through them at strategic points under the floor joists. Seven hydraulic jacks are placed under the I-beams before being connected by hoses to a pump on a truck. Coordinated by a man watching the dials on the side of the truck, the house is slowly raised a couple of feet in one operation. Next, the workmen place two sets of dollies under the I-beams so that when the house is lowered onto them by the truck's pump, it appears to be sitting on a giant flatbed.

That evening, as we're eating a takeout meal in the kitchen, a tug enters the harbour on the high tide and pushes a sixty-foot-long by thirty-foot-wide barge against the beach in front of us. On it is parked a tractor unit.

In our effort to organize things so that we don't spend a single night out of the house, we have bought a port-a-potti, the kind people use for basic campers, and the Hendricksons next door have lent us their camping stove. I have already tied most of the kitchen cabinet doors tightly together so that nothing will fall out of them, and the glassware is packed in boxes.

At low tide the following midday, the boss calls through the back door, "Everyone out!"

After shutting the cat in the spare room and fitting our nine-month-old daughter into her Snuggli around my neck, I hang the camera over my shoulder and climb down from the house. The workmen walk around the dollies, constantly checking their position, while the tractor unit pulls the house slowly and shakily off the old basement, across the grass and up the ramp. Within half an hour, house and tractor are up on the barge, which now looks like some bizzare, two-funnelled ship.

With the danger-ous part over, we cross the ramp and inspect the chimney.

"It's okay," I shout.

"What did you ex-pect?" Dick asks smugly.

Upon further in-spection inside the house, he tells me that every-thing is on schedule for tonight, adding that since he'd had to postpone this

Our house being loaded onto the barge in Gibsons Harbour.

morning's beachcombing rounds to keep an eye on the house move, he'll do them now.

The mid-afternoon sun hangs over the busy harbour, its rays trapped by the surrounding hills and bluffs. Not a whisper of breeze reaches us from the light-aired, fairweather westerlies out in the Strait. Even though every window is open, sweat drips off my brow, and Patricia's cries have almost reached critical mass. She does not want to be in the playpen.

From my new high vantage point, I gaze through the veranda door screen and watch the *Snark* rise to a plane as Dick leaves for Gambier Island.

And so we wait for the high evening tide to float us off the smelly harbour mud. Slowly creeping up since lunchtime, the calm water is little more than halfway along the length of the heavy wooden barge.

Patricia grabs the playpen rail and tries to climb out. She's been walking for a month now, far too early for her own good.

"No," I tell her, shaking my head. "We can't go outside. It's not safe."

Deciding she needs a change of scene, I lift her up and show her the tractor unit below us, perilously close to the edge of the barge. Then I point east to the government dock and floats packed with pleasure boats and commercial fishing vessels. "See the boats?" And in the distance, above this tangle of masts, boats and creosote pilings, the Coast Mountains stand guard, their snowy crowns now vanished, revealing their age-furrowed brows.

Followed by the cat who, like Patricia, yearns to be set free, we check the view from every window in the house. From the back bedroom, our old property looks as if it has been hit by a bomb. Only the cement basement survives, built the year World War II began. "Look," I point, "at those holes in the walls."

She listens, occasionally responding with sounds of acknowledgement. Then I carry her to the northeast window, the one that overlooks my father-in-law's creation, the half-acre meadow with its two apple trees and the stream-fed trout pond. I point out the glistening water that falls gently from the dam into the little creek and down to the harbour. "That's where the otters play in the evening. Otters with tails like Puss."

"Pa!" says Patricia, reaching for the black and white shorthaired cat perched on the window ledge. I put her down, and she toddles ahead of me, past the locked door that only two days previously had led to the basement stairs, then runs under the chimney-protecting cable and into the kitchen. I catch up with her as she stops to play with the cutlery box. Apart from the camping stove—also on the floor—the essentials for tonight and tomorrow are wedged in the double sink: an oil lamp, gallon of water, and three thermos flasks of hot water.

Sitting at the kitchen table, we watch a tugboat refuelling at the Boatworks' float, now almost alongside of us. "See that silver boat?" I tell Patricia, pointing to the *Silver Streak*, a twenty-foot aluminum work-boat also tied to the gas float.

"Ba," she says.

"Boat. That boat's going to help Dick pull us off the beach."

In spite of being overdue for a nap, she jumps down, runs to the back door and tries to reach the handle, but she's not tall enough. I shut the cat in the spare room and climb into the playpen with Patricia with one of her favourite books. Within five minutes she loses her fight against sleep and I place her gently on the blanket beside me. As I gaze at her peaceful expression, I cannot see a hint of the strong mindset that has driven her to walk so early. But the fact that it's there gives me hope that she will never be a diffident and indecisive teenager like her mother. Not if Dick and I have anything to do with it ...

Three hours later I step out onto the veranda to check the tide, which has almost reached the end of the barge closest to the beach. Another few feet ... another couple of hours.

Our house is so high I can see over the government wharf across to Keats Island shore and our Shelter Island storage grounds nearby. Then I spot the *Snark* speeding straight past Keats wharf and out to the Gap in Shoal Channel where as many as thirty sports fishermen are either anchored or trolling. Even seen from two miles away its jet wake is unmistakeable.

It disappears behind the bluff, only to reappear moments later when Dick steers for the Boatworks to refuel. Ten minutes later he is in the kitchen, holding two pale yellow roses under my nose. They are from the bush near the beach steps.

"Midsummer roses for madame," he says and gives me a hug.

I sniff them. "Mm-m," I say appreciatively. "Find any logs?"

"Couple of small fir," he replies, placing the flowers in a mug with a couple of inches of water in the bottom. "Shouldn't have bothered going … Someone had been around earlier." He hears Patricia's mutterings as she awakens. "How about you?"

"Hot," I say.

He laughs. "You can say that again!" he responds, following me into the living room with the mug of roses. He wedges it beside the hearth, while I check on the sweaty baby in the playpen. I pick her up and offer her my breast, but she is not interested. She's weaning herself. Right now she only wants apple juice.

He glances at the clock. "Ready?"

As soon as he's fed the cat, we leave for his parents' place. "They do know we're going to eat and run?" I ask, packing a couple of diapers.

"Don't worry," he reassures me. "It's another Bingo night."

An hour later Patricia and I are back on our barge island and the sun is already drawing close to the top of the hill—the early sunset a trade-off for the bowl-shaped harbour's protection.

Thankful for the new cellulose diaper liners, I take one of the thermoses into the bathroom and wedge it in the sink beside the "Mothercare" changing pad. Last time I tried a cold water wash on her during a diaper change, her barrage of angry screams informed me that such treatment was totally unacceptable.

Back in the kitchen with her, I check the tide table for the umpteenth time. Give or take perhaps fifteen minutes to account for local conditions, we have twenty more to go.

From the window I watch Mike climb into the *Silver Streak* and drive it behind the barge to connect his thick towline to one outside corner, while Dick ties the *Snark* to the barge's other side.

"Look," I point out the window. "Two boats. See Dick?" But her attention only lasts for a couple of seconds, and as if showing me she knows what a boat is, she grabs the little wooden canoe on the table, the one her grandfather Hal had carved and given to her that week.

Simultaneously both boats take a run from the barge. Their parallel towlines snap tight and the two men keep their engines revved to maintain horsepower, while under their hulls the milky-brown harbour mud boils up to the surface, but the barge doesn't move. After ten seconds, they signal for each other to stop, then try pulling at a different angle, a little to port and the government dock.

Why aren't we moving?

After five more minutes without success, Mike drives *Silver Streak* into Smitty's, the privately-owned marina between the government floats and the foreshore.

The sun, its gold rays now almost orange, touches the hill behind the harbour, but above us the sky is still a pale blue. Fishermen returning in pleasure boats from the Gap or Gower Point stare and point at us as they round the bluff.

Keeping my eye on Patricia, I consider the situation. Whenever I have seen houses barged—as happened soon after 1968 when the federal government expropriated most of Sea Island for the YVR airport preserve—they were loaded at launching ramps or from gravel or rock beaches. Our beach is mud, the result of years of sediment brought down by the creek, and the weight of the house and tractor has caused the barge to sink into it. We are stuck. We desperately need more horsepower.

Have we missed the tide? It's unlikely tomorrow's will be any higher and I don't relish another day up here. The throbbing growl of a diesel engine catches my attention, and the blue tug *Moonfleet*, owned by Smitty's son, John, emerges from his marina and steers straight for us. Mike and Dick connect the towlines to John's diesel power and retire their boats to the gas dock.

The line tightens and the engine bellows with increasing intensity. The *Moonfleet* holds the tension, swings a little to port, then to starboard. But limpet-like, the barge's flat bottom clings fast. John abruptly cuts the revs, and the echoes from the ear-shattering roar resound around the harbour. He reverses, almost touching the barge with the tug's stern and readies his boat to aim further to starboard. But there's a little speedboat in his way and he has to wait for it.

At last he takes a run. This time he uses even more throttle ... and maintains it. The barge moves slightly. It pivots a few inches to starboard, but there is still no forward movement. The tug reverses again, steers toward the float plane dock and repeats the persistent, taut, pulling manoeuvre until we're facing that direction. But have we moved forward? Or is the barge burying itself deeper into the mud?

No, the tug is holding, pointing slightly toward the fuel dock again. The throttle reaches its upper limit. Mud churns under the prop. The unremitting roar evolves into a scream and I turn to the vertical pilings alongside our floats for reference. They appear to be moving. This illusion becomes reality as the mud slowly relinquishes its grip. I glance at my watch. We're twenty minutes past high tide. How will this affect our unloading?

While the sun has disappeared from the harbour, across Shoal Channel the grass field and surrounding trees on Keats Island are still a gilded green. There are a couple of hours of daylight left. At soon as we clear the harbour, John hands over the barge's towline to Dick and leaves for the marina. We are now on our own.

As if having second thoughts about an early night, as we move out of the hill's shadow, the sun shows itself again. There's a slight breeze out here in the channel—the fair-weather wind is taking its time to die down tonight. But it's warm and there's only a ripple on the water's surface.

Patricia runs for the two yellow roses as soon as I lift her out of the playpen. She grabs one and drops it, crying as she learns the hard way that things are not always what they seem. I retrieve it from the floor and show her the thorns. "Smell," I suggest, showing her how it's done. "Beautiful yellow roses." She stares at them but does not touch. I place her in her playpen again and present her with the basket of coloured wooden blocks, which she promptly tips over.

Once more at the bedroom window, I'm compelled to remind myself what we're leaving behind—the urbanization of Gibsons. I suppose most of its inhabitants would choose to regard it positively, to say it has gained the status of a town. But not I, nor Dick. Where last year rushes grew, perches for red-winged blackbirds, habitat for hake and sculpins, ducks and eels, a playground for otters, even a respite for the occasional wayward snow goose or trumpeter swan—both of which I have hand-fed—there, in front of our property, the ugly dirt esplanade now covers the new sewage pipes. It saddens me. But while, from my vantage point in Shoal Channel, I see the slow, fungus-like growth of houses on the shaded hillside as a hint of things to come, I still feel regret at leaving. However, it is better we go now than later.

Returning to the unfinished living room, I stand by the sliding door and focus my eyes on the little black and grey fibreglass *Snark* at the other end of the two-hundred-foot towline. Dick turns, waves and blows a kiss. We don't seem to be moving very fast. Ideally a barge should be towed by a displacement-hulled boat with a propellor that can move a lot of water. But, although unspoken, I think Dick's reason for insisting that he tow us instead of a stranger in a tug might be something to do with his Grandfather Jack moving his family to Nelson Island by raft in 1902.

While we won't run into a thick fog as the earlier Hammonds had done, we have another problem—a strong tide. But where their tide had helped them to reach their new home, ours is running fiercely against us. Even though the spring freshet has already peaked, the glaciers on the Coast range are still melting under the hot June sun, and the Squamish River and tributaries are torrenting down the mountains into Howe Sound. It is adding to the already large volume of water from the highest tide of the year that is now starting to pour out of the inlet, slowing us down. I doubt we'll reach our destination before dark.

A ray of sun shines through one of the smaller windows and falls on my favourite painting, the Lady in Green. The colour of her face is richer, the green of her dress deeper and as vibrant as the trees on Keats Island. Most of all, though I'm struck by the way the rays accentuate her eyes, imbuing them with an alertness I'd never noticed before.

Away from the shadows against the shore, the sea shimmers a rich gold. Then, just above the darkening mountains to the southeast, the first star of the evening emerges, and for the second and last time that evening, the sun sinks behind Mount Elphinstone.

As I light the charred edge of the lamp's wick, the smell of kerosene unlocks a particularly vivid memory from my grandmother's place. She heated her apartment with it. Paraffin oil, the English call it. As soon as I entered her apartment, I'd smell the familiar odour and know I was safe. At night she kept a tiny oil lamp burning in the hall, and feeling blissfully secure, I would fall asleep watching its halo through the golden dimpled-glass pane of the bedroom door.

Patricia's baby talk interrupts my reveries. I close the veranda doors and let her wander around the kitchen while I chop a banana and butter some bread for her. As she looks up and stretches her tiny hand toward the lamp, its warm glow highlights her face, casting gentle shadows around her eyes and under her chin. It is a shame she's too young to remember this day.

The *Snark*'s engine drops in pitch. Ahead of us, the workmen, their lights flickering on the shore, ready themselves for our landing, and *Silver Streak* arrives to assist Dick to push the scow against the beach as the ramp is put in place. With Patricia on my back and a flashlight in my hand I climb down to the barge deck and wait.

Just two seconds before my feet touch the beach, something black and white flies past me, across the shallow water and up the bank.

"There's a cat!" a woman shouts.

Puss must have slipped out the door with us. Her near-drowning memories as a kitten have left her with a fear of boats and docks.

A figure leaves a crowd of about thirty onlookers and approaches me. "Your cat just ran in there," the young woman says, pointing to the blackberry patch with her flashlight. "If you want to grab it, I'll hold your baby."

Warning her that Patricia will most probably start crying at any minute, I hand her over and shine the flashlight into the brambles. Seconds later, a pair of cat eyes reflect at me and I seize the trembling Puss by the scruff of her neck. Shivering, she doesn't struggle as I carry her up to an empty room in Olaf's summer house.

By the time I rejoin the crowd and collect the overwrought Patricia in my arms again, the tractor unit—still on the barge—has started to back the house down. It is halfway down the ramp. Then suddenly, a shout from one of the workmen, "HOLD IT! GO BACK! GO BACK!" Flashlights wave frantically, relaying alarm to the tractor driver. Something is badly wrong.

Even though the two boats are still pushing against the barge, it is no longer parallel to the beach. As the foreman on the shore continues to yell and gesticulate, the tractor pulls the house back up the ramp. The strong tide pouring out of the inlet past Soames Point promontory is partly causing the problem. That, coupled with the weight of the house descending the ramp, is forcing one side of the barge offshore. Ramp, house and truck had almost fallen onto the beach well below the high-tide line.

Once more, Dick and his friend push the barge square-on with their boats, but as soon as the tractor reverses the house down again, it starts to angle out as before. This time, I can see in the searchlight that the upper end of the ramp is a mere two inches from disaster. More shouts, and the house is pulled up yet again. The two little boats do not have enough thrust to counteract the pressure.

Olaf marches his imposing bulk over to the foreman and in a loud but calm voice tells him, "I get my Cat machine. I tell you, I fix de problem. No danger."

He positions the Caterpillar thirty feet from the barge and attaches the line from the offending corner to his machine's rear winch. For insurance, the workmen tie the other corner to one of the fir trees. Slowly the Cat pulls the barge until it sits parallel to the beach the way it was intended. While Olaf keeps his machine's revs up and the line taut, the house rolls down the ramp, followed by the reversing tractor unit.

The onlookers cheer. Beaming, Olaf turns the tractor engine off and faces the audience. "See, I told you it vould turn out goot."

By half-past midnight the crowd has dispersed and the workmen leave for their motel. While Dick tows the barge back to the harbour, I collect Puss from Olaf's house and put Patricia to bed. The night is so hot that we keep all the windows open.

As I fall asleep beside my husband, I sense a different kind of breeze easing itself through the house; a welcoming breeze smelling of trees and mountain air, gentle and caressing on my face. And amongst it, the evocative redolence of kerosene ...

I awake early to the sound of unfamiliar heavy breathing. Still in sleepy stupor, I nudge Dick apprehensively. "Can you hear someone breathing?"

"It's waves ... breaking on the shore ..."

Of course, there had been no waves in the harbour, except during an exceptionally wild Squamish. I lie there for a while listening to the rhythm, trying to breath in time with them. Gradually, the wave leit-motif from the *Hebrides* overture overlays itself so naturally in my mind that I find myself humming the tune instead.

"That reminds me," Dick interrupts, "I've seen seals off this beach. Several times."

Patricia chatters from the spare room down the hall.

"Jo," he says, "if you're not too tired, how about all of us doing the morning rounds together for a change."

"Only if I can go back to bed afterwards," I insist.

As soon as the three of us are settled in *Snark*, now at its new per-manent anchor in front of our house, I find one of the yellow roses in the carrycot. Patricia must have dropped it in there with her stuffed cat.

She watches as I sprinkle its petals upon the sea.

Around ten, Nickel's men return with their hydraulic jacks. They remove the truck and wheel assemblies and lower the house onto cribs—stacks of timbers—where we will have to stay for as long as it takes Olaf's Estonian builders to complete the basement underneath.

Later that morning, Olaf connects our fridge to a very long elec-tric power cord that leads from his summer house. We can safely plug in one more item, which usually has to be either an electric kettle or the electric frying pan. Any more draw on the power means a trip to the summer house to reset the circuit breaker. We also have access to an outside water tap that Olaf had installed prior to our move.

Halfway through August, it appears that Dick's intuition about developers overextending themselves has been correct. When we begin to receive bills for materials and labour connected with the move, Olaf apologizes profusely.

"Dis is only for the time being," he says. "Like I say, it vill only be until my other defelopments work themselves out. I do my best."

Without electricity, water, septic tank hookup and heat, we have no other option but to borrow from the bank and take over the bills. Nothing more can be done until our basement is finished and inspect-ed. Only then can the house be lowered onto it and various hookups permitted. Dick now expects the worst—that we will eventually have to remortgage the house.

Meanwhile, Patricia fusses more than usual during cold water diaper changes, since hot water is only available from a recently boiled kettle, and a weekly visit to the local laundromat with work clothes is a given. However, while housekeeping is easier after Nickels have lowered us onto the new basement, our furnace isn't hooked up until long after the cold weather has settled in. An electric blanket solves the problem of warming up after a wet and frigid boat ride.

On a cool October morning following the move, we meet a friend—a backhoe operator—at our old harbour property, where we excavate Dick's father's two twenty-foot-high apple trees from the meadow. That same afternoon they're planted into well-manured, five-foot diameter holes near our new septic field and my husband makes sure they are well watered.

Hal continues his daily fishing trips from our old harbour float, but one November morning that same year as he walks up the incline from the Boatworks to his home, he collapses from a fatal heart attack. Dick says little about his father's death, but it's only when he shows me the poem he has written about it that I realize how deeply this event has affected him.

The Shark

Newly freed from the grasp of night
The sea is calm and the morning bright.
Where the tides meet, a boat drifts,
The oarsman rests as the mist lifts.

Through the surface a sharp fin slides,
Makes no sound as it smoothly glides.
The fin moves by, and the watcher knows
That, black as the depths from which it rose,
Under the surface, with grinning face,
Death is there in that peaceful place.

Mirthless grin and soul-less eye,
The shark will grin though the world should die,
And the watcher feels, with a pang of fear,
That we never may know what thing is near.
And, down below, where it's cold and dark,
Patiently waits—a grinning shark.

And, we who sail on the seas of life,
When we tire at last of the noise and strife,
May look around for a place of rest
As the red sun dies in the distant west.
But there's nothing to see, no harbour near,
And we feel the touch of the hand of fear,
For faintly, out of the shrouding gloom
Comes the dreadful beat of the wings of Doom.
And all we can see in the waning light
Is the shark's grin,
And endless—
Night.

The death of my father-in-law makes me ponder over my relationship, or lack of, with my own father. As soon as my mother and stepfather had disowned me at age twenty-one, I had made a point of contacting him for the first time after he'd "run away." Forewarned of my visit, he and his second wife had welcomed me politely enough, but I had been shocked and surprised when they had introduced me to their own children as a friend. Even though I had written to him several times since then and have learned that he, too, enjoys singing and appreciates classical music, I still feel very much abandoned by him.

But I have no fear that any child of ours will ever lack paternal love and attention.

22

Winter Storm

The harsh Arctic wind throws itself against the lone group of fir trees, clutching, ripping branches, hurling smaller ones toward our house, while off the point, angry whitecaps foam and spit, drawing trails of bubbles along the surface of a frigid viridian sea. This is the winter outflow wind, the dreaded Squamish that roars down from the icy north in its search for the Pacific, howling a path across the Rockies and Coast Mountains before forcing its way through steep valleys and fjords to gain strength and speed.

I draw myself away from the kitchen window, check on fifteen-month-old Patricia, now playing with tinker-toys on the living room floor, then visit with Dick, who lies soaking in a hot bath. He has just returned from a morning of brutal, icy work, pulling logs off the Gower Point beaches west of Gibsons. The following two hours spent towing in the open *Snark* while drenched in sweat has further chilled him.

"Did you catch up with the tug?" I ask.

He shakes his head. "Not a sign of it. The captain must have been trying to beat the wind."

"What kind of logs was he towing?"

"Mostly fir … I had to fight a strong tide all the way back," he complains, sloshing hot water over his body. "But at least they're safe inside our grounds."

"Shall I phone BC Log Spill?"

"I'll do it," he says. "I need to talk to them anyway."

Patricia toddles in and points to the bathwater. "Dad, dad, wa-wa."

"Dad-Dad is in the water," I echo. "Dick is in the bath."

Grunting noisily, she tries to climb over the rim. Such efforts to communicate her needs should not go unrewarded and so I undress her and lower her in.

"Why don't you join us?" Dick invites.

And the three of us squash into the wide bath and play with the tiny hand-carved canoe her grandfather had made for her the previous summer ... until it dawns on me that I haven't yet made lunch. Fully dressed again and in the kitchen, I glance up from the half-made sandwiches and stare at the roiling sea, out to the anchored boat ... But where is it?

On high alert, I scan southwest and west until I see the *Snark*. Driverless, its fluorescent red anchor buoy still attached to its bow line, it's travelling fast, too fast to be dragging its anchor. If it is damaged, it could take as much as a month or two to repair.

"Dick!" I yell, rushing into the bathroom. "*Snark*'s loose ... Going toward Gibsons!"

Splashing water everywhere, he thrusts Patricia at me, leaps out of the bath and tries to draw on his jeans, but they grip against his wet skin. He hops through the kitchen, managing to yank them up by the time he reaches the back door, zips up his fly, jams feet into boots, skids out and down to the beach. He's topless.

"Nah! Dada! Ba!" Patricia protests, scuttling back into the bathroom. I grab her, shut the door and watch Dick's progress from the kitchen window. She screams disapproval at having her water play cut off. Her father is right: she is a challenge.

Still running, he pulls our ten-foot aluminum skiff down the gravel and throws it into the water. It's a little calmer here because our south-facing beach is protected by the rocky point. He jumps in and, helped by the wind, waves and current, rows as if the devil is chasing him. Tiny snowflakes materialize, blown almost horizontally by the Squamish. The water is now a dull khaki.

"Look at Dick!" I point to his retreating pale torso and bowed, balding head, now beaten by the clouds of fine snow. Regardless of weather, he always wears a cap. Not today.

Patricia struggles and I set her down. At her age she can't concentrate on distant objects. Naked, she runs to the bathroom door but her attempts at opening it fail because the handle is covered with a childproof sleeve. I ignore her frustrated yells.

While the skiff seems to be flying along like the snow, it's going to be touch-and-go which vessel will reach the rocks first.

But how long can he keep this topless activity up? He's only twenty feet away from his target when a gust and a swell gives the *Snark*—it has more surface area than the skiff—a boost so that now it's almost ashore. But at the last moment the two boats collide and Dick leaps aboard.

Now, will the engine start?

Even with binoculars it's hard to see through the snow, but I know the routine. Dick's blurred shape bends, crouches as he loops the skiff's rope over the *Snark*'s stern cleat just as the *Snark*'s heavy fibreglass hull hits the shore side-on. He jumps out and shoves it off the large boulders, points the bow offshore before it's swamped.

I hate to watch. Will it start?

Boots full of water, he climbs aboard. No time to empty them now. Then I see the bow rise, and with the skiff behind it, the *Snark* begins to move—slowly at first—toward Gibsons. I take a deep breath, dress Patricia in a warm sleeper, grab her and Dick's jacket, then drive the Citroën to the Boatworks' fuel dock in the harbour.

By the time I reach the parking lot, the Citroën's heater is working at full blast. Dick opens the car door and I shove his jacket at him. His teeth are chattering so hard he can't talk.

"Dad, dad!" Patricia shouts. "Wa-wa!"

He can barely bend his legs to sit. "B-b-blasted b-b-boat!" he manages then blurts out, "Home!"

"It's the first Arctic outflow on our new property," I remind him as we turn onto the main road. "No wonder you wanted to wait a while before building a beach float."

Such a float would never survive a wind like this. Our skiff will have to remain our access to our permanently anchored work boat. But why had the anchor failed today?

I wait a few moments for his face to warm up. "So what happened?"

"Anchor chain broke … the link just under the buoy. Worn through."

"You only installed it last June," I point out. He had set it up the day after the solstice, one of the highest and lowest tides of the year, the day following our house move.

"That chain was new …" After a pause he postulates, "It might be something to do with the higher oxygen content near the water's surface."

"Sounds likely," I agree.

The snow beats against the windshield, mesmerizing me, and I have to force myself to concentrate, particularly steering in second gear down the steep winding Grantham's Hill. I'm thankful that nobody is trying to drive up it.

Dick is still shivering as we draw into the carport. "Hope you left the water in the bath," he says.

"Of course!"

Patricia runs ahead of us into the bathroom and tries to reach the hot tap. "Wa-wa! Dad!"

While it's all one big game to her, for Dick and me it's another typical day in our lives, another day of learning to expect the unexpect-ed, including the weather. He often complains—and I heartily agree, particularly out on the water—that when the unexpected is linked to the inexplicable, it causes the situation of "the perversity of inanimate objects." We usually run into this when speed is essential, as it might be under threat of a boat being in danger, while one of us is trying to free a heavy pulling chain and line that for some unknown reason has trapped itself between two rocks. But unlike me, he never wastes time swearing.

23

Parenting

Our new cement seawall—built to Dick's specifications the following spring—is two feet higher than that of our summer neighbours who, we suspect, have never seen a high winter tide combined with a storm surge. It is around this time that Patricia, now eighteen months old, refuses to take an afternoon nap unless she is with me on the boat, in which case she will fall asleep for the rest of the trip and make up for lost time by staying up later that same evening. Inquisitive like her parents, she probably fights sleep because she is afraid of missing something.

One day I leave her playing in the sandpit outside the basement door and return to the kitchen to make lunch.

When it is ready, I call down the stairs asking Dick to collect her from outside. He's mixing and refilling the grease gun with his own bearing mix. "Where did you say she was?" he shouts back.

"Sandpit!"

"She's not!"

I check from one of the living room windows, then from the veranda. There is no sign of her on the beach either. I sprint up the long driveway, peer behind the carport then the workshop ... She can't be far away, probably right under our noses, even in the house. I alert Dick who immediately runs down the new beach steps and turns left toward the point.

I remove the scorched soup from the stove then search in the book storage area under the stairs. Having exhausted all possible hiding places in the house, I rush to the water's edge and look both ways around the gently curved bay. Since my main concern is the nineteen-foot-high rocky promontory of Soames Point at its east end and the sharp boulders beyond in the next bay, I follow the tideline to the base of the outcrop. It's here that I am met by a barrage of angry screams from the other side.

As I glance up at the jagged granite, Dick's silhouetted figure emerges carrying a small child, head down, under his arm. Legs kicking and arms flailing, the ear-splitting racket issuing from the child's mouth overrides even the screeching calls of the gulls. He pauses there, atop the highest point, then delivers three sharp smacks to the child's upturned backside and in a stern tone admonishes, "You are NOT to go on the rocks again!" There is no anger in his voice. The order is clearly and fairly delivered, a warning simple enough for a bright eighteen-month-old to understand.

At first I am amazed at my own reaction upon watching this scene. In spite of having been strapped often and well into my teens, I feel no hysteria nor the fear I had expected. But my own punishment had always been delivered in anger with cruel words on bare skin.

Dick calmly lowers the wailing Patricia onto the gravel at the base of the cement steps and watches as she runs into the yard and through the open basement door.

"We'll have to give those fencing people a call," he says to me in a normal voice that sounds nothing like it had when he'd been confronted with the Forestry bureaucrats and policemen in the grey boat. "She was halfway across the next bay, climbing over all those boulders when I found her."

"Do you think she'll remember her punishment?" I ask him.

"She's too young to understand the dangers of falling and drowning off rocks. She might remember what the spanks are for, but I'd just as soon not take the chance."

"How can you keep so calm with her?"

He shrugs. "What's the point in being otherwise?"

"Well, how did your mother cope with you?"

"She used to warn that catastrophic things would happen if I disobeyed her. It didn't take me long to learn that she was wrong."

"So you did disobey her?"

"It started with tree climbing. When I found out I wouldn't fall and break my neck, it made me want to try other fun things like swimming because I knew I wouldn't drown." He pauses then shakes his head. "She never understood how a child thinks. I remember being six or seven and had just got home from school … she told me to bring in the firewood. I asked her if I could play outside first, and she said something like, 'Take your own time, why don't you.' I didn't know then that she was being sarcastic, that what she really meant was 'do it now,' so I went on playing."

"She must have been furious!"

He waits for me to go through the basement door ahead of him. "She grabbed the axe and chased me around the yard, screaming, 'I'll kill you! I'll kill you!' I was just lucky that Father happened to be coming off work at that moment."

"But she wouldn't really have killed you?"

He nods. "I'm sure she would. But when she saw Father, she just collapsed … I think she was having a 'nervous breakdown,' as they called it back then. She just wasn't suited to the isolated life on the Coast. When something annoyed her, she reacted, never stopped to consider if it made sense."

As Patricia calms down in her bedroom, it occurs to me that my own mother must have had a nervous breakdown that lasted several months after my father's infidelity and their subsequent divorce. I was only four or five at the time, and it is only now that I remember her frightening misery and frequent tears, and how one morning I had escaped my kindergarten class to check on my parents at home. For the first time in my life I ask myself what had prompted that reaction. But the answer only hits me later that evening while Dick and I are listening to some Schumann. The day before my kindergarten escape had been a Sunday, and I see, in my mind's eye, my mother and me sitting on the hot dry grass near the beach. Over the stones, past the sand, an unending row of scaffolding projects out of the water to prevent—so I was told—the bad Germans from landing on our Bognor beach. My mother has been showing me how to make a daisy chain, but I haven't been able to pierce the holes through the wilted stems. I know, somehow, that she is thinking of other things.

Frustrated, I glance up. She stares out over the town.

"Where's Daddy?" I ask. The heat rises from the baking turf, hitting my chin. "Mummy!" I plead louder. "Where's Daddy?"

She stares at the sky above the town. "He's run away…" And the rest of her words fade on the breeze.

"Where's he gone?"

A strange silence falls between us.

"Mummy, where's he gone?"

She's shivering, in spite of the heat. "Don't know … He's … run away." Her voice makes me think of the cracked earth beneath the arid grass.

She was never the same after that.

At the end of the Schumann, I tell Dick about my memory and he empathizes.

24

Red against Blue

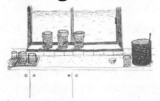

Over breakfast one warm August morning, I remark that it must be close to cranberry time.

"How about today?" Dick suggests. "We can't ask for better weather."

"We can't take Patricia through all that rocky brush," I object, "And your mother's gone to the city."

"No problem," he says. "That's what George's baby carrier's for."

George is our log scaler. He was the Adonis look-alike in Gib Gibson's red truck at Langdale that first day Gordon and I set foot on the Coast. George and his wife often give us their children's hand-me-downs, and their aluminum-framed toddler carrier is the latest welcome donation. But when it's loaded with Patricia, it cuts into my shoulders, while Dick, well-padded with logging-jack muscles, has no problem at all.

We pack two large buckets, one small one, lunch, and the carrier in the Citroën, and drive northwest up the Coast highway. After sequestering the car beside a logging road we start burrowing straight into the dark forest.

This annual destination, one of our favourite haunts, had been discovered by Hal in the 1920s while grouse hunting on his own. It is a meandering, hilly, forested hike, with no hint of a path and no apparent landmarks, so that only a true woodsman could find the way there and back. It had been on my first expedition to this secret place (secret enough that we never tell any of our friends or acquaintances where it is) that I saw my first western tanager, one of the most exotic-coloured birds in our area. With its reddish-orange head, bright yellow, black and white body, it looked like an escapee from a tropical aviary.

But most of all I recall from that first time how frustrated and exhausted I had felt climbing over the bramble-covered rocks and saplings, pushing past branches, never sure of what I was going to find with my feet after setting them down. If I hadn't been paying attention to my new partner's interesting tales about his past hiking trips, I would have collapsed under the tangle of trees and undergrowth and refused to go any further.

The most vivid story he told me concerned the time he and his father had taken some family friends there. Apparently one of the men was a little portly. "Poor man," I'd interrupted. "How on earth did he manage?" Panting and sweating profusely, I stopped for a rest.

"He wasn't complaining," Dick had explained, "and his wife was with him. But near the top of this hill ... just about where we are now, I noticed he wasn't looking that great."

"I understand how he felt."

"I doubt it," said Dick dryly, "because he suddenly collapsed, and when I felt for a pulse, there wasn't one."

"What did you do?"

"I left the others and drove to the police station. They sent two RCMP officers with me dressed in uniform and wearing leather shoes! Would you believe it? Smooth leather soles!" he said. "Totally useless in that terrain. And when they tried to take the stretcher out they kept tripping and falling. I had to do most of the carrying because they just weren't up to it."

"I guess you were wearing your old running shoes?"

"Naturally. Cheap rubber soles ..."

Since then, each year at cranberry time we make a point of visiting the lake, and when we reach the point where his friend died, I always think of that story. Even this time with Patricia slung behind her father's back, with me following behind, I remark aloud, "Poor Mr. Gray." Dick turns around and responds with, "But it was the best way to go."

At the crest of the rocky hill there's yet more dense forest and a steep climb downhill. It is a dangerous descent amid projecting tree roots, low salal branches, old fir cones, twigs and rocks, all of them potential bone-breakers. But as I glance occasionally through gaps in the trees, little bits of lake appear like scattered pieces of jigsaw puzzle, and by the time we reach the bottom they have somehow fallen together into one complete picture.

Emerging from this hillside forest during my first visit, I had been a little disappointed because I had expected a large lake with pale blue or green water, glassy water that mirrored its surroundings, not a strange boggy area with tiny dark pools glistening in the sun. But I had paused and, inhaling deeply through my nose, quickly discovered that there was something different about this place, something I'd never experienced before, a special smell that bonded to my skin and clothes. And each time we arrive, the moisture-laden, primordial perfume is here, trapped within the tree-edged basin. The scent, so redolent of life, is always spread protectively over the warm bog like an invisible blanket.

Today, as usual, there is not a sound of human activity. Dick takes Patricia out of the carrier and sets her down, and for a few magnificent seconds the three of us remain motionless, isolated from the rest of the world ... until the hum of a distant plane reminds us of the silence surrounding us.

To our south at the base of a shady treed bank lies a small but deeper part of the lake sectioned off from the shallower areas by a large fallen cedar trunk. Today it is occupied by two pairs of fluttering, squawking mallards. A few more skinny cedar trunks lie here and there across the whole basin, but they are just resting on soggy ground and are safe to stand on. Sooner or later, however, one has to take the first step into the bog itself, a hodge-podge mixture of various types of sphagnum mosses, carnivorous sundew plants, masses of low bog cranberry plants, and the tallest bushes—no more than a couple of feet high—Hudson's Bay tea, sometimes called Labrador tea.

That first step always takes me off guard. I'm afraid of sinking further than the four or five inches of "sponge," but once I'm used to the squishy, soaking feeling I don't mind in the least. Patricia, whose light body has little effect on the almost floating moss, seems to accept this new experience as another normal part of her interesting life. She immediately spots one of the myriad orb spiders that have built their spiralling, dew-covered webs all over the lake, mostly on the Hudson's Bay tea plants. Unafraid of these large, benign creatures, she quickly discovers that if she touches the glistening web, the "bider" and its pretty web will dance. It's strange how, when seen in this particular environment, their dull-brown rounded bodies and well-proportioned legs give them an entrancing, almost loveable quality. Dick points out that they're industrious, too, building a new web each night by feel.

As soon as we begin to pick cranberries, Patricia joins us, throwing the occasional berry into her small bucket, but she soon loses interest and amuses herself by playing with pieces of moss and twigs. I stop for a moment to show her how to feed bugs to the sundew plants.

The meaty, tart berries are small, averaging five-eighths of an inch diameter, and so close to the ground they're almost hidden by the other plants. Their skin colours are not an evenly distributed red like the cultivated ones. Instead, a single berry will usually be covered by a variable mixture of shades: purple, red, pink, yellow and green according to the amount and direction of the light that has fallen on it. And some might have a dulling bloom on their skins. I'll walk over to where I expect to find a patch, yet only see a couple of them until I bend down and start picking. Then, wanting to feel even closer to nature when I gather the berries, I usually sit on the soggy ground.

Once on the bog, Dick and I separate, and because the low vegetation seems to absorb our voices like an anechoic chamber, our conversation ceases. But I still sense a strong connection with him, not by speech, but through the interwoven, water-suffused mass of living plants in the bog itself. From time to time I will look up from my picking to turn my head toward him, but my gaze will be caught by a dew diamond on one of the spider webs between us, and I sit there, transfixed for a moment, moving very slightly to change the sun colours that the drop refracts back to me … Again the alien quietness of this place instills itself in my thoughts, until Patricia, puttering about between us, chatters for a few moments, usually to herself. Or once in a while I'll be startled by the first of a series of piercing tree frog croaks from the forest's edge. It's so easy to forget that most of my days are spent alongside the sea, that the sound of it is constantly in my ears, unless it is masked by cars, voices, music …

An hour or so into the quietness, a deer wanders onto the bog, stopping barely twenty feet away from Patricia, who gazes at it without saying a word. After exchanging stares with her for a few seconds, the deer bends down to drink. It hangs around for several minutes but idly meanders into the woods when we settle down on one of the cedar logs for lunch.

We leave the secret lake with one and a half bucketfuls, the larger proportion, I'm sure, picked by Dick. And as we drive past Davis Bay beach that early afternoon, our thoughts of the hunting and gathering expedition return to those of the more usual kind. We both comment on the signs of an untimely rising southeasterly, something that might yield a few logs, particularly if a tug and boom has tried to beat the wind to a mill or sorting ground.

Back home Dick peers out of the kitchen window with the binoculars, and says, "Better take *Snark* for a run. Whitecaps in the Gulf."

I watch him zoom past the harbour and charge out through the Gap before turning to port around Salmon Rock.

Settling Patricia with some crayons and scrap paper on the kitchen table, I rinse the inevitable scraps of moss and Hudson's Bay leaves out of the berries, dump half of them in the jam pan with two cups of orange juice and some grated orange peel, and store the rest in the fridge for another day. That spring Dick had carved me a giant jam spoon from a sunken gumwood log his father had found in the mud at zero-tide years ago. It's just perfect for my oversized jam pan.

As they simmer in the orange juice, the cranberries pop and spit alarmingly, releasing their rich, luminous-red juices into the mix and occasionally beyond. I only add enough sugar until it's tangy but not overly sweet. The perfume is priceless.

At last I have a row of eight Kerr jars of the jam cooling on the window ledge, a vibrant red against a backdrop of churning dark green-blue sea. The wind is now blowing over the seven-hundred-foot ridge of Keats Island, stirring up Shoal Channel. In a little while it will find its way around Keats Island's Observatory Point and really make waves.

Around suppertime the phone rings. It's Dick. Will I pick him up from the Boatworks? No explanation. Presuming the jet boat has broken down, I fasten Patricia in her car seat and drive the Citroën to Gibsons.

I find Dick standing at the top of the Boatworks' driveway gripping an oil-soiled rag in his right hand. As after all boat breakdowns, I have to press for information.

"What happened this time?" I ask, driving for home.

"I'm pretty sure it's another piston," he mutters. "Right off Worlcombe. Worst southeasterly we've had in a long time."

"How did you get to the Boatworks?" I ask.

"I was lucky. The island caretaker saw me drifting. He towed me into one of the bays. But as you know, things are never that simple."

"What do you mean?" I don't care for his hesitation, or his tone of voice.

"There were complications …" he adds.

"What kind?"

"He had to call Mike on his radiophone to tow me to Gibsons."

Knowing my partner's tendency to understate certain situations, I know there's something more afoot. "Oh?" I mutter.

"There was an accident …"

I knew it. "What kind of accident?"

"My thumb. Lost it overboard."

In spite of his occasional black-humoured jokes, this time I take him seriously. I slam on the brakes and make a three-point-turn. Shades of the flying dog and pickup line, I think, and visions of the red thumb falling through the water become linked somehow in my mind with the red cranberry jam against the blue sea backdrop.

"What are you doing?" he asks.

"Driving to the hospital."

"Take me home first," he demands.

"What on earth for?"

"Can't go like this. I'm covered in oil."

It dawns on me that he's holding the filthy rag over his right thumb. Blood has seeped through it.

"Please, Jo, I want to go home." He pleads so earnestly, then again more forcefully that I do as he asks, speeding all the way to the house, where I hand him some clean clothes. But he will not show me what's under the dirty rag. He just grips it tightly.

During the drive up to the Sechelt hospital and obviously in pain, he tells his story. "The caretaker towed me toward the float, but the waves were pounding in there and he came in far too fast. I warned him to slow down because of the *Snark*'s inertia, but he left it too late. Wasn't used to towing, I guess. The swell lifted that flat bow of ours above an expensive-looking boat moored ahead of us. I slammed my hand down on the other boat to protect it. The next thing I saw was the top of my thumb sinking under the sea ... I suppose the crabs'll have eaten it by now," he adds ruefully. "That sharp fibreglass edge was just like a razor."

I feel sick, almost faint. Have to keep driving ...

The whitecaps are even higher as we drive past Davis Bay beach for the third time that day.

"Dick!" yells Patricia from the back seat. "Dick took me to the lake."

"Dick has to see the doctor," I explain. "He hurt his thumb."

Looking rather the worse for wear a couple of hours later, he emerges, hand thickly bandaged, and surprisingly, his left forearm covered in tape.

"I could have done without that," he mutters settling himself on the passenger seat. "Did you know that bones have nerves in them?"

"I'd never thought about it," I say, buckling up Patricia's safety belt. "How did you find that out?"

"There was only bone left. Everything else had popped off, so he had to chop the bone down to the joint. He used a horrible tool called a nibbler."

"You mean ... you were awake?"

"Of course. And it hurt like blazes because you can't put freezing in bone. Had a hard time controlling myself."

I feel faint again so I delay starting the car. Patricia struggles to get free. "Want to go home," she urges.

"How come your arm is bandaged too?"

"That's where they stole the skin to cover what's left of my thumb."

"I'm hungry!" moans a voice from the back seat. "Want to go HOME!"

"So now you'll be like Gib Gibson."

Dick nods. "Except it was his left thumb he axed off."

That was something I'd not considered. Dick is right-handed. It will be difficult to write, and difficult to pick up nails and screws.

"I did learn something that might interest you," he volunteers as I drive onto the highway. "The doc gave me a kind of option, but it didn't sound like a good idea to me. Apparently there's a way of fixing a skin-less thumb—or finger—into an incision somewhere near the front side of your chest. They'll tie it and tape it there for a few weeks while your own skin grows around and onto it. Then they'll separate the hand from the graft area with the extra skin on it and sew around the top. But if you stop and think about it, it really doesn't sound practical."

"Because it'll only be a bone covered with skin, no padding, mus-cles or nerves."

He nods. "And with my job I'd always be damaging it."

I was correct about him being handicapped by his missing right thumb end. It takes months to heal because he constantly forgets and tries to use it. When he discovers it's hypersensitive to cold, I make a sheepskin thumb cover that ties onto the wrist with elastic, and a spare for when one gets wet.

His stoicism doesn't fool me.

25

To Choose What We Want

Just before my daughter's second birthday I'm suddenly aware that I am feeling normal again. My vague but constant fatigue of the last couple of years as a new mother seems to have disappeared almost overnight. It is time for Dick and me to bring out our fly fishing rods for an August hike up Mission Creek. But I return from that particularly romantic trip with more than our limit of fish.

A month later, when both store-bought and clinic tests reveal that I am pregnant again, I panic. Those first two years of motherhood had not been easy. In spite of being breast-fed, Patricia had suffered from colic for at least eight months, and even though she's only two, she is getting by on less sleep than I. Aged almost forty-five, Dick is old enough to be a grandfather, and when I tell him that I am considering not going ahead with the pregnancy, his seemingly uninvolved comment, "If you feel that way, well, I guess it's up to you," disturbs me. Perhaps he doesn't want another child. He never seemed to connect with Patricia when she was a very young baby, although now that she is older, he insists on reading to her every bedtime, and he backpacks her on our hikes.

I think of my tiny collection of incubating cells in the same way I had whilst gazing through a microscope at a prepared slide of similar cells in embryology class, visualizing them as a collection of conjoined dead amoeba, still undifferentiated and without a brain. Not too late … Hadn't I regarded my grandmother's death, anyone's death, in that same dispassionate way? Perhaps that was different. I hadn't seen her die. For all I knew at the time, she might not have died because I only had my mother's word for that. Why didn't I cry when my grandfather or other relatives had died? Is something wrong with me?

I talk to a doctor, a stranger, who explains in a surprisingly casual—or is it unemotional?—manner, that removing these few cells will be simple at this earliest stage. He phones a couple of days later and gives me the date for the procedure. The moment I hang up the phone I realize I have acted too rashly. If I have them removed, will I cry? Should I? What if they were in a dish and I—or anyone else—threw them down the drain? But my love for my husband is immeasurable. Our cells are the purest symbol of this everlasting state. That night, as my overactive imagination shows me lying on the operating table, I shudder. How can I allow such life be jettisoned when it stands for so much?

That weekend I go on a quest, solo. One at a time I visit four friends, all mothers with children about the same age as Patricia or younger, and after telling them my news, I ask them how their feelings of

In the winter we rarely went out on the water without good rain gear and our yachting boots.

motherhood compare to mine. They are very patient with my probing questions, and while they speak from their hearts, none of them moralize. Religion and ethics are not discussed.

As I dawdle home from my last visit, it strikes me that each of my four friends seems to have accepted motherhood as a temporary state, and none of them feels threatened or frustrated by it. "It doesn't last forever," they'd reminded me, a fact that I'd been unable to grasp during Patricia's first two years. "If *she* was a problem," said one woman, "your next baby should be easier."

"She'll be out of diapers by the time the new one's born," another pointed out. "And as for money," she continued, referring to my lament about irregular paychecks, "whoever has enough of that, kids or not?" How true. "Besides," she added, "we always manage somehow." And we do.

It is during this long walk that I realize the other mothers seem content and able to accept most child-rearing problems with equanimity, whereas much of the time I had been resentful that Patricia seemed to reject my efforts to provide what she needed. Could it be a backlash from my girls' grammar school education where motherhood was totally ignored? Or perhaps there's a deeper reason that goes back to when I was even younger.

At home again, I turn to my Green Lady miniature beside our bed. Even though her face has an open reflective quality about it, there is nothing about it that affects my thoughts one way or the other. Instead, I'm struck by the insistent silence that surrounds me ...

Where is Patricia and where is her father?

I find Dick watching Patricia collect crabs from beneath the rocks at the water's edge. A playful wavelet chases her a few inches up the beach ... And as I gaze at the *Snark*, incessantly undulating on the gentle swells, it suddenly dawns on me that I'm already thinking of those cells—our future baby—as a fait accompli. This time, I'll tell myself to copy the sea and its tides, go with the flow like the other mothers, and our second child should be easier.

That night over supper I remark to Dick, "You know that saying— the one we used to argue about?"

"Which one?"

"The one about free choice: 'we can do what we choose to do but we can't choose what we want to do.'"

"What about it?"

"My choice has been made for me, but you probably won't like it."

He holds Patricia's hand to stop her messing with her food, and a flash of alarm passes across his face. "You're going ahead with the surgery?"

"No," I mumble. "Do you mind?"

"Mind?" he exclaims in such an uncharacteristically loud voice that Patricia stares at him and quits fighting with his hand. "Why on earth should I mind? I always hoped you'd want another child."

My jaw drops. "Why didn't you say so? You know how I hate having to make decisions."

He grins. "I wanted you to figure things out on your own—without me twisting your arm. Besides, you've been making yourself pretty scarce this weekend and we've hardly seen each other—"

"But I thought you didn't want to talk about it!" I burst out. "What would you have said if I'd chosen not—"

He leans over the table and squeezes my shoulder. "I'd have thought of something," he replies far too confidently. Then he asks, "What made you change your mind?"

"Oh," I mumble contentedly, "lots of things."

26

Searching

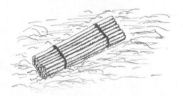

The following morning I leave Dick to catch up on a couple of hours' sleep after his early rounds and take Patricia out in the *Snark* to tow some logs from Gambier Island to our storage grounds. But on my return a couple of hours later, as I approach the mooring buoy in front of our house, I see him on the beach, dressed for work and beckoning impatiently. I turn the engine off and allow the boat to drift against the shore.

"Hand me the Sprout," he calls. "I have to go out."

I pass Patricia over to him and jump onto the gravel beside her.

"Fraser River Pile Driving's lost a large bundle of sixty-foot-long creosote pilings," he explains. "They could be anywhere between here and Nanaimo." He shoves the boat back out, leaps aboard and he's off.

I know creosote-treated pilings are expensive, so he could be searching for hours … unless he's lucky.

Moments later Mr. Scott, the man in charge of the BC Log Spill office, phones to inform me that the piling owners have already sent a plane to search for it. "I guess Dick still doesn't have a radiophone?" he asks.

"Nope," I tell him. "But it's not for want of me bugging him."

He laughs because he's heard my complaint before. "Tell him to give me a call when he gets back."

Six hours later, Dick returns, approaching from our storage grounds—a good sign.

As soon as he enters the kitchen, I hand him a sandwich.

"Thanks. Always thinking, aren't you?" he says appreciatively.

"Well, it took a while, but I found it … four miles off White Islets."

I relay what Mr. Scott had told me about them hiring a plane.

"No wonder," says Dick, dialing the Log Spill office. "That bundle should be worth at least twelve thousand dollars."

After Dick has reported his find, Mr. Scott congratulates him for succeeding where the plane had failed.

"What I can't understand," Dick remarks after their conversation, "is why they didn't see me towing … unless they never bothered to fly this far."

"They probably lacked your tide expertise," I suggest. He agrees. Then I ask the leading question. "How much do you think they'll pay you?"

He shrugs. "I'll bill them six hundred, although it's not really enough."

We wait weeks, six months. Eventually Mr. Scott tells us that he's done his best and three hundred is their final price.

After putting the receiver back, Dick mutters he'll eventually get his own back on them.

"How?" I ask.

"If they lose another bundle—"

"You'd feel justified in breaking it up so you can charge for the individual logs?"

"Unfortunately, yes." He sighs. "If my father hadn't brought me up to be so honest, I'd be a richer man today."

I know for a fact that unless the regular log bundles he finds are in poor shape, they will reach their buyers' mills intact, thanks to him. However, I suspect it will be a long time before he catches up with the pile driving company because they seldom work this area. [Author's note: Much to my chagrin, he never did.]

Not long after the piling incident, we participate in a search of a different kind. It begins as I take Patricia for a walk down to Hopkins wharf, half a mile from our house, partly to check for any fresh logs along that beach. Sometimes, when in the boat, it's easy to miss a good log if it's lying on a flattish beach behind a larger diameter cull. As we lean over the dock walkway to look at the ducks, we watch Frank, the German stone mason and Gambier Island resident who built our fireplace, mooring his twelve-foot aluminum outboard boat to the floating dock below. He tells me he is on his way to the hospital in Sechelt to visit his young son who's just had an operation on his leg after a complicated break.

I point to Gap at the long, white, dense line of fog lurking beyond in the Gulf. "Doesn't look good," I remark.

"It'll probably be gone by late afternoon," he says.

I tell him I hope he's right. He and his family live directly opposite the Langdale ferry terminal, and when commuting to Hopkins, they always have to be cognizant of the constant marine traffic, ferries, self-loading log barges, deep-sea freighters, tugs, log booms and water taxis, not to mention log salvors with and without their tows.

Frank is wrong. Within an hour or so the fog has invaded the Howe Sound area and becomes as dense as it had been in the Gulf.

Because it is still over us at sundown, I call Frank's wife, Ursula, to see if he's arrived home. He hasn't, and when she'd last phoned the hospital, they had only been able to tell her that he was no longer in the building.

Later I check in with Ursula again, offering to drive down to Hopkins to see if her husband's truck is parked there. The fact that it is puts a different light on the matter, and when I inform her, she tells me he still hasn't arrived home. It's almost eleven o'clock.

With Patricia—still awake in her sleeper—clasped against me, I open the window and shine our one-million-candlepower searchlight in the general direction of the *Snark*.

"Fog," I tell her. "It's hiding the boat."

She stares quietly at the formless white curtain outside, then demands, "Where's the boat?" Her body stiffens at the way it muffles her voice. "Boo!" she calls into it.

"Boo!" I echo, hearing in my mind the diaphone foghorn of the Owers lightship that used to scare me as a child until my grandmother explained what it was.

"Vrrrr-oomph! Vrrr-oomph!" I call. She gives me a puzzled glance. "Lighthouses make that noise in the fog," I explain, "so the ships won't crash into the rocks."

She tries to imitate the sound.

Dick stands behind me. "It's getting worse," he mutters. After a pause he says, "Give me the searchlight. I'm going to look for Frank."

I know better than to object. It worries me that Dick will be in a small vessel with only a hand compass as a navigational aid ... And, of course, no radiophone.

"Where will you go?"

He gives his customary shrug. "The obvious places. Check the currents, try to put myself in his shoes ..."

"Boat, you mean," I joke.

He smiles.

Patricia sleeps soundly but I don't. Dick returns about an hour after midnight. "Not a sign and no boat tied to their dock," adding as he snuggles down beside me, "Bet Frank'd give anything for a warm blanket."

I stay awake for ages before falling into a dead sleep, so deep that I don't wake until the sound of *Snark*'s engine starting up interrupts my dreams. It's almost six, dark, and the fog is still over us. I hope Dick will find enough clear patches to keep him out of trouble.

The first ferry of the day blasts its horn to signal its departure so that the high-pitched tugboat's foghorn that immediately follows sounds almost comical. Where is the *Snark* now? A foghorn blasts from the ferry. Now set on automatic, it reminds me of my long sleepless week sailing north up the California coast aboard the constantly blaring *Canadian Star*. Hoping the fog would lift, I had propped myself up against a pile of ropes on deck, intending to photograph the Golden Gate Bridge en route to the San Francisco docks. But I was so tired I'd fallen asleep. One of the officers eventually wakened me, pointing about a mile ahead of us to what my sleep-dulled mind saw as four swags of a lacy drape silhouetted against a blue sky. Entranced, I watched as it gradually metamorphosed into a delicate, silvery-grey bridge.

"But it's supposed to be red," I'd mumbled.

"The Golden Gate was socked in," the officer explained. "This is the Oakland Bay Bridge ... the western end."

And as we passed underneath, its form revealed its true nature to me, a wide and sturdy structure, strong enough to withstand massive weights and whatever the weather might throw at it. But when, moments later, I gazed back at the functional sculpture glittering with moisture in the morning sun, it appeared even more ethereal than it had at first sight ...

The bedside phone rings and Patricia shouts, "Dick! Mum!"

"Wait!" I call and lift the handset.

"Could you pick me up at the ferry terminal?" Dick says coolly.

I feel the first signs of panic. "Are you okay?"

"Naturally."

Naturally? What the hell's wrong with the Snark? "Did you find Frank?"

"Never had a chance to look."

At the intersection between the coast highway and the ferry turn-off, the fog is still patchy enough to hide the illuminated ferry slip.

Happy to see her father, Patricia yells "Dick!" At least he's whole and not limping though perhaps a little sweaty.

"Blasted starter!" he growls, sliding into the car seat. "I stopped to pick up a log, shut the engine off and couldn't get it going again."

"Where's *Snark?*"

"Down there," he nods his head toward the Gambier and Keats passenger ferry dock, adjacent to the big ferry dock. "Should have known better than to buy a rebuild."

Particularly when our job entails starting the engine several times a day, I want to add.

Back at home in the kitchen, I phone Ursula, who tells me that Frank has only just arrived home. A passing tug had spotted him going around in circles and waving his flashlight off Hood Point, six miles from their Gambier home. Apparently Frank had heard the *Snark's* engine around midnight, but his own flashlight wasn't powerful enough to break through the fog, which explains why Dick had missed him.

It's not until I have handed Dick his omelet that he feeds me his story ... in spoonfuls. "I can't say I care for being stranded out there in front of a ferry that's about to leave ... even in daylight, never mind fog and dark."

Here comes the truth. "How long were you broken down?"

"Far too long. It took a while to find out what was wrong." He keeps me waiting while he chews. "I heard the ship leave, then its fog-horn. I knew I was in its path so I kept sounding my horn—in between paddling like mad. You know what that hull's like when you're paddling."

It zigzags and fights forward motion. You have to keep changing sides or it'll go in a circle. "How close were you when it missed you?"

"Put it this way: I'm glad you two weren't with me."

Remembering my pregnant state, I correct him. "Three, you mean!"

For the first time this morning he grins. "Frank was lucky he didn't do what I did some years ago. He could have ended up halfway to Nanaimo."

"How on earth did you find yourself out there?"

As Patricia listens to her father, I wonder how much she understands.

"I was coming home from the inlet … Defence Islands. It was quite amazing really … as if someone had dropped a blanket over Howe Sound. That's when I discovered my compass had fallen out of my pock-et … must have happened when I dogged a log. I steered in the direction of what I thought was Gibsons but obviously had aimed a couple of degrees too far south. Drove clear through the Gap and ended up in the middle of the Gulf."

"Didn't you have any clue where you were?"

"With no land to refer to and without a watch on me, it was difficult to judge."

"How did you get home?"

"I was lucky. The wind cleared enough of the fog that I could see Roberts Creek."

Now I know why he keeps a compass in the coffee can under the gunwale.

27

Booming

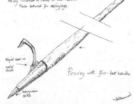

Peavey invented in Maine in mid-1800's.
Never bettered for rolling logs.

Peavey with five-foot handle.

Rigid hook on metal shaft

heavy iron spike

Erik, named partly in memory of my art critic grandfather, surprises everyone, me and the doctor included, by arriving at some ungodly hour of the morning, breeches first. When he starts screaming blue murder at two on his first night home, I order myself to take my friends' advice to calm down and relax. Like his sister, he's colicky, and while I don't obsess about it as I did with her, his crying troubles me, particularly when he loses a fair bit of weight during his first month. I still suspect that both siblings' rowdy nature has something to do with their prenatal exposure to the 4,200-plus rpms of the *Snark*'s Ford 351 HO engine. Although Erik slumbers through my towing trips, during the dark evening hours at home he is even noisier than Patricia had been at a similar age.

Once again, our borrowed carrycot comes in so handy for boat work that I wonder if it will wear out before Erik outgrows it. Not only do I take both offspring towing, they accompany me during certain booming operations at our Shelter Island storage grounds.

Since I started helping Dick with boom work after Alan left, we have always worked together, but now that we have a family, things have to be done differently. Instead of using the tug for pulling the hefty sixty-four-foot-long swifter logs over each boom section—an operation that cinches the sidesticks together and also helps prevent the logs from bouncing out during transit—we have to use the *Snark*. And because it isn't nearly as powerful as the tug, we make use of elementary physics—pulleys, which in this case are called "blocks."

Of course, nothing in this business is ever straightforward or predictable, one of the reasons being that all logs are different. Cedar is less dense and higher floating than most species, some logs might have a twist or a bulge in them, or their bark may vary. There will certainly be variations in diameter and length, too. Making up a good flat boom often reminds me of working on a jigsaw puzzle, except that nothing will ever fit perfectly. But Dick is a third-generation boom man and prides himself on his neat and expertly made-up booms, most of which, when finished, show hardly any water between the stowed logs. Now that my family tasks are more time-consuming, he prepares booms for swiftering by himself. Then, when he needs my help, he can pick me up from the beach with Erik in the carrycot and Patricia suitably dressed and wearing a life jacket, and we can set to work immediately.

Today each of the four swifters are already tied outside their appropriate section, with a block, ropes and a logging peavey already laid out on the logs nearby. I give Erik a final few moments at the breast and wedge him securely under the bow. Patricia already knows the drill: sit down as soon as the engine starts and hold on.

Leaving me to drive, Dick alights on the boom, picks up the looped end of the long pulling line off the sidestick and slips it over the towpost. The rest of it lies loosely across the width of the boom to where the swifter floats, its one end already choked by the chain. Dick leaps to somewhere in the centre out of harm's way where he has a good view of the action.

From my standing position in the boat I make a mental note of the forty-or-fifty-pound boomchain that projects from the middle hole of the sidestick. Not only is that where the far end of the swifter has to come to rest, the toggle of that same boomchain will eventually have to be pulled up through the swifter's end hole.

"No block?" I yell, even though I can see that it looked slippery.

"Don't need it," he replies.

I start the engine and accelerate, turning the *Snark* away from the boom. Checking over my shoulder, I increase the revs as if pulling a log off the beach. The swifter swings around, its choked end hits the far sidestick and stops. Now I know that my next attempt will need more acceleration in order to pull the swifter across the boom. This time it jumps onto the sidestick and slides at an angle across the boom, but even though I change course slightly and keep the revs up, it halts, leaving about twenty feet of its far end jutting out over the water. It is not quite as slippery as I'd expected.

Dick gives the crossed arms signal, and I cut the engine. He rechokes the swifter, putting a slight roll on it and points the direction he wants me to pull so that it will end up at right angles to the sidestick. "Short and sharp!" he shouts before raising his right hand to give me the wrist-twisting go-ahead signal. If I am overzealous, the swifter could overshoot and slide off the boom. So as a result I almost err on the slow side, but it works.

After tying *Snark* to the nearest sidestick, I make my way onto the boom and hand Dick the peavey—the thick wooden-handled logging implement invented in Maine during the mid-1800s to manoeuvre logs. With its heavy iron spike at one end and longer, hinged, hooked "thumb" fixed just above that, it has never been bettered for the job.

Using the peavey like a pry, he half-slides, half-rolls the swifter about a foot so that its hole and that of the sidestick are almost lined up—give or take a few inches—a perfect position for the next procedure.

"Okay, do your bit," he says.

I lower my hand through the top of the swifter hole, grab one end of the chain toggle that lies beneath it on top of the sidestick, turn it lengthwise so that it fits into the swifter hole, and carefully draw it up and out, making sure that once through, the toggle lies across the outside to prevent it falling back. This procedure is not easy for Dick because his hands are wider than mine and tend to get stuck.

With the peavey he lines up the other side and we repeat the chaining process. "I'll plug 'em later," he says, meaning that he'll hammer a cedar wedge into each swifter hole to prevent a boom chain jumping out in a swell.

For the third swifter, an ugly old heavy beast scarred with barnacle shells, he needs the block. Usually kept in the boat, ours is metal, about ten inches long. He quickly rigs it up, laying it on its side between the boat and the floating swifter. It needs constant attention because with each pull, it jerks, and the rope around its grooved wheel tends to twist, sometimes slipping out of the grove. And if I happen to pull before he's reset it, the rope may jam.

It never ceases to amaze me how much extra power this simple device generates. And I am always surprised at the huge discrepancy between the distance the *Snark* has to travel in order to move that swifter a far shorter length.

Eventually we have the heavy brute almost where we want it, except that it needs to be rolled slightly to align one of the chain holes. I tie the boat and, leaving Patricia holding a stick fishing rod over the gunwale, make my way across to the middle of the boom not far from Dick who's dismantling the block. Standing against the swifter, facing it while I watch him, I pay scant attention to the growl of the slow passenger ferry that has just passed between our grounds and Keats on its way from Keats Wharf to Gambier Harbour.

The *Snark* is hidden by a swell after coming to a sudden stop between two booms.

Seconds later, Dick yells, "Watch out!"

As the sharp and violent swells pass alongside our small, unfinished boom, the *Snark* slams against the sidestick and Patricia falls, screaming, inside the boat. Dick runs toward her. Unprepared for the swells that continue to churn inexorably through the midst of the boom where I'm standing, I overbalance and fall backwards. From my prone position, I can see the unchained swifter is lying on top of my foot. Why doesn't it hurt? My shin is bloody and has been bruised by the barnacles. Examining things further, I see that while the swifter is touching my running shoe, its weight is not actually on it. By some lucky fluke I happened to have been standing with one foot slightly forward on a lighter, smaller diameter log that floats a little lower than the ones on either side. Those two logs that are supporting the swifter have saved my foot from being badly squashed.

"Jo!" he yells, comforting Patricia in the *Snark*. "Are you okay?"

"Just about!" I ignore Erik's whimpering from under the bow.

Relieved and unhurt, all I can do is swear at the ferry. At that speed it had no business taking this inside route, which is shown on the charts as non-navigable water.

As soon as Dick has aligned the swifter, I pull the chains through and climb back into *Snark*. Once the last swifter has been dealt with, we head home. The chains will be plugged later.

That night I write a letter of complaint to the Department of Transport. They respond within a week … The only future swell problems we will have to contend with will be those generated by water skiers and the occasional thoughtless pleasure boater.

28

Gathering the Tows

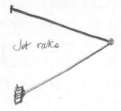

Jet rake

The roar of *Snark*'s reversing engine is better than any alarm clock. From our bedroom, I hear Dick returning from his early morning round, and as I open my eyes, the reflected light from the hall floor tells me it's another sunny day. I'll try to forget the hour of sleep I had lost earlier, thanks to being awakened by my subconscious mind. Even though Erik—about to turn two—is sleeping through the night, old habits die hard.

Dick marches into the bedroom and immediately answers my unspoken question. "Ten logs, all good ones," he says. "Five in the bays, five in the river freshet." Then he pulls the blanket and sheet off me and gazes at my nakedness.

"Surely you're bored with that sight by now," I tell him.

"Do I ever get sick of Callebaut chocolate or fresh macadamia nuts? Or my favourite 5 puttonyos Tokaji?" [The highest grade of sweet Hungarian wine.]

"Flattery," I say with a bashful smile.

"You know me better than that," he says and leaps, fully clothed, on top of me. His face smells so strongly of the sea it makes my mouth water.

Patricia wanders in and drops Puss beside us.

"Ah-ah!" says Dick, and jumps off the bed. "Time to get up. We have too many logs tied around the islands."

Which means that if a strong summer westerly—the fair-weather wind—starts blowing later this morning, two of our vulnerable tie-up buoys might drag anchor or the pickup lines attached to them might pull themselves out of the logs. It is amazing how certain peculiarly shaped logs will do that, perhaps those with a little flair in one side of their butt or with a slight curve along their length. They will catch the wind and current and spin endlessly in one direction until their pickup lines have turned into balls. By that time, the tension is sometimes so great that the metal spike—the dog—pulls out, and the log escapes. We will often find that the strands in one rope have separated themselves permanently, each one forming a ball. In that case, only the dog and the "cold shut," the metal link used to join it to the rope, can be reused. "Blame the perversity of inanimate objects," Dick will say. "But there has to be another agent," I'll argue, to which he'll declare, "Well, it's beyond my control."

He works in the basement while I make breakfast. "Keeping an eye on the tide?" he yells up the stairs, a subtle sign that he's feeling pressured by natural constraints. And it's true that a mere couple of extra minutes can transform a potentially reasonable day into one fraught with difficulties.

After breakfast, I cram a diaper bag with the usual mothering items, sun hats, diapers, band-aids, a baggie of Cheerios, a couple of sandwiches, crusts for seagulls and some ice water in a thermos. While I row out to the boat, Dick, followed by the two toddlers, packs the carry-cot down to the beach and waits until I drive the *Snark* against the shore. As soon as the bag and cot have been stowed aboard, he hands me the two small passengers then pushes the boat off the gravel. I start the engine and drive a couple of hundred feet off the beach before settling the children down. "Get some sleep!" I shout to Dick. "No reading!"

It's 8:10. I have, at most, a couple of hours before the wind starts.

Towing on a morning like this is a holiday. There is less to go wrong when the sea is "flat calm," as my storytelling father-in-law, Hal, used to say. He would always pronounce the "A" in that word, calm, as in the word cat. Both Dick and I suspect this and other strangely accented words were a remnant of Hal's mother's Irish heritage. She had come with her parents from Monaghan to live in isolated Nimpkish River on Vancouver Island. That is where she met and married Dick's grandfather, Jack. I remember Hal's three younger sisters speaking the same way, too, but with an even stronger accent, quite understandable because their mother spent far more time with her daughters than her sons.

All three of us are wearing ear protectors, so there is very little talking. Patricia has brought a book with her because she's already begun to read. I'm afraid that her precociousness will pit her against school when she starts kindergarten.

The usual and logical way to collect the tows from the Pasley group of islands is to start on the buoy furthest from our storage grounds. Today, however, I have to travel beyond that, to the shore south of Bowen Island's Cape Roger Curtis where Dick has anchored one extra-large log. So I am glad that earlier this morning he has simplified things for me by amalgamating four of our island tows into two. Thoughtfulness is one of the things I appreciate about him.

Instead of taking the Shoal Channel route, I wheel the *Snark* toward the north shore of Keats, turn down Collingwood, past Bowen Island's Tunstall Bay and head straight for the automated beacon on Roger Curtis. It is on the other side of this cape that Vancouver and its trademark, the Lions Gate Bridge, suddenly shows itself. My reaction to the sight proves how much I have changed over the last few years, so that instead of hankering after choirs, concerts and restaurants, I now pity the inhabitants of metropolis who live and work in their noisy stacked boxes, breathing exhaust fumes and doing their bosses' bidding.

The log, forty feet long with a diameter of four feet, is tied to an iron spike that had been driven into the granite some years ago. It is only a stone's throw away from a twelve-foot-wide fissure about forty feet high that slashes through the cliff at a drunken angle. I cannot forget the first time Dick showed this cleft to me, driving the *Snark* right inside it. After turning the engine off, he'd used the pike pole to push the boat along the thirty-five-foot-long passage until we reached the far end, where I had disembarked, flashlight in hand, onto a gravel beach only big enough for one pair of feet. When I had shone the beam inside the thirty-inch-high cave opening, all I found was a mound of dried seaweed and some empty clam and mussel shells. But the visit had always left a small question mark in my mind, and since our usual rounds rarely extended this far south, I'd never found time or opportunity to check it again. And I don't have time today if I really want to get this towing job done before the wind reaches us. I give a mental shrug. So what if the wind makes things more difficult for me? Curiosity wins. Besides, the children would enjoy a diversion.

Today, the reflected midsummer light from the top of the cleft is so bright that I can see a small log partly aground at the far end. While it's not worth salvaging, it has another use.

"Want to look in the cave?" I ask Patricia.

She is game, and naturally her young brother wants to go with her.

I pole the *Snark* the full length of the passage, dog the small mooring line from beside the gunwale into the log and help the toddlers out, handing Patricia the flashlight. Small enough that they don't have to crouch far, they poke their heads expectantly into the fireplace-sized opening and aim the beam inside. For a few seconds the only sounds I hear are the gentle swells mounding against the cliff, slapping partway into the cleft, lapping their way along the granite corridor.

Erik screams. Both children back up in alarm as something scuttles past them. In a shaft of light, I catch sight of a shiny, almost black, streamlined body and tail for a second as it slithers into the water.

"Animal!" yells Erik.

"With big eyes!" Patricia shouts, obviously shocked by the suddenness of its move.

They certainly hadn't expected to see something alive in there.

"That's an otter," I tell them, helping them off the ledge and into the boat. "We must have given it a scare."

With the large log on a long towline behind the boat, I drive toward Pasley. Within two hundred yards of the tie-up, I glance out at the Gulf behind me and see a boat, perhaps a twenty-four-footer with dark planing hull and towpost, approaching purposefully from a southerly direction. A log salvor. Perhaps he's spotted something. From the direction he's travelling—toward Gower Point—I'd guess he's seen a log or has been informed of some drifting logs. But how could Dick have missed them?

Deciding to investigate, I grab a folding anchor from under the bow, fasten the big Bowen log to its long line and throw it overboard. It's close enough to Pasley Island to be out of the way of passing boats.

By this time, the salvor further out in the Strait has passed me. However, Dick hasn't built the fastest boat in this area for nothing. "Hold on!" I yell to the children.

We usually cruise at 4,000 rpms, but now I edge it up to 200 beyond that. As I cut a corner around Popham, the engine pitch suddenly roars upwards, revving to 4,700, the jet cavitates and loses power. I turn the key off immediately.

"Damn!" I curse, recognizing the symptoms. It's not electrical, not the engine. It's the jet. The two children eye me a little apprehensively. What will Ma do now?

Under the hull about two feet from the stern is the Achilles' heel of jet boats—the jet's water intake, a rectangle of longitudinal metal bars half an inch thick and half an inch apart. Rattling my hand around in the bow for the second time that morning, I eventually find the jet rake. Unfolding it until it looks like a half-sized metal garden rake with a ninety-degree angled bend halfway down the handle, I lean far over the stern on my stomach and use the rake to feel backwards for the grid, hooking and scraping it vigorously. Something soft catches, I pull ... and again ... and lift. A large thatch of japweed, *Sargassum muticum,* is now entangled in the rake. "Bloody weed!" I yell, yanking it off and throwing it as far behind the stern as possible. Patricia laughs. I suspect she enjoys watching me lose my temper. It's drama, something her father rarely dallies with because he sees no point in it. Raking again, I pull out a much smaller wad. At least it wasn't a polythene bag, a stick, or a dreaded piece of rope. Once we had to take the boat out of water and disassemble the jet to remove a small piece of polypropylene pickup line that had wound itself irretrievably around the spline, and even then we had to slice it off with a stiff, sharp blade.

My competitor now has the advantage. In the distance, the dark horizontal line of the approaching westerly has deepened, so that the half of the Strait closest to me is pale and the distant sea is a disturbing navy-blue. Speeding won't be so easy after the wind has reached us.

The tachometer hits 4,400 and we're flying. At last, after passing

Popham to starboard, I spot some logs—all grouped together—floating about half-a mile ahead.

With 4,500 on the tach, the *Snark* overtakes the larger boat. "Go, Ma!" shouts Erik. Not only does he love speed, he's already showing the unmistakable signs of a keen hunter-gatherer.

The logs—ten of them—are on pickup lines. They look familiar. Drawing closer, I notice the dogs have the triangular-shaped "cold shuts" connecting them to the ropes. Not many salvors make their pickup lines that way. Seeing that he hasn't a chance, the salvor wheels around and doubles back. I don't recognise the LS number on his boat, so it can't be anyone local. It's likely he'd been following the freshet from the Fraser.

I stop the engine and check the LS stamps. They're ours. But what infuriates me most is that the long, new, yellow connector line, the seven-eighths-diameter rope that had earlier fastened that tier to our standing boom, has been cut two inches behind the bowline knot holding the ten pickup lines and logs together. Strange that the person who had cut it hadn't known how to undo a bowline. Will the other end still be at the boom? I doubt it. Boaters have stolen such ropes from us before and couldn't care less what happens to the logs.

The wind arrives as I'm anchoring the tier at Keats' Cable Bay. They will be easier to gather from there when I return with the island tows behind me, rather than from the cramped rocky bay behind Salmon Rock that's so vulnerable to westerlies.

Erik's diaper change will have to wait. Perhaps his soggy discomfort will convince him that I am not always available to take care of him. It might even speed up his toilet training, a better method than the barbaric way his father had been taught—pinned down to his child's pot seat with a broom handle until he produced.

Back at Pasley, I raise the Bowen log's anchor and aim for the arbutus tree tie-up where I linger just long enough to change the diaper and to share sandwiches with the children who delight in hand-feeding crusts to the seagulls on the *Snark*'s bow.

Today this tie-up is so different from that icy winter evening I had been scared by the sea lion. Hermit and the two Popham islands shelter us from most of the warm westerly, but some of it sneaks over and around them, falling in little gusts, obliterating their mirror-like reflections as it ripples the water surface. The tranquil ambience of the early morning is gone, while further out in the Gulf to our south, whitecaps litter a dark sea. They'll become higher and the swells further apart as the day progresses. Around suppertime, if the high pressure area is weak or further out in the Pacific, the wind will retire for the night.

Beneath the red arbutus trunk, three of the fourteen logs Dick had left me to gather have already worked themselves crossways to the others. Towing logs with even one at right angles to the direction of travel will slow our progress noticeably and use more fuel, so I slide the pike pole from under the gunwale and, from the stern, manoeuvre the offending logs parallel to the others. Then I rush back to the wheel and start the engine, stepping on the accelerator to tighten the long towline that floats in lazy loops on the water. As it straightens, I slow the engine so that the pickup lines don't jerk tight; I do not want a dog to pull out. The plan is to start towing before any of the logs have a chance to turn crossways again. As my partner often growls, "never expect things on the water to cooperate." He's usually right. In the blink of an eye, they'll get themselves and you fouled up or tangled in seemingly impossible ways.

It is against my nature to move speedily, but now that I've won, I aim for the next tie-up, off Popham. There four logs have worked themselves crossways. Another seven minutes and we're on our way to Salmon Rock. But I have learned my lesson, and rather than taking such a wide tow of unknown depth through the narrow shortcut between it and Keats, I choose the longer way around.

The Cable Bay logs are already being buffeted by swells, so much so that I throw the big tow off first, before grabbing them and raising their anchor. At least the wind is blowing the larger tow in the right direction toward the storage grounds. Working as fast as I can, I catch up to them and slip their towrope back onto the stern cleat.

Half an hour later all is accomplished and the tows are tied inside the standing boom perimeter. However, I am still irked at the thought of having to pay $120 for a replacement rope. Perhaps the next would-be thief will ignore the dirty old connector line I have used today.

On the way home from our grounds, the children have a ritual.

They expect to ride on *Snark*'s flat bow in front of the windshield. Since they wear life jackets and hold on to the mooring line fastened just behind the bow spotlight, I'm not usually concerned about them falling off. But today I tell them that the swells are too sharp and uncomfortable for that game. They don't argue because they have been trained not to argue with their parents in any boat. The thumb story, the flying pickup line story and other marine dramas have had their effect.

As I accelerate from Shelter Island and aim for Soames Point, I sense that something strange is taking place out in the middle of Shoal Channel, the one we're crossing. Small whitecaps fleck the water, but the surface I'm staring at has some larger whitecaps and accompanying swells and swirls that seem to be moving in a different direction. An extraordinary water disturbance. Something splashes. A large fish? A harbour seal slapping its pectoral flipper to communicate? Then, only fifty feet away from the *Snark*, a puff of vapour from the sea, and another … and five more. Black fins arc upwards from below the surface and down again. I slow the *Snark* and yell, "Killer whales!"

Patricia leans over for a closer look, while Erik peers at them a little more guardedly. I don't think he's heard the term "killer" used in front of the word "whales" before. Both children are very quiet.

There must be about seven or eight whales—including two younger calves with smaller fins—passing through from the direction of Gambier Island. Now that we are no longer planing, the animals appear to be aiming for us. Could they be attracted by the black hull? While it looks flat from above, the front part underneath is streamlined, and I wonder if the whales might regard the *Snark* as a strange and noisy sea creature. They surround us but don't touch the boat, at least, not in a way that I can feel or witness. I sense their presence, smell their fishy breath and understand their curiosity, but I'm sufficiently in awe of them to speed up just a little.

Then, as if they have had enough proof that the *Snark* is not a live animal, their dark presence moves off toward the Gap.

Dick meets us on the beach. "How come you took so long?" he asks.

"Otters," and "killer whales," are the children's first excuses, but when Patricia tells him the bad news, he is not at all happy. "Blasted tourists!" he mutters. "I forgot to tell you last week that someone dropped my pile of boomchains off the boring machine float."

But his mood quickly changes when he learns that I have beaten the competition. After all, that's one of the reasons we had the hot engine installed. "Good for you," he says. "He'll think twice before coming up here again."

Later that year, we, along with some other log salvors, are audited by the taxman. Apparently a couple of salvors had been less than honest with their income, and one of them—recently killed in an accident—now owes fifty or sixty thousand dollars in back taxes. "It must have been over a long period," Dick had remarked when we first heard about it. While I have been responsible for paying bills and keeping records, I have left most of the red tape for our accountant.

. When we meet with him, he addresses one of the auditor's queries to me directly. "He's wondering why you, Jo, can claim the percentage of profits you've been paying yourself when you have a baby and a young child to care for."

"In other words," interrupts Dick, "he's suggesting she's not out there in the boat working with me, and that we might be lying."

Our accountant nods. "That's about it."

"There are two or three things he should know about," I explain, trying not to shoot the messenger. "Carrycots, breastfeeding and cellulose diapers."

Shortly after this, we learn through the harbour grapevine that the tax auditor has indeed been so conscientious that, after speaking to our accountant, he paid a visit to the marina owner in Gibsons to ask if he had actually seen me alone in the *Snark* with our offspring aboard. I'm glad that it had been during summer and the marina owner had indeed witnessed such an unbelievable sight, not once, but several times, and that I had been wearing not a swimsuit but work clothes.

It is around this time that, by way of compensation for failing to live up to his side of our house-moving contract, Olaf signs the deeds of his vacant summer cottage over to us. "Unusual for a developer to have a conscience," Dick comments. I remark that Olaf's apparently idealistic nature is probably what got him into trouble in the first place.

Within that year we exterminate the rats, pay the back taxes, some remaining mortgage on it, and sell it as soon as we can. Since both of us hate owing money, we sleep more easily.

Curious and ever hopeful of establishing some kind of emotional connection with my biological father, several years later I visit him and his wife again in the south of England. As before, he tries to let me know that he has made a success of his life, takes me around the house, tells me about his choral performances, shows me his car and his bike. And when he brings out his childhood Meccano set, I tell him I would have loved a set like that as a child, but he doesn't say a word. Is he genuinely incapable of seeing things from another person's point of view? Or is his remoteness just armour against guilt? It's while he's talking to the young female guide at the famous castle we're visiting that his wife suddenly drops a bombshell. "It's not been easy living with a man like that," she confides. "He's often been unfaithful to me, you know."

When I commiserate and ask why she hasn't left him, she shakes her head. "One of our daughters asked me that. But it's just not that easy."

A question of balances? A beautiful detached house in a desirable part of south England, enviable garden, new car. It is a high price.

Considerably older since my last visit, I find myself examining their artwork more carefully, although I know my own children will never inherit it. After admiring a life-sized bronze bust of my grandpa Eric, I follow my father into another room and stop at a framed letter hung beside the doorway.

"Oh, that's to my new wife from my mother," he explains. "We really treasure it."

"I consider how lucky my son is to have won you, and congratulate myself also, in its consequence," his mother writes.

I feel as if an ice-cold knife blade has been laid against my face, drawn full circle around my neck and down into my stomach. As its icy shards pass through to my extremities, I hold my breath the way I had done in Mr. Evans' car when I learned I had to call him "daddy."

Treasure it? "That's nice of her," I hear myself remark. Has he no idea how I might feel? This final blatant lack of empathy now explains why he has never asked me how I felt when he disappeared and never bothered to reconnect with me, never troubled to find out for himself how I was being raised. I feel a deep anger. But even if he hadn't left, would my childhood have been any better? Different, yes, but not necessarily an improvement.

And so, without having found a way to break through to him, I have to let go, to leave gently and without any kind of bitter confrontation.

As my Wardair plane passes over Howe Sound and circles over the Strait on its approach to Vancouver airport, I try to photograph our log salvage area, but with my misted eyes it's not easy to focus through an aging single-lens reflex camera.

Owing to some overzealous customs officers who find a gift-wrapped, store-packaged bonsai starter kit that my sister has laid on top of my carry-on bag for Patricia, I am detained for an extra hour while they examine the rest of my luggage—even the contents of my toiletry bag—in detail. But the sight of Dick and our two effervescent children impatiently waiting beyond the swinging doors of the reception area gives me a new sense of perspective, even to the extent of crossing "father" off my want list: I have been living with one for years.

Dick and I embrace, and I can smell the familiar scent of the sea on his skin.

"We thought you'd missed the plane," he says, his face showing lingering concern.

"Bloody bureaucrats!" I growl.

He shakes his head.

And I know that in about four hours I will enter our living room—Dick's work in progress—and like me, it will look the same as it had before I left.

So will the view of the Gulf.

Epilogue

April 2009

This year spring arrived much later than ever before. The sudden change to warmer, dry weather gave me a chance to try my hand at apple grafting, something I wouldn't have attempted otherwise. Working with a knife in temperatures hovering around freezing would have been asking for trouble, particularly in my present state of mind. As it was, I cut my fingers and thumb several times that first afternoon.

Now, a week later, I wander outside to check my experiments. Of course, it's far too soon to see if the little sticks have taken, but I'm impatient. While it's a character trait Dick sometimes found amusing, he'd usually chide me about it.

But as I climb the gentle slope behind our house I'm distracted by a strange blue haze under the fruit trees. I blink twice. Blue? Perhaps not … I draw closer and it deepens to a periwinkle, then, closer yet, intensifies into a true violet. They *are* violets, masses of them, every one of their upturned faces staring at me, their petals set off by dark olive leaves flattened against the ground. Where have they come from so suddenly? I've never seen them in the orchard before and they certainly weren't there two days ago. The sight brings another spring morning to mind when, after returning from his job of searching for stray logs in the local waters, Dick had crept straight into our bedroom to thrust a bouquet of violets under my nose. "Found these on the islands. One of my favourite flowers," he'd said.

"So, you sent these to jog my memory, did you?" I remark aloud, self-conscious about talking to myself in the orchard.

I see him, as I often do in the months since he died, almost as clearly as though he were standing there. He's grinning, even laughing at me sitting there on the carpet of damp violets under his favourite apple tree. It's a familiar vision, but so real. And when a hummingbird, just arrived from the south, buzzes noisily past to warn me off its territory, the evocative sound connects me to the first time he and I declared our love beside the mountain forest, aeons ago.

It has only been a few months since the doctor on duty in the local hospital had met me in the hall. "I'd like to have a word with you," she'd said. "It's not good. He's in so much pain we had to give him the maximum amount of hydromorphone. He's not really conscious." She pauses. "I—we—don't think he would choose to prolong his life under these conditions … I think he would want us to remove all his medications except the analgesic. No IV, no insulin. You understand I'd like your agreement on this?"

I was stunned. Although he'd been suffering from a serious kidney infection as a result of having had his malignant bladder removed the previous year, neither he nor I had thought that he would be dying in the near future. Then the truth hit. Physically. We would never communicate with each other again. Unimaginable. Throughout our marriage it had been as if we'd had some kind of mental telephone connecting us, and now, without warning, the line had already been cut.

I felt nauseous. Barely able to breathe. Wanted to join him wherever he had gone or was going. This was the moment I'd dreaded but never considered because I was convinced he was going to get better. He always had before, just as he returned a stronger man from his quadruple bypass ten years earlier. Even up to the previous day he and I had never talked about him dying, and neither did the doctors. Why not? Why didn't anyone in the medical profession phone me and tell me in a slow, clear voice, *"He will die soon. This week or next week. Do you want to talk to him about anything before we give him extra pain medication? Because by then it will be too late."* Surely they knew?

The duty doctor had continued, "We'll wheel him into the palliative care ward and remove his IV, and you can stay with him."

Until he dies, I wanted to scream. *Why don't you doctors use that word? DIES! DIES!*

I handed my cell phone to my daughter, Patricia, now a classical singer visiting from London. "Phone your brother."

At the nurses' station I asked if I could talk to his family physician. "Sorry," they said, "it's his weekend off."

Abandoned. I had been abandoned … with him.

Dick lay there, tense, eyes closed, face drawn. He had aged thirty years during the previous few weeks. Gone were his well-cut muscles from four months ago. He didn't appear to sense my presence.

As we waited for Erik and his partner, Jen, to drive the half-hour journey from their home, I persuaded Patricia to accompany me to the Sechelt Nation's art store opposite the hospital.

Leaving her to wander around inside the museum area, I stared at the glass display case crowded with silver and gold First Nations' jewellery. I didn't know what I was doing here.

Gradually, my answer was revealed. Dick had always given me jewellery for my birthday, choosing it himself. But since he had been in hospital on my birthday the previous week, he had asked our son to buy me a spa treatment voucher, but that item wasn't Dick's style. But *this* gift I was about to find would be his last. It would have meaning, but I didn't know what. There was no question that he, in his twilight mind, would be choosing it.

Without consciously studying the hundred or more pairs of earrings and other jewellery, my blurred eyes stared at the display. I could see, but nothing registered in my brain. And then, in less than thirty seconds they presented themselves. Unique and not at all feminine, I don't think I would have chosen the earrings for myself. They weren't the usual flat type with an incised design. They were silver, but three-dimensional, solid. Each polished bird's head was, as Dick had been, a remarkable combination of power and grace. The saleswoman—from the Sechelt Nation—explained the significance of my choice as she handed them to me, but I didn't hear her. I had been sensing their weight and smoothness, feeling how they seemed to melt in my hand to become part of me. The way he had done.

Trying to hide my tears, I paid and left. While we waited for Erik and Jen in the parking lot, I hooked the earrings on and read the accompanying card. *Thunderbirds, believed by the Squamish Nation to be one of the special messengers of the Creator.*

Creator, but also Destroyer.

Oblivious to the other three behind me, I ran to the palliative care ward, leaned over Dick and lifted his hands to my ears so that he could feel the earrings. "These are what you gave me for my birthday," I told him.

He must have known I was there. With his remaining vestige of strength he let go of the earrings and slid his arms slowly, barely perceptibly, up around my neck. I held him close. Gradually, his arms fell back onto the bed.

Patricia took hold of his hands and sang to him. Although she performs in concert halls, opera houses and cathedrals, she regularly entertains patients in hospitals and rest homes, and I was unprepared for the emotional onslaught that her voice had on me and on her father who managed to signal for more by dragging his trembling hand to his ear. Even patients in wheelchairs gathered outside in the hall to listen as her voice eased though the open door.

"Ma," she said after three songs. "It's your turn."

I started singing a Scottish folk song, *Caller Ou*, but gave up after five words.

That night the westerly wind increased, unusual for that hour, and a strange intermittent wailing started up, a cross between a harmonic yodel and mournful howl. It took me a while to discover that the first floor's external architecture was the cause. The eerie sonics were produced only when the wind blew at a certain angle and speed, hitting a series of perpendicular wooden posts that projected outwards from the walls between the windows.

The other sounds were the moist rales of my husband's breath as it pushed past the liquid gathering in his lungs. I tried to view his body as a faltering machine with a computer that was in the process of freezing. But it was a mental trap that always ended with the age-old unanswered question. Where had *he* gone?

Every three hours a nurse would come by to administer the narcotic and check on the oxygen flow, and I would ask naïve questions: "What is it like when people die? Is it horrible to watch? Do they have their eyes open? How long will it take?" One nurse in her early twenties told me, "Sometimes people hang on for weeks," and, "No, they don't die with their eyes open."

I could not sleep. The story of Gluck's dramatic opera, *Orpheo ed Euridice,* became an obsessive reality. That night I *was* Orpheo, the musician-god who had mourned so desperately for his forest nymph wife, Euridice, killed by a snake. The relentless rhythm of my husband's breathing drove the music's familiar melodies further into my brain, leading me to some kind of unknown world, a place I had to search as Orpheo had searched the Underworld of Hades for her. Would I find Dick there? And if I did, would I be unable to resist his pleas for me to look back at him and talk to him as Orpheo had been forbidden to do upon pain of his reborn wife's death? For when Orpheo did glance back and Hades took Euridice, he still did not give up on her. Using his musical powers he eventually persuaded the gods to bring her back yet again so that he could be with her forever.

As someone who'd always regarded the plot as a mere fairy story, I was now assaulted by its real meaning and there was no release. How could anyone do justice to the role of Orpheo without having experienced the death of their partner? This was no longer a Greek myth. It was real, and with my memory of the music to reinforce it, the emotion was concentrated and absolute. I'd always sneered—in public—at Orpheo's apparent stupidity for gazing back at his revived Euridice, but now his motivation for doing so regardless of the consequences was now utterly clear to me.

The story would torment me for the rest of my hospital stay, and to a certain extent, still does.

I wanted to flee and yet to stay. I was watching a man being tortured. Not even a dog would have been left to die like that. Dick's intermittent horrified cries led me to suspect he was reacting to the painkiller the same way he had done years ago when it had been prescribed for his back spasms. Hallucinations and nightmares had been its side-effect.

For four days in that room, I never slept. Not once. Outside the window a sodium light kept turning itself on and off every few minutes. The hospital seemed to be more active during the dark hours than in daylight. One night the hallway sounded as if it had been taken over by some drugged thugs. The male nurse was threatened. And when I investigated, he told me the dramas must have been the result of the full moon. A bizarre distraction that only added to the surrealism of my surroundings.

The glowing Indian summer weather only made the dying process more poignant because it was Dick's favourite time of the year. I'd occasionally lie beside him, willing him to react in some way, waiting for improvement. Not that I expected any. When the nurses came to wash him each day, he moaned every time they moved him. And the devastating part was that I wasn't able to comfort him.

During the fourth night, his breathing eased, quietened. He seemed more relaxed. At dawn, he took a fairly deep, quiet breath and gave a long sigh. I sprang up and felt his pulse, but there was none. His eyes were closed as the young nurse had told me they would be, and he was warm. I looked at the tide calendar that Patricia had pinned to the cork board on the second day. "Check the tide when he dies," she had said, "It'll be almost low. You'll see."

She was right. Perhaps his subconscious mind had remembered Dickens' character, Mr. Peggoty's commonly held views as the taciturn Barkis lay dying: "People can't die along the coast, except when the tide's pretty nigh out."

I kissed his lips, now so thin, one last time, then clipped off a lock of his hair, but even as I let my gaze linger on his barely recognizable face and shell of a body, I had the oddest feeling that something was not dead.

Erik, who lives with Jen on our property, had taken time off his log salvage work and the refurbishing of the original *Snark* to come to the hospital. He drove me home and there was no tiredness, no tears. As I stepped out of the car, he, Jen and Patricia showed me their surprise: While I had been staying with Dick, they had coped with the emotional crisis by demolishing the old rotten cedar walkway leading into the house, and replacing it with a new one. This would be the first of many renovations and improvements undertaken by my children to finish or fix all the unfinished projects Dick couldn't get to because of his gradual deteriorating health. He had been unwilling to deal with any of them, telling me to be patient, that he would get to everything as soon as he felt stronger. During each of the two pre-dawn ambulance trips earlier that summer, I had cringed as the paramedics had pushed Dick in the gurney over the thin plywood patched planks. If they had known there had been a five-foot drop underneath, they would never have risked it.

Although I had planned to go to bed immediately after Jen's pancake breakfast, my body had other ideas. Within that same hour, I was in the undertaker's office. The owner was on leave and his temp was an older man from Nanaimo.

Without prompting, I handed over the pertinent documents, he filled in some forms, I signed them. So trite, so anticlimactic. What bathos. Dick had never said, "I want to be cremated." He'd never said, "I don't want a ceremony." He'd talk about such things as if they were meaningless, that funerals were for the relatives and friends, that he was never going to attend one, that cremation was the sensible thing to do. He was the one who had dealt with his own mother's cremation. Without me. It was this enforced bureaucratic link that made it so pointless for me and for him. We would deal with it in our own way.

The man from Nanaimo interrupted my thoughts. "Now I have to take you into the back room … It's part of my job," he added almost apologetically as I followed him down the corridor.

There, on a white shag carpet, reminiscent of some kind of upscale basement rec room, was a bizarre sight. So many caskets, some closed and gleaming, others lined with shimmering white silk, somehow reminiscent of giant clams, mouths open, ready for a good meal.

That's when I thought I heard a snicker. *"Now you see how silly it all is!"*

I almost laughed aloud. The voice and speech pattern was so familiar, so typical, but they weren't mine. I reminded myself I was exceedingly short on sleep. Besides, if I could hear music in my head, why not a voice with familiar tone and pitch?

The Nanaimoan pointed at a few caskets, "This one's three thousand dollars … or you can have this for ten thousand … and here's another at five hundred."

I stared at them. After an uncomfortable silence I had to ask, "And you put the body in them and burn them immediately?"

"That's right!" said the familiar voice in my head.

"Yes," the undertaker agreed, "That's what happens."

"Well," I continued, "to me, it doesn't make sense to buy a beautiful wooden box that's taken time and effort to build, then just burn it up. Never mind that it costs a lot."

Normally I wouldn't be that rude to someone who has a job to do, but I swear that at that moment I was being aided and abetted.

"My sentiments exactly!" the voice chimed in.

I pointed to a cardboard box that seemed to be a display plinth for a glossy burled model. "What's that one?"

"Oh," he said dismissively, "that's the cardboard one. It's the cheapest. Twenty-five dollars."

"That's what I bought for my mother," stated the firm voice.

"We'll use that one," I said.

"I bet he never expected you to choose that!"

I almost told Dick to shut up.

Back in the office the man asked if I wanted the ashes put in one of the urns displayed on the bookshelf.

"No thanks," I said. "Years ago we bought a replica Egyptian coptic jar. We used to joke about who would be put into it and where it would stand."

He didn't smile. "We could put the ashes into it for you," he offered.

"No, it's okay, thanks. I don't mind doing it," I said, hoping that they wouldn't mix his with anyone else's.

"Don't forget my mother," came the warning.

"While I'm here," I added, "I may as well pick up my mother-in-law's ashes. My husband should have done it years ago, but he kept putting it off."

"That's right. Blame me!"

I stifled a laugh.

The undertaker left the room briefly, then returned, telling me he'd found them and would give them to me after Dick's cremation. "Are you sure you don't want a ceremony?" he asked.

"No thanks. His death was ceremony enough. He was a recluse," I explained, "and I don't think he'd care for people being around his dead body."

"You did nobly," congratulated the voice.

Still unable to sleep, the next morning I searched for various documents, including our wills, then filled in some more forms, one of which was an application for death benefits—money supposed to help defray funeral expenses. However, when I read the small print informing me that I wouldn't be receiving the funds for at least twelve more weeks, I was very relieved I hadn't chosen an expensive casket.

"So why didn't you bury me under an apple tree?" the smart-assed voice whispered.

"You mean, the way you did with the cat?"

"You would have saved fifteen hundred dollars."

"Oh, sure. Then the undertaker wouldn't have given me the death certificate for the benefits."

"Might've been worth a try," he said, sounding a little disappointed.

I knew he was joking. He often joked like that, and just as often I'd think he was serious. "Easy for you to say. You who always left the form-filling duties to me."

"You should be thankful. Now you're an expert." Trust him to rationalize one of his shortcomings—his refusal to deal with bureaucracy—as benefitting me in the long run.

"Doesn't mean I like it," I growled.

Returning home a couple of hours later, I found Patricia manically ripping the stinky, worn forty-five-year-old carpet off the plywood living room floor. Outside, Erik and Jen had begun to clear the land of ivy and brambles, starting where the invasive species were making inroads on the repositories of various piles of iron, stainless steel, aluminum, nuts and bolts, wire, boat parts, styrofoam, timbers, blue plastic barrels, old engines, staples, ropes, shackles, pieces of plywood, cans, bottles.

"I'll get one of my friends to prune the apples in January," Erik promised as I stared helplessly at the orchard's intertwined mat of branches overhead. "And," he added, "We will finish the living room. This winter and spring. Promise."

That afternoon when Jen prodded me to accompany her in their twenty-four-foot work boat, *Dejavu*, while Erik worked the beaches in his small boat, I didn't even have the energy to refuse.

Out on the water, I felt alive, in a time warp. I forgot history, forgot the hour. Was this the other world I had craved so much? With the constant activity and a slight chop on the water, there was no time to think about personal comforts or food. While Erik used his small boat to go ashore to put the pulling chain and rope on the beached logs, Jen and I hooked the other end of the long rope onto the *Dejavu*'s towpost and pulled them off. It was only now that I realized how much Dick must have missed working out on the boat over the last three or four years. But he had never complained.

Steering off Gower Point to our storage grounds with the tow of logs behind us, I caught sight of a dark shape gliding under the water only three feet from the stern's port side. It crested, and a large dark-brown Steller sea lion looked me straight in the eye for at least twenty seconds before sinking below the surface. As it rose a second time and followed alongside the boat for about five minutes, it stared at me again, and I thought of the first time Dick had taken me out in the *Snark* to show me their kind on Worlcombe Island. Even they, like the logs and the salmon, have dwindled in numbers since that time.

That spring, after Erik moved the sound system into the almost finished living room, I tried playing a recording of a solo piano work composed by Beethoven played by a virtuoso who died young of a progressive disease, but there was something wrong with the sound. The piano notes were muzzy. Wondering if Erik had hooked a wire up incorrectly in the midst of all the renovations, I searched among the files in the bedroom for the brochures that came with the huge speakers.

These stacks of papers contained Dick's handwritten book

manuscripts from the last fifteen years. He couldn't type, and thanks to my grammar school education, neither could I. A friend of ours, Professor Walter Hardwick, gave me his old Mac Plus, which had a writing program on it. And so Dick set to work, writing in longhand in the quiet bedroom, while I taught myself to type on the Mac Plus in the kitchen, deliberately not reading his handwritten stories ahead of time so that I could treat their ending as the proverbial carrot. It worked. I sent a story to Howard White at Harbour Publishing, who sent me a postcard with "Send more!" on it. This was an incentive to Dick, who hated the physically constraining act of writing, and also to me, who equally hated the idea of learning to type. Stacks of encouraging postcards later, Dick had written enough stories for almost two books, and still held at least another book of tales in his brain.

In amongst the old manuscripts I discovered the diagrams for the sound system under a file containing Dick's original handwritten manuscript of *Haunted Waters*. As I lifted the whole drawer out, I also discovered two pages he'd written to me in that same year—1998—something unique for him who kept the deepest of his feelings very much under his hat. I had remembered its existence and its sentiment, but had not seen it since hiding it far too safely away.

The handwritten pages told me volumes about the man. His romantic actions were usually more indicative than his words and he was never very easy speaking of love, claiming the word had become so overused that it had lost its meaning. But his letter and poem communicated far more now than when he handed them to me a few days after his quadruple heart by-pass. Perhaps he wrote it then because he had just survived death.

Dear Jo,

You have accused me, only too truly, of never having written you a poem or a letter. Henceforth you will have to reproach me for other reasons. I will doubtless make this easy for you, as always.

The poem is not to be read in the spirit of facile adulation which mars so much of Victorian—and other—poetry. It is intended, rather, in the spirit in which Sir

Conan Doyle's hero Sir Nigel—in Doyle's eponymous historical romance—vowed to fight to the death any man who refused to acknowledge Sir Nigel's wife as the foremost beauty of the world. (She was renowned, but for her temper, not her beauty!)

Don't mistake me here! I draw no invidious comparisons! But one of the truest sayings is that beauty "lies in the eye of the beholder."

So, if read in that spirit, these verses shouldn't embarrass you. But remember also as you do that they don't stray all that far from the truth!

From your admiring husband, with love:

This Friday, Dec. 10th, 1998—being the second day returned from the hospital, and writ with the new pen.

Poem to Jo

Mist-snow by morning light in cedar forest;
Rainbows spiralling over blue-spruce branches:
Radiant armadas of pollen descending in golden strings:
I have seen all of these things, and
—you are more beautiful.

The iridescence of a leaping trout in a morning pool;
Wild columbine be-dewed by flashing spray;
The last dew-drops glistening on perfect rose:
I have seen all of those, and
—you are more beautiful.

Mountain blue-berries with their bloom unbroken;
The comet's hair, the butterfly's wing, untouched by flight.
And pool-deep moss, more brilliant than the emerald's green:
All of these things I have seen, but
—you are more beautiful!

Out in the orchard, the purple carpet of six weeks ago has now been covered by lush grass, buttercups and dandelions. The only apple grafts that have taken are the ones on the pre-potted tree I had bought first. But the far cheaper tree that I'd purchased from a well-known franchise the following day has died. It had been mistreated—stored outside in freezing temperatures with several others in loose wood chips. I should have listened to Dick. He's always telling me that buying "cheap" is false economy. Now I'll have to wait until early next year to try again. But it will be the perfect time to plant a new tree, to begin a new graft. That's when our first grandchild is due.

Dick tightening a swifter wire.

Dick and Patricia on a hike to Mt Steele.　　Eight-year-old Erik learning to boom logs.

In 1962 I was studying piano and voice at the college in Liverpool. My instructor needed a trumpet player for the college orchestra, so I used the money from my farming job to buy the trumpet and take lessons.

Acknowledgements

Thanks to Betty Keller for her inspiring help, and to her garden of writers for their unfailingly constructive comments. I am thankful, too, that my author husband encouraged my writing efforts while keeping (I suspect) most of his critical thoughts about it to himself. He did, however, give my technical descriptions a "pass." I also thank Rebecca Hendry for her sensitive editing, and publisher Vici Johnstone for her encouragement and excellent guidance.

And last but not least I am very grateful to our admirable children, Patricia and Erik, and my equally admirable daughter-in-law, Jennifer, who have rallied round helping to repair my property inside and out. Their single-mindedness has enabled me to finish writing this book in a warm and dry home with a view of Howe Sound behind my computer instead of a mass of invasive vines and bushes beyond mildewed and misted windows.

As for the unique jet boat *Snark*, it lay in the garage for twenty-six years as a broken and battered wreck. But by a strange coincidence it will be ready for its relaunching around the same time as this book thanks to our son Erik, who has restored it as a testament to his father.

Soames Point, August 2010